A FOOT WIDE
ON THE
EDGE OF NOWHERE

OLIVE AND THEO SIMPKIN
Sharing Good News in China

BY HELEN JOYNT

A FOOT WIDE ON THE EDGE OF NOWHERE
Olive and Theo Simpkin — sharing Good News in China

First published in 2019 by Helen Joynt

Copyright © by Helen Joynt 2019

The moral right of the author has been asserted.

Cover design and maps courtesy of Joy Lankshear

Interior design courtesy of Sandra Joynt

ISBN 978-0-6483849-0-8

Printed and bound by Ingram

To Mary
without whose selfless love
and prayers
this book could not have been written.

One of Theo's favourite hymns

Jesus, Rose of Sharon, bloom within my heart;
Beauties of Thy truth and holiness impart,
That where'er I go my life may shed abroad
Fragrance of the knowledge of the love of God.

Jesus, Blessed Jesus,
Rose of Sharon, Rose of Sharon,
Bloom in radiance and in love within my heart.

Ida Augusta Guirey (1874-1957)

CONTENTS

LIST OF ILLUSTRATIONS

SPELLING OF NAMES IN CHINA

The way Chinese names are written for Westerners has changed considerably over the decades. The names in this story (whose spelling has changed over the years) are included in the table below. The names in the left-hand column are as Theo and Olive wrote them. The names in the right-hand column are the current Pinyin spelling, and the spelling used in most cases in this book.

Older spelling	Current spelling
Akumi	Aguomi
Anhwei	Anhui
Anking	Anqing
Canton	Guangdong
Chiang Kai Shek	Jian Jieshi
Chungking	Chongqing
DaChing	Daqing
Hankow	Hankou
Hsia Kuan	Xiaguan
K'eh t'i	Keti
Kopu	Gebu
Kiating	Jiading (now known as Leshan)
Kuling	Guling
Kuomintang	Guomindang
Kwangluchen	Guanglu Zhen
Kweichow	Guizhou
Luh Ch'üen	Luquan
Pehtakai	BaitaLu
Szechwan	Sichuan
Taku	Taogu
Tsu Yung, also Tsu Hsiong	Chuxiong
Wuting	Wuding
Yangchow	Yangzhou
Yunnanfu	Kunming

Olive and Theo Simpkin

ACKNOWLEDGMENTS

A story untold

They were just old letters.

My parents, Theo and Olive, had written volumes of letters.

This seemingly insignificant box had passed, from Theo's sister Mary (who kept them) to his sister-in-law Nell, and on to my brother, David—who had been too busy to attend to them. I don't blame him; we had all assumed we knew what they would say.

On retiring from private practice, David had more leisure to discover what the box contained—an astonishing opportunity to get to know our parents better, decades after their death—a treasure trove of previously unknown gems and reflections from a lifetime of fascinating experiences. Using voice-recognition software, he 'read' them onto his computer and then passed them on digitally to his sisters.

What a privilege was mine, more than half a century after the letters had been written, to pore over my parents' letters, and 'listen in' to their struggles, their longings and their joys. As I read them, I, their younger daughter, came to know so much more of my parents' 'inside story', this time from the perspective of being an adult—and I longed for others to hear their story. I decided to write their story, based primarily on all the letters and old photographs we had received, as well as from my own memory and personal knowledge of my parents, to round out the story and bring them to life.

The Epilogue tells of the trip that proved the catalyst for commencing the writing.

To begin with, I had no idea how to start. My previous writing experience had been either for academic purposes, or the practical writing of educational sessions in Christian Religious Education for use in government primary schools. Neither of these seemed the right model.

After signing up with a local Writers' group for a term or two, I decided I had better start and learn on the job. Friends, like Elizabeth Braithwaite and Lyn Gee, to whom I showed my first attempts, encouraged me to continue, giving me helpful hints in the process.

As I discovered more about my parents, I realised I wanted to know more about their ancestors. How had they come to be in Australia? Were any clues to be found there regarding their characters and the direction their lives would take?

I am deeply indebted to my husband Robert, who took on the challenge of genealogical research, unearthing unknown stories about their families while supporting and encouraging me throughout the writing process, proof-reading and making many timely suggestions.

The deeper I delved into the letters, the more I longed to share the story more widely. A church friend, Mavis Ford, kindly read an early draft, assuring me that others would find the story engrossing. I was fortunate to be put in touch with Trix Wilkins of OMF, who is a writer and enthusiast for the writing of such missionary tales. She spurred me on to streamline my account, keeping in mind who I hoped would read it. Her help and encouragement has been invaluable, and she gave of her time and assistance most generously.

I am extremely grateful for the prompt and always encouraging responses of my editor, Andrea Lundgren. Her meticulous work and attention to detail was thorough and particularly prompted me to keep the story flowing, to be consistent and to identify antipodean and other special references that might otherwise be incomprehensible to readers.

For a project like this which has explored so much family history, it has been a delight to have the contribution of more family members in the final production. Thank you to two artistic younger relatives – my niece, Joy Lankshear, for the cover design (as well as the maps and a lot of helpful publishing advice) and my daughter, Sandra Joynt, for the interior design (and many other valuable proposals).

Most of all, I owe the story to my father's sister, Mary, who supported and encouraged my father throughout his life, and whose preservation of his and my mother's letters meant we could all share his adventures.

I give sincere thanks to all who have helped and encouraged me. Without you, this story would never have come to light. I am sure there have been times when I ignored all advice and followed my own impulses. I apologise for the times when this has spoilt your reading experience.

I hope that, like me, as you read this story, you may echo the words of Fanny Crosby, the hymnwriter, *'To God be the glory, great things He has done'*.

Helen Joynt (*nee* Simpkin)

The map of China used by Olive and Theo in deputation

PROLOGUE

We lay on the wet ground beneath the bright stars and prayed that somehow the Lord would undertake for us, as every road seemed blocked.

I felt led then to lead the way up on to the city wall. We lay on top of the wall for half-an-hour or so, hiding amongst some brambles while the bullets whistled overhead. During this time the whole city had been overrun by the 'Reds', the Yamen taken, and, as we learnt afterwards, the Magistrate and family killed...

From letter written by Theo to the Melbourne Bible Institute,
dated 9 May 1935.

In the spring of 1935, the Chinese city of Wuding in the province of Yunnan had the misfortune to be in the path of some of the soldiers of the Communist Party's Red Army[1], who were embarking on what came to be known as The Long March.

During the previous four years, Chiang Kai-shek, the leader of the Guomindang[2], had launched a series of five military encirclement campaigns against the Chinese communists, in an attempt to destroy their base in

---

1   Mao Zedong adopted Marxism–Leninism while working at Peking University and became a founding member of the Communist Party of China. He helped to found the Red Army, the military forces of the Communist movement in China. The People's Liberation Army traces its roots to the 1927 Nanchang Uprising of the communists against the Nationalists. Initially called the Red Army, it grew under Mao Zedong and Zhu De from 5,000 troops in 1929 to 200,000 in 1933. Encyclopaedia Britannica, People's Liberation Army, n.d., viewed 24 October 2016, www.britannica.com/topic/Peoples-Liberation-Army-Chinese-army.

2   The Chinese Nationalist Party

south-eastern China. This had proved quite successful, and the Communist troops, out-manoeuvred and out-gunned, fled westward.

At this point, Mao Zedong was not leading the army. When he established his dominance early in 1935, he employed totally new tactics. He split the army into smaller units, and used twisting movement patterns so that the army's progress was much harder to predict. His goal was to join a communist enclave in the northern province of Shaanxi. This would involve a gruelling journey through some of the world's highest mountains. Not only would the armies have to contend with natural obstacles, but there would still be the Guomindang (the Chinese Nationalist Party) and local war lord soldiers in their path as well.

A unit of the Red troops turned southward and entered Yunnan, coming within ten miles of the capital, Kunming. Nationalist troops rapidly moved in from Guizhou province in pursuit, but the Reds pressed on. It soon became clear that this was merely a diversionary tactic, and that the

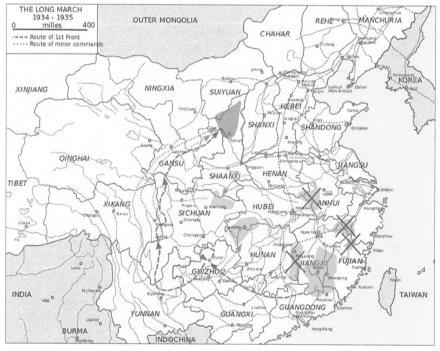

Map of the Long March[3]

---

3   Wikimedia Commons, *Map of the Long March,* viewed 2 November 2018, commons.wikimedia.org/wiki/File:Map_of_the_Long_March_1934-1935-en.svg#file.

intention of the main body of the Red Army was to cross the Yangtze river, so they could proceed to Sichuan and the north. Despite the Nationalists having manned each crossing point, the Red Army managed to cross the Yangtze and continued their march north.

However, fewer than ten per cent of those who started out in the Red Army arrived safely in Shaanxi Province.

This was how, during the period of October 1934 to October 1935, one section of the army (which had set out from Jiangxi towards Hunan) circled back south and west through Guizhou and Yunnan, before turning towards the north again. It was a unit of the Red Army which was marching through Yunnan, and was forcing its way into Wuding, where Theo Simpkin lived, that fateful May evening in 1935.

But who was this young Australian, Theo? How had he come to be in the path of this history-making army retreat in western China? Who were his companions? And what happened to them?

He is one of two remarkable people to whom this book will introduce you. The other was a young Melbourne office worker—the daughter of the local police constable in Gisborne, Victoria.

Educated, dedicated, enthusiastic and zealous, these two young people went to extraordinary lengths to do what they believed God was calling them to do, no matter how dangerous or controversial.

> *...we wandered around the tops of the mountains all the morning, and towards lunch time we got down to the main road, but as soon as we had had lunch by the roadside we once more struck out onto an unknown path, and for the whole of the afternoon climbed up and up and up — and still up. Would that mountain never come to an end! It was an awful climb over more awful tracks or no track at all. Sometimes we seemed as though we were coming to the end of nowhere, with just a huge precipice of rock in front of us, but even there hidden away in those mountain fastnesses we would come across a little mountain village, making one realise just how many millions of these villages there are in China. On looking out over range after range of hills— no villages at all visible — yet you know there are thousands of them all there if you are only at the right angle to see them all.*

From Olive's letter to her mother dated some time in 1950.

Chapter 1

A NEW CENTURY STARTS

and two babies are born

Theo in Lexton, Western Victoria

B orn into the new world of Australia one wintry August day in 1903, a squalling baby boy was saddled with the impressive name of William Theophilus Simpkin: William after his father, and Theophilus probably after the first Secretary of the Lexton Road Board, Theophilus Daubuz Nicholls, for whom the baby's father was working.

William and Elizabeth, the proud parents, looked adoringly at their new baby son. Another boy to join their firstborn, Jonas (named after his grandfather), after a string of five daughters, would provide an extra pair of hands to help provide for the family. He was a welcome addition. What was in store for this little mite in this strange land of Australia? And how had they come to be in Australia?

Jonas and Sarah Simpkin emigrate from Wicken

Theo, as the baby very soon came to be known, was a grandson of Jonas and Sarah Simpkin who had emigrated from Wicken in Cambridgeshire, England, in 1853. The living conditions for people in Wicken, in common with many areas in Europe in the first half of the nineteenth century, were poor.

Consequently, when the Colonial government offered subsidised passages to Australia for skilled tradesmen, agricultural labourers and domestic servants, many labourers jumped at the opportunity for a new start in a new land. Sarah and Jonas were two such emigrants. They arrived in Australia on the ship *Confiance* in April 1853, and went straight to Lexton, a very small township in Western Victoria.

The Colony of Victoria was very new, having been founded on 1 July 1851. The first successful British settlement in Victoria had been established in Portland, nearly two decades earlier, in 1834. Squatters, land speculators and indentured servants followed from 1835, eager to seize this 'empty' country, at huge cost to the land's indigenous inhabitants.

Twenty years later when Jonas and Sarah came to Lexton, already only a few Aboriginal camps remained in the area. One group, led by an Aboriginal man known as 'King Billy'[1] was encountered there from time to time. He was the last of a tribe centred on this region. There were no government handouts to the Aboriginal people at that time, but most big stations gave them an occasional ration of flour, sugar and salt, in an effort to maintain good relations with them. 'The King' was one who was given supplies from time to time by the people in the broader Lexton area.[2]

In those early years of European settlement in Australia, the settlers and squatters were vital to the opening up of the vast lands outside the government authorised limits of location. Squatters were usually either free settlers or ex-convicts, who occupied tracts of Crown land in order to graze livestock on it, initially without legal rights. They were often the first Europeans to enter parts of inland Australia.

The growth of the wool industry was linked to the growing prosperity of the squatters, and the government finally decided to legalise squatting. Following legislation, squatters were required to pay a licence fee, which, in turn, allowed them to refuse passage through their land by any other grazier and his flock. After fourteen years on the land they were permitted to purchase it.

Lexton (or Burnbank as it was originally known), being at the junction of squatters' tracks, became a centre for settlement and government administration. For the settlers, the grassy areas were ideal for grazing stock or

1   Oulton, M 1995, *A Valley of the Finest Description – A History of the Shire of Lexton*, Australian Print Group, Maryborough, p. 36.

2   Oulton, M 1995, op. cit., pp. 36-37.

planting crops. By 1851 the township of Lexton had been surveyed, and the first official gold discovery was made at nearby Clunes. [3]

Like many early settlers, Jonas probably tried his hand at different jobs, including gold prospecting. Prospecting was unreliable as a way to support his family, though, and soon Jonas had taken up a regular position as a labourer, working for the local shire, making and repairing roads and bridges. At some stage he was able to purchase a small block of land on which he built their home out of local materials. A small kitchen garden enabled them to grow some of their own food. They were true pioneers. [4]

As with many pioneers, their lives were not long. Jonas died before he reached 49 years of age, and Sarah died later, aged 56. On their death certificates, Jonas' death was attributed to 'tuberculosis and dropsy', and Sarah's to 'chronic liver disease and exhaustion'. It was a harsh life, and the medical resources were limited.

By the time of their deaths, they had had seven children, three of whom did not survive infancy. Yet their home was one of music and laughter. Jonas and Sarah, being Wesleyan Methodists with a strong faith in the goodness of God, had brought a pedal organ with them from England for worship services. In fact, they commenced Methodist services in their own home. [5] Their children were all able to play musical instruments and sing in quartets. [6] Jonas played the violin, and it is likely that William, who was to become Theo's father, played the portable organ his parents had brought with them from England, as well as the violin.

Since the children were now fatherless, the eldest surviving son William took over the role of head of the house. He was not yet eighteen years old. Until her death five years later, his mother Sarah did sewing for other families in the district to supplement their income, but it was up to William to provide for the family. Like his father, he worked for the shire as a labourer. [7]

On the death of Jonas and Sarah, the surviving sons, William and Jonas continued as leaders in the Lexton Methodist church. Their older sister, Mary, married and eventually moved to Western Australia with her

---

3   Oulton, M 1995, op. cit., pp. 2, 19 ff.

4   Oulton, M 1995, op. cit., pp. 36-40.

5   Oulton, M 1995, op. cit., pp. 88-90.

6   Oulton, M 1995, op. cit., p. 59.

7   Oulton, M 1995, op. cit., p. 37.

husband, for the couple to try their luck on the goldfields of Coolgardie and Kalgoorlie. Their younger sister, Sarah, also married and moved to Western Australia. Jonas, who worked for the shire as the collector of rates, also married and settled down in Lexton.

Whenever William was able, however, he was learning what he could from neighbours and friends about keeping animals and growing fresh food. There were other new settlers also struggling with providing for their families in this different country with its peculiar climate. He was quick to learn what he could from them, storing it away in his mind until such time as he would have his own small farm.

One local, who would later become his father-in-law, Martin Martin, was an experienced farmer, having learnt the trade in Tasmania. It is probable that he gave young William invaluable advice during those early years. No doubt there were a few failures, but by the time William was 25 years old and was setting up his own home, he had a wealth of knowledge and experience to help him become self-sufficient for food.

Martin and Mary Ann Martin, and what brought them to Hobart, Tasmania

Theo's maternal grandparents, Martin and Mary Ann Martin[8], emigrated to Australia two years after Jonas and Sarah Simpkin sailed to Australia. The Martins and their daughter, Mary Ann, were registered members of the Church of England, and came from Spratton in Northamptonshire on board the *Startled Fawn*. They arrived in Hobart, via Sydney and Melbourne, on 21 August 1855.

The convict connection

Martin and Mary Ann came as Bounty immigrants, having been sponsored by Martin's brother John who was already in Tasmania.

John Martin had got on the wrong side of the law in England by the time he was twenty. He had been convicted in Spratton, in 1840 for 'burgulariously entering a dwelling...and stealing a caddy with silver teaspoon and glasses'[9].

---

8   See limited family tree, page 36 below.

9   Northamptonshire Quarter Sessions minute book, January 1840. The court case is reported in detail in the *Northampton Mercury*, 11 January 1840. Source quoted in E Binns, *John Martin and Mary Ann Martin (nee Harriman)*, unpublished. Elizabeth Binns is John's great granddaughter.

Since he had already served a previous sentence for being caught with a stolen horse[10], his sentence this time was transportation for fifteen years. After spending some time in a hulk, he was shipped out in the *Lord Lyndoch* and arrived as a convict in Tasmania in February 1841.[11]

John's convict record shows that he was found guilty of several misdemeanours until April 1847 when he was assigned to work on a wheat farm in the Macquarie River region in northern Tasmania for a Mr R O'Connor of Oatlands. John married another convict, Mary Ann Harryman, in 1852. Soon after, he was recommended for a conditional pardon, which was finally approved in June 1853.

Two years later, John brought out his brothers Peter, and Martin (with Martin's wife Mary Ann and child Mary Ann) as Bounty immigrants to join him in Tasmania.

Neither Martin nor Mary Ann was educated. Neither could read or write. Indeed, Martin could not understand how they had arrived in Tasmania, since he believed the earth was flat.[12] The ship must have slipped off the edge overnight, he declared!

After working as farmers with John in Tasmania for about ten years, the brothers split up. John went to Queensland where his convict past was unknown, and he became an exemplary member of the local community.

Martin and Mary Ann with daughter Mary Ann (later called Maria to distinguish her from her mother) moved across Bass Strait to the Australian mainland where Martin commenced work as a carrier, transporting groceries and other supplies to settlers in Western Victoria.

Not long after this, Mary Ann became pregnant with their second child. When the time for the birth was close, Martin was away on one of his rounds. His wife and eleven-year-old daughter were alone at Mt Elgin, near Nhill, with no other white people nearby. Nhill was a sparsely settled area

---

10 John may have been, like many other uneducated and unemployed men at the time, simply hanging around the market, looking for any opportunity to earn money. Perhaps when the actual thief saw the police arriving, he quickly handed the horse over to John with a coin, asking him to hold the horse for him. The thief then disappeared leaving John to face the music.

11 It is probable that the convict connection was not spoken about in the family. Whether or not Theo knew it, this story has been included as a comment on the unexpected ways in which God's purposes are worked out in human history.

12 As recorded in the personal reminiscences of Theo's oldest sister, Sarah Young. A copy is in the author's possession.

in Victoria's far north-west. Squatters had reached this area by 1845, and there encountered a group of Wotjobaluk Aboriginal people[13]. It was some of these local Aboriginal women who helped Mary Ann through the birth of her second daughter, Elizabeth, on the 15 March 1866, in this unfamiliar new land of Australia. The Aboriginal women were enchanted with this little white baby[14].

Soon after Elizabeth's birth, the Martin family moved to the region of Lexton, where they began to put down roots. Initially working on another settler's property, Martin eventually acquired his own land and settled into a farming life. Having learnt farming skills in Tasmania, Martin now was able to grow his own grain, and this is where his daughter Elizabeth grew up.

William and Elizabeth Simpkin and the birth of Theo

A local school had early been established in Lexton, churches had commenced services, and somehow in all this, William Simpkin and Elizabeth Martin met. They grew to adulthood and were married on 9 February 1887 in Lexton. And so began a new family line in a relatively unknown continent.

Elizabeth and William Simpkin
on their wedding day

If William were ever to be free from his back-breaking role as a road maker for the local council, he would need more land than his parents' small block. So, some time after their marriage, William and Elizabeth selected land about a mile out of Lexton on Mile Creek which flows into Burnbank Creek. The creek would provide a small water supply. William's parents' old home was moved out to this site and became their first home,

13 Bruce Elder, n.d., *Aussie Towns: Nhill, VIC,* viewed 2 November 2018, www.aussietowns.com.au/town/nhill-vic.

14 See Sarah Young's reminiscences.

The Simpkin house at Burnbank. An early photo and with later (1931)
additions. (Photo supplied by Nell Simpkin)

while the small block of land that the old home had been on was given to
the Methodist church.

Their house had a bark roof with hessian[15] walls. Some of the walls were
papered to keep out the draughts and the insects. At first they had just
two rooms, a bedroom and a living room which incorporated the kitchen.
During this era, simple necessities like stoves and cooking equipment were
not easily obtained. People needed to be self-reliant and innovative and
make what they needed. In the living room, there was a large open fireplace
with a swivelling crane over it. From this, they could suspend a kettle, a
boiler, even an urn with a tap, depending on what they were cooking.

As the years passed, they added more rooms and outbuildings and
extensions to the house, making their own mud bricks, using local clay
mixed with dry grassy tussocks added from the vast paddocks.

More important than extra rooms was the establishment of a kitchen
garden, and then an orchard and farm. The ground had to be cleared and
broken up, a dam dug[16], and vegetables and fruit trees planted. When he
could afford it, William purchased his own pigs, cows and poultry.

William's orchard became more productive until it became the family's
prime source of income. Eventually, he grew many kinds of apples, pears
and cherries, as well as walnuts and almonds which he sold locally, and
then further afield.

Whenever paid work was available, such as making the Lexton to

---

15 Burlap—a plain woven coarse fabric of jute or hemp.

16 In the uncertain Australian climate, the creek sometimes ran dry, and rain could not be
depended on. Dams were essential to ensure water for crops and animals.

Amphitheatre road, William would be away working on the construction, leaving the animals, the garden and orchard to Elizabeth to tend. In a good season, she might have extra vegetables or fruit to take into Lexton to sell, but there were plenty of mouths to feed as their nine children were born over the ensuing 24 years.

This was an era when people survived if they were resourceful. Making a living depended on their ingenuity and industry. There were few stores where supplies and household equipment could be purchased, and people had to be self-reliant and able to improvise. They had to bake their own bread, very often growing the grain first.

Elizabeth made her own yeast by boiling up hops, potatoes and sugar and leaving it to ferment. She used this with their own flour (ground from their own wheat) to make bread. William would cut a kerosene tin in half to make two bread tins, and eventually he built their own scotch oven in which to bake the bread. After milking the cow, separating the cream from the milk to make butter was just another of the regular daily chores.

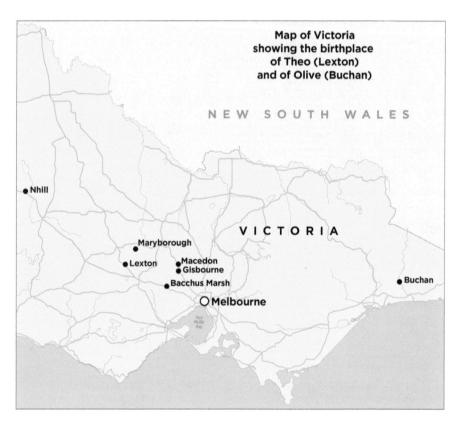

Map of Victoria showing the birthplace of Theo (Lexton) and of Olive (Buchan)

It was essential for all the children to help as they were able. The older children were expected to be up in time to milk the cow, feed the pigs and poultry, make the beds and get a cooked breakfast before walking three or four kilometres to school. By the time the children were twelve or thirteen years old, they would join the workers, learning farming or taking on labouring jobs in the wider community, and helping with the younger children.

This is how Mary, the third oldest of the children, was taken out of school and given special responsibility for Theo who was thirteen years younger than she. She learnt the value of keeping her mind on the job when one day she took baby Theo out for a walk in an improvised pram.

Her steps took her past the dam. She saw a splash of colour above the dam and ran over to gather some flowers to grace the meal table that night.[17] As she bent to pick the flowers, there was a flicker of a movement. Looking back, she saw the pram bumping and careering down the bank towards the dam. Her heart in her mouth, Mary leapt down the bank, fear lending wings to her feet. Just before the pram reached the water's edge, its wheels struck a bump and it overturned, depositing its precious, and now howling cargo into the muddy verge of the dam.

A final flying leap landed Mary next to the baby whom she snatched up from the shallows. Was he alright? Another loud squawk reassured her as she squeezed him in a relieved embrace. 'Thank you, God', she murmured as she comforted the crying child. It seemed that there was a divine plan for this baby's life, which was to be marked by God's miraculous care for decades more.

Her muddy clothes and those of the baby had to be explained when they got back home, and it was a chastened Mary who went to bed that night.

Perhaps this was what started the very special relationship that grew up between big sister Mary and Theo from that day, a bond that was founded on and grew together with their faith in a sovereign God.

---

17 The story of Mary 'tipping Theo into the dam' became part of family lore.

Weekends at the Martins' home

Theo with little sister Myrtle
(Photo from private collection)

Grannie and Grandfather Martin delighted in their grandchildren, at one stage having two of the children, Jonas and Mary, living with them for a few years to give Elizabeth some relief. Elizabeth and William were so grateful for this, especially since the Simpkin grandparents were no longer alive. Regularly they all ate Sunday dinner together, either at the Martins' house, or at Elizabeth and William's house. Every evening, before going to bed, the family would gather and read a chapter from the Bible together.

The Martins went to church regularly, and Grannie set a great example of neighbourliness, helping whenever anyone was in trouble, or sick. In fact, it was during an influenza epidemic just a year or two before Theo's birth, that she went to help a sick neighbour and herself succumbed to the 'flu' and died. Despite her death, Theo's Martin grandparents had such a significant impact on the tenor of Theo's life, that he later named his firstborn son David Martin. Theo was thirteen years old when his Grandfather Martin died.

Trained ministers of any persuasion were few and far between. Ministers endeavoured to include Lexton on their rounds, but local worship services were often led by lay people, and most churchgoers would turn up for the service if a minister of any denomination happened to come to Lexton. A United Sunday School grew, along the lines of the early Presbyterian Sabbath School, and was a centre for local community and fellowship. William was one of the leaders in the Methodist community, taking the role of lay preacher as well as being one of the church trustees, and his son, Theo, would have been expected to be a regular attender at Sunday School.

Olive in Buchan, East Gippsland

Just two weeks before Theo made his noisy entrance to the world in 1903 in the Western District of Victoria, about 500 kilometres east, in Buchan, East Gippsland, Victoria, a little baby girl was born. Olive Hilton Kettle arrived on the scene in the Police House at Buchan where her father, Henry Kettle, was stationed as the local police constable.

The house leased for the police constable and family was a small old house with four equal-sized rooms off a central passage, surrounded on two sides by the wide veranda, so typical of Australian houses. The kitchen, toilet and police lock-up were all outside. In 2016 the house (now known as 'Connorville') was still standing and lived in, having had rooms added including an inside kitchen and bathroom.

Buchan was part of a very isolated farming community in a mountainous region of East Gippsland situated on the Buchan River. The first European settlement and station was established in 1839 and the town was proclaimed in 1873.

Olive's father, Henry Kettle, was newly married when, as a police constable of about three years' experience in Bacchus Marsh, he was moved to Buchan sometime around the end of the nineteenth century. The first four children of Henry and his wife, Susie, were born there: Gertrude, Howard, Olive and Garnet. In the Buchan region, Henry served the scattered

The house now known as 'Connorville' in Buchan (Photo: H Joynt)

farming community, often needing to ride long hours on horseback over the mountains.

A church had been built in Buchan as a community church around 1894 and was consecrated as an Anglican church the same year. Anglicans, Methodists and Presbyterians alike worshipped in this little church. Henry Kettle's family soon became staunch members of the Methodist fellowship in Buchan, and Susie took the position of church organist, playing for all the services held in the church, whatever the denomination.

John Flynn

An intriguing connection with the Kettle family from their Buchan era has been discovered.

Towards the end of their time living in Buchan, a young Presbyterian home missionary came to minister to the parishioners there. His name was

Constable Henry Kettle
(Photo from private collection)

Rev John Flynn[18]

18 Wikimedia Commons, the free media repository, 2018, *John Flynn*, viewed 1 February, 2018, commons.wikimedia.org/wiki/Category:John_Flynn.

John Flynn. He was just 23 years old. There was nothing particularly striking about this young man who had been appointed as a student pastor to the pioneering district of Buchan. Like Henry Kettle, John travelled many miles into the mountains to places that are still very isolated, ministering to his parishioners there, including the Kettle family.

Yet he went on to become most well-known for his development, over a decade later, of the Royal Flying Doctor Service, serving people in Australia's vast outback.

Did his brief service in Buchan and the East Gippsland region contribute to his growing sense of call to serve people in lonely and isolated places? Perhaps, even at that early stage it set an example to the Buchan parishioners, including the Kettle family, of concern for others and single-minded determination to follow in the footsteps of the Lord.

Gisborne where Olive's father meets a gangster

Henry's next police station was a move, in 1907, of over 400 kilometres back to his parents' and grandparents' home territory of Gisborne, 55 kilometres north-west of Melbourne, about a hundred kilometres from Lexton.

As the years in Gisborne passed, Olive's father, Henry Kettle, began to find his role (as Policeman in Charge of the station at Gisborne) quite stressful. (Indeed, he could sometimes have said, 'When constabulary duty's to be done, to be done, a policeman's lot is not a happy one'[19].) The story was told that one day Gisborne was visited by the notorious criminal, Squizzy Taylor.

A very dapper figure in his boxer hat and shiny patent leather shoes, Squizzy was standing beside the fountain near the Post Office. Others were gathered around, and they were tossing coins. It was a game of two-up, illegal in Victoria. They had been to the races at Woodend or Kyneton.

Somebody sent for Constable Kettle who arrived shaking in his boots. He knew that as like as not he would get a bullet from Squizzy, but, being the only policeman in the district, it was his duty to go.

When Squizzy saw the policeman, quick as a flash he unrolled a £10 note (a very large amount in those days) from a roll in his pocket. He approached Mr Kettle with the words, 'Ah, Constable Kettle—for your little church'

---

19 From the lyrics of the 19th century comic opera *The Pirates of Penzance*, by W S Gilbert, 1879.

and put the note in Henry's hand. He and his friends had their last toss and then got into their car and drove off.[20]

One wonders how, or indeed if, Henry explained the presence of such a high denomination note in the offering plate the next Sunday!

Despite this, Henry was held in very high esteem in Gisborne during the twenty years he was Policeman in Charge. He was a 'real country police-man'. It was said that he never locked up a person unless it was absolutely necessary.

Often if he was called to deal with a drunk, he would avoid charging the man, and instead would lift him into his jinker and drive him home where he could sober up overnight. If he had kept him in the cells overnight, he would have had to charge him the next day.

Joining 'The Army'

Olive's mother, Susie, had come from a Salvation Army family in Bacchus Marsh. Her father, William Hollis, had been a strong Wesleyan Method-ist. When the Salvation Army started operations in Bacchus March, Susie's mother Elleanor Hollis was immediately attracted by the Army's emphasis on practical Christianity. Elleanor and the family became active members of the Bacchus Marsh Salvation Army corps. This meant she tried to bring up her children to live Christlike lives.

Elleanor was a strong-minded woman with robust views on the role of women in society.[21] Her name is one of nearly 30,000 signatures on a peti-tion that 'women should vote on equal terms with men' which was pre-sented to the Victorian Parliament in September 1891.

In Gisborne, the court house was next door to the police station and police residence, with the lock-up behind the house. Olive remembered many occasions when her mother had cooked a meal for the prisoners,

---

20 Keith Flack, in *The village that was*, compiled from Gisborne Shire Oral History Collection by Lesley Soulsby, pp. 76-77. There was no comment on what Constable Kettle did with the money.

21 Elleanor came from Kyneton, where Caroline Chisholm, the progressive 19th century cam-paigner for female immigrant welfare, lived for some time during Elleanor's childhood. It is intriguing to note that Elleanor's name is on the 1891 Women's Suffrage Petition. Was she influenced by the opinions of Caroline Chisholm regarding the rights of women, which would have been discussed in the town as Elleanor grew up? Further, Caroline's renowned concern for the well-being of the less advantaged in society—in particular, of women—would most likely have had an influence on people of faith in Kyneton at that time, even those not identi-fied with the Catholic Church.

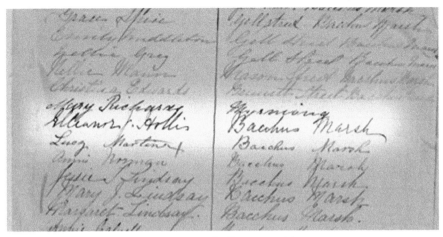

The Women's Suffrage Petition
showing Elleanor J. Hollis from Bacchus Marsh[23]

which she, Olive, was asked to carry out to them in the lock-up[22]. Serving meals to people, whether deserving or not, helped introduce her to practical ways of following Jesus by helping others.

Olive attended the local Methodist church in Gisborne with her family, since there was no Salvation Army corps there. As she grew up, she regularly heard the challenge to follow Jesus. When she was twelve, there was a mission conducted in her church by the Methodist Conference Evangelist, Rev. George Beckett[24], at which she made a public declaration of her faith in Jesus, as did her older sister and brother.

On looking back to this occasion later, she would say that, despite this public declaration, her Christianity was still fairly nominal at that time[25]. She followed her parents' example of Church attendance and good works, but there was little personal motivation for her faith. Her life was proceeding in an unremarkable and traditional trajectory. All this was to change, however, for God had other plans for Olive.

---

22 In later life, this was a story Olive frequently told her children.

23 Parliament of Victoria, *Women's Suffrage Petition of 1891*, page 681, line 19, 2010, viewed 2 February, 2018, www.parliament.vic.gov.au/static/WomensPetition/pdfs/681.pdf.

24 Interestingly, George Beckett's grandson, Robert Joynt, would later marry Olive's younger daughter, Helen.

25 As she wrote in her application to join the China Inland Mission (CIM), file held in the Melbourne School of Theology (MST) library.

Limited family tree

William ROBERTSON (1795-1890)
married
Marion McGILCHRIST (1793-1866)

They had 7 children including

William HOLLIS (1809-1897)
married
Ann JACKSON (1806-1853)

They had 2 children

Marion ROBERTSON (1821-1858)
married
Henry KETTLE (1812-1842)

They had 3 children including

Ann HOLLIS (1839-1921)

William HOLLIS (1841-1921)
married
Eleanor HILTON (1851-1947)

They had 9 children including

Robert MARTIN (1787-1854)
married
Ann CRANE (1794-1874)

They had 9 children including

Henry KETTLE (1838-1926)
married
Ann PATTERSON (1851-1913)

They had 10 children including

Susannah HOLLIS (1878-1970)

Jonas SIMPKIN (1794-1844)
married
Mary HAUGHTON (1792-1856)

They had 8 children including

John MARTIN (1816-1897)

Martin MARTIN (1834-1916)
married
Mary Ann LANTSBURY (1833-1901)

They had at least 3 children including

Henry KETTLE (1872-1931)   *married*   **Susannah HOLLIS** (1878-1970)

They had 6 children including

Jonas SIMPKIN (1830-1879)
married
Sarah JENNINGS (1828-1884)

They had 8 children including

Elizabeth MARTIN (1866-1939)

Olive KETTLE (1903-1988)

William SIMPKIN (1861-1933)   *married*   **Elizabeth MARTIN** (1866-1939)

They had 9 children including

Theo SIMPKIN (1903-1978)

married

Olive KETTLE (1903-1988)

They had 3 children

Mary SIMPKIN (1890-1979)

David SIMPKIN
married
Marjorie JENKINS

Dorothy SIMPKIN
married
David STRACHAN

Helen SIMPKIN
married
Robert JOYNT

Chapter 2

HORIZONS BROADEN
BEYOND SCHOOL

Theo moves in with his sister Mary in Maryborough

Over a hundred kilometres north-east of Gisborne, Theo was coming to the end of his primary schooling. William had always valued the 'Three Rs' for his children, encouraging them to improve their skills by reading aloud to him during the evenings. Although Theo never had any music lessons, he was naturally musical, and was quickly able to play by ear the piano or pedal organ. His parents must have realised his potential. Instead of expecting Theo to join the work force immediately on leaving Lexton School—perhaps because his school results had been good—William encouraged Theo to go on to high school in Maryborough, about forty kilometres away from Lexton.

By this stage, Theo's older brother and sisters were all married and living in various western Victorian towns, except for Mary, who at about thirty years of age, was still single. There was a family rumour that she had had her own 'young man' who went to the war (the first World War) and died on the battlefield. She had obtained a paying job in Maryborough at the Maryborough Knitting Mills, and was living nearby. So, Theo went to live with her while he was at High School, thus further cementing their strong bond.

Theo was an able and interested student. He returned to Lexton when he

Theo with his family in Lexton
Back row (left to right) his older sisters Ethel, Sarah, Mary, Mabel
Middle row: brother Jonas, father William, mother Elizabeth, Theo
Front row: younger sister Myrtle, brother Ray (Photo from private collection)

could, at weekends—possibly riding a bicycle, walking, or taking a Cobb & Co stagecoach—to share some of what he was learning with his family and to attend church with them. There may occasionally have been an acquaintance with a horse and buggy or gig travelling towards Lexton, from whom Theo could beg a lift. (In later years, after the advent of motor vehicles, Theo's uncle and cousin ran a bus service from Lexton.) Sometimes Mary came back to Lexton too, though she was developing strong links to the Methodist Church in Argyle Street, Maryborough, near where she lived.

I'm OK as I am, thank you!

Even then, Theo knew that his life was not his own. Growing up in a devout Christian family, he had gone along with his family's practice of regular attendance at Sunday worship as well as regular family devotions. Most of the folk in his little Victorian home town of Lexton were connected with one or other of the local churches.

Theo's family had a leading role in the Methodist congregation where his father was a lay preacher. Theo had continued regular Sunday morning attendance at worship in Maryborough where he went to high school, and then in Melbourne, where he went to continue his education.

'Going to church every Sunday was surely enough' had been Theo's attitude. But all that began to change when there was a mission at Lexton run by the Victorian Open Air Mission. Theo attended, as expected, when he was home at a weekend, but strongly resisted attempts to have him 'make a decision for Christ'. What did they think he was? He was an honest, upright member of the community. He didn't join in the drinking and carousing at the local pub. He was OK as he was, thank you.

But the Lord had laid this young man on the heart of the local minister. The next time Theo was back in Lexton, the minister called round to plead with Theo to declare himself unashamedly on the Lord's side. The path of peace was just to agree, which Theo did, and after the minister left, Theo breathed a sigh of relief.

But in the following days his mind was in a turmoil. Was there really something more required than simply 'living a good life'? If, indeed, Jesus was the Son of God, and had died for him, then surely, nothing less than a total life commitment was owed to Him. And so, somewhat reluctantly, Theo made the decision to live his life for this One Who had died for him. [1]

Making that decision didn't seem to change much, however. His temper flared up as often as before; his thoughts still strayed into forbidden territory; he had nothing convincing to say when questioned about his faith. What had been the use of 'making a decision' when it made no difference?

Theo's high school results gained him entrance to the Melbourne University science degree course with a view to becoming a science teacher, and he threw himself into his studies enthusiastically.

Olive moves to Thornbury

Meanwhile, at the Higher Elementary School in Gisborne, Olive was developing a keen ear for correct English Grammar and pronunciation under her head master's strict teaching. He also introduced his students to Esperanto—a language devised in the late nineteenth century, to become, hopefully, a universal international language. She had no way of knowing that her ear was being trained to detect variations in tone and grammar that

---

1   This is recounted in Theo's application to join the CIM in 1928, file held in the Melbourne School of Theology library.

Olive Kettle as a teenager
(Photo from private collection)

would one day help her discern and express meaning in a very different language: Chinese.

Later, she recalled how every day at school started with mental arithmetic. The teacher would call out a series of numbers for the children to add up in their heads. Olive remembered that, by the time she was in the upper classes, the numbers might be amounts of money (in pounds, shillings and pence), and that there might be a dozen or more to add up mentally. She revelled in the challenge! [2]

Perhaps this was where her interest in figures started, for when she had turned fourteen years old and had completed her Merit Certificate[3], she was able to leave school and pursue an office career.

So, while Theo moved away from home to live with his sister in Maryborough to attend high school and then go on to Melbourne University, Olive was moving from Gisborne to Melbourne where she enrolled in a business course for office workers She studied at Zercho's Business College in Melbourne, learning shorthand, typing and bookkeeping.

For the first time in her life Olive had to live away from home, finding board in Thornbury, from which she could conveniently travel to and from the college. How she missed the clean air and open spaces of Gisborne, and the family and friends there. She missed the horse rides over the hillsides with her brother Howard. She missed knowing everyone in the town where she lived.

---

2   Related by Olive, years later, to her children.

3   The Certificate of Merit marked the end of state elementary education at this stage. Later, the Proficiency Certificate, and then Intermediate, Leaving and Matriculation Certificates were added by the Education Department.

To begin with, she returned home to Gisborne for weekends, and was glad to take her place in the Methodist Church with her family on Sundays. As time went on, though, Olive started attending the Methodist Church in Thornbury, and developed friendships there as well.

Typing trials and thrills

On graduating from Zercho's, Olive went on a trial week to work at the Dunlop Rubber Company. Her first day in the office proved a baptism of fire when she was given a long invoice to type out (with twelve carbon copies). The invoice listed dozens of items giving the number of articles at the price per article with the total cost listed as well.

Laboriously and painstakingly, she typed out the list, getting all the pounds, shillings, pence and halfpennies correct. At the end, with great relief, having checked and re-checked that there were no errors, she took the papers out of her typewriter, only to discover that all the carbons were in back-to-front. She had the whole job to do again! When the tears were dried, she sat down to repeat the job.

She failed the trial week, but it was a lesson she never forgot.[4]

After her disastrous start, Olive found another position in the office of a chartered accountant, Mr Alan J Hutchison FCA(Aust), in the Stock Exchange Building, 426 Little Collins Street, Melbourne. She quickly settled into the work routine of the Accountant's office. Very soon, her work came to be highly valued by her boss.

Olive enjoyed her responsibilities there, and the added independence of having her own small income. She could now afford an occasional treat for herself, or a gift for her family.

A challenge for Theo: Are you fair dinkum?

Meanwhile, in another part of Melbourne, Theo attended an Easter Convention at the Albert Street Baptist Church East Melbourne, which proved a turning point in his life. The speaker, Rev D. H. Moore from England, had a challenging message about revival and the secret of victorious Christian living. Theo felt it was directed at him and how he had failed to live up to his profession of faith.

When Mr Moore appealed for those willing to consecrate themselves

---

4   This is a story often told by Olive to her children, and also referred to, decades later, in a letter from Olive to the author, dated 18 March, 1962.

fully to the Lord to stand, Theo's heart lurched, and his stomach seemed to have leapt into his throat. God was speaking to *him*. Was he prepared to be 'fair dinkum' about following the Lord wherever He might lead—even to the ends of the earth? There could only be one answer.

Deliberately, and with fast beating heart, Theo stood, publicly confessing his faith in Christ and consecrating his life to Him.[5]

This meant that he was declaring his willingness to offer his life to God for service wherever the Lord should lead him. In the ensuing months, he began to hear about the needs of people in other countries and decided he should not waste time studying.[6] He transferred directly into a Teacher Training course so he could be free sooner to go wherever God might lead him.

He was appointed as a Junior Teacher in the Gisborne Higher Elementary School, where he taught from 1925–1927. Commencing teaching had simply been, in Theo's eyes, the next step in preparation for overseas service for the Lord. He expected to work out his bonded years of teaching and then get on with training for the business of serving Christ overseas. During his training, he was rated as follows:

> *A fair teacher. Needs more experience. A keen student who is doing his best and has more than average ability. Not an impressive personality.*[7]

A subsequent report declared the following about him:

> *A good worker at all subjects who will do well. Needs to widen his interests more. Unimpressive personality at present. No interest in College activities.*

It seems that his supervisor was not attracted by Theo's deep spiritual commitment and lack of interest in what Theo now saw as the 'worldly' pursuits of the college's extra-curricular activities.

---

5   See Theo's application to join the CIM.

6   In later life, when giving his testimony, Theo encouraged a different attitude, commenting that '…circumstances in SE Asia today make it almost imperative that would-be missionaries complete their courses and gain one or more certificates or degrees. The better trained you are the more doors of service are opened to you'. Recorded in a hand-written testimony in the author's possession.

7   This quote and the next come from his Victorian Education Department record, No. 22961, where each year a separate report was made on his progress.

His teaching, if not his personality, gained a consistently good report from the Inspectors.

Theo was quickly involved in the life of the Gisborne Methodist church while doing his best as a new school teacher. He had much to learn, both in the school and in service within the church andwhile he was teaching in Gisborne, he met someone who was to have a significant impact on his life and future.

One Sunday morning, on walking to the Methodist Church to worship, he found himself entering the church with a slim young lady with blue eyes and long brown wavy hair[8]—Olive Kettle. Over his next three years in Gisborne, his friendship with the family of her father, the local police constable, Mr Henry Kettle (or 'Copper Kettle' as some laughingly called him), grew.

'Miss Kettle…'

While Theo was embarking on the challenge of teaching, Olive had become a member of the fellowship of a local Methodist church in Thornbury, a suburb of Melbourne.

On those weekends when she returned home to Gisborne, she heard more about and then met this new member in the church—a young man called Mr Theo Simpkin. He had been appointed by the Education Department to teach at the Gisborne Higher Elementary School, where Olive's younger brother Murray and sister Marjorie were still students.

Mr Simpkin seemed to be a very serious and earnest young man. Marjorie showed some interest in the new young teacher, but Olive wasn't particularly attracted, not even when he began to find excuses for walking and talking with her. He was so earnest.

He was invited to become a lay preacher in the Methodist church, occasionally leading the services in Gisborne, though more frequently at outlying posts such as Toolern Vale or Macedon, often walking for hours up and down the hills to reach his appointed preaching place.[9] He taught in the Sunday School, as Olive did when she was at home, and eventually he became Sunday School Superintendent. It was natural, then, that he would seek Olive out to discuss Sunday School arrangements.

---

8   Theo's letter dated 10 April, 1933, to his sister, Mary, recalls his meeting with Olive on the way to church.

9   See, for example, Theo's letter to his sister, Mary, dated 20 June, 1926.

'Dear Mr Simpkin' ... 'Dear Miss Kettle'

When it became necessary for new materials to be purchased for use in the Sunday School, Olive offered to find them in Melbourne and post them to Gisborne. And so a very formal correspondence ('Dear Miss Kettle...' 'Dear Mr Simpkin...') commenced[10], quite sporadic and disinterestedly from Olive's side, but with growing frequency and feeling from Theo.

Now there was an elusive figure appearing and re-appearing in his thoughts and dreams. However, although Theo's eyes were beginning to light up whenever Olive came on the scene, she lived in Melbourne, working in an accountant's office. As the days passed, Theo found himself wondering if (hoping that?) Olive would be back in Gisborne for the weekend. Often she was, and for him, Gisborne was all the brighter for it.

The Kettle family stayed in Gisborne until eventually, because of heart problems, at the relatively early age of 55, Olive's father decided to retire with his wife, Susie, and family, to Melbourne.

There was no reason now for Olive to return to Gisborne. The town seemed greyer for their loss. Was it time for Theo to move on from Gisborne too? Where did the Lord want him to be?

At the same time, Theo began to read about men and women who had left their home countries to tell people in another country about the love of God. When he found a little book, 'Lotus Buds', about missionary work in India, Theo sent a copy to Olive to read, as a gift from the Sunday School at Gisborne[11].

He also read many articles in the CIM magazine, *China's Millions*. One book that made a special impact on him was the life-story of Hudson Taylor, the founder of the China Inland Mission. In 1926, while Theo was reading this book, he wrote to his sister Mary,

> I don't think I have ever read such a book – what times of heart-searching I have had as I have read. I have felt that I am not worthy nor fit to be a missionary – how little is my faith, how little I have ever really suffered for Jesus[12].

Another year was to pass until Theo had fulfilled his three-years teaching bond with the Victorian Education Department. It was then Theo sensed

---

10 For example, Olive's letter to Theo dated 3 August, 1927.

11 See Olive's letter to Theo, dated 3 August, 1927, acknowledging the gift of the book.

12 From Theo's letter to his sister Mary, dated 20 June 1926.

God leading him to move on, this time to the Melbourne Bible Institute (MBI) for a year's concentrated Bible study to equip him for service. But the Kettle family still featured in his thoughts and prayers, especially one member of the family.

He applied to study the Bible at MBI during 1928, supporting himself by teaching half-time at Northcote High School. The Melbourne Bible Institute had been established only eight years earlier to train missionaries to serve with the China Inland Mission (CIM) in China.

While at MBI, Theo heard many missionaries speaking about service in China and other countries. In fact, from 1900 to 1920, around 12% of active workers in the CIM in China at any one time were from Australia and New Zealand[13]. Australian CIMers were congregated in five provinces along the Western borders of China as the dedicated 'Australian provinces'.

Theo at MBI
(Photo: WT Simpkin collection)

As the year went on, the conviction strengthened that God was calling him to leave home and kindred to go to China, to share the Good News with the people there. Although civil war in China during 1927 forced the evacuation of many missionaries from China, still the call went out for more to join their ranks.

In 1928, Theo applied to join the CIM to serve with them in China. Very soon he received the news that his application had been accepted. God willing, he would be leaving Australia shortly, to travel to a land he had never visited and had only read of, and whose language was totally foreign.

---

13 Welch, I 2014, *Mary Reed of Australia and the China Inland Mission*, Australian National University, viewed 2 November, 2018, openresearch-repository.anu.edu.au/bitstream/1885/13040/1/Welch%20Mary%20Reed%202014.pdf.

Olive hears about missions

While this was happening for Theo, Olive was participating actively in the fellowship of her local Methodist church in Thornbury. She joined the Christian Endeavour group as well as the Young Women's Missionary Movement (YWMM)—an organisation of the Methodist Church established to encourage the interest and support of young women for the church's foreign missions—where she heard about her own church's concern for people in the Pacific islands who did not know about Jesus.

Olive heard about Theo's belief that God wanted him to go to China to share the Good News of forgiveness with the 'heathen' in that land. She learnt that he had resigned his teaching position in Gisborne to study at the Melbourne Bible Institute.

However, he applied, not to his own Methodist Church's overseas missions department, but to an inter-denominational missionary organisation, the China Inland Mission. He was accepted for service and was about to sail to China. It must have all seemed a bit strange to Olive, in whose family no-one had ever done anything so out of the ordinary.

Or had they?

Chapter 3

MOVING OUT INTO THE UNKNOWN BY SAILING SHIP

More about pioneers and Olive's ancestors
(for those interested in such things)

If Olive had known more about her great grandparents, she would have known that they had done something just as adventurous as Theo's endeavour. Perhaps there was a streak of the adventurer and pioneer in *her* blood too.

1833 From Scotland to Tasmania

A century earlier, in 1833, Olive's paternal great grandmother, Marion Robertson, at the age of twelve, had accompanied her parents and siblings from Scotland to Australia. Marion had embarked on a sailing ship. Her trip was to take six and a half months. Who knows what that 12-year-old lassie from Edinburgh made of her journey and re-location?

Marion's father had been a tailor and draper in Edinburgh[1]—so she had been used to wearing fashionable clothes, and having a relatively comfortable life, albeit in the bracing Scottish climate. Her father was a Justice of the Peace and a diligent churchgoer. He took his religion seriously. He

---

1   This chapter relies substantially on information in the book McGilchrist, Stevenson 1968, *William Robertson, Victorian Pioneer, 1837-1890*, Melbourne.

gathered his family night and morning to read the Scriptures and pray together, thus starting and ending each day with God.

Marion's maternal grandfather was a minister (appointed to the West Linton Presbyterian church near Edinburgh) and there would have been many long and earnest discussions between her father and her grandfather. Marion's family were dissenters and sensed opposition—both personal and economic—because of their views. Perhaps it was this that prompted them to respond to advertisements seeking settlers to go to the new colonies. Yet, how could they leave Scotland, the land of the heather, of the banks and braes, the land of their ancestors? But after Marion's younger sister Johana died in the chill Scottish weather, no doubt the thought of warmer climes became very attractive. Whatever the reason, they embarked in 1833 as steerage passengers on the sailing ship *Thomas*, from Leith, Edinburgh, bound for Sydney, Australia.

At first, it must have seemed quite an adventure to Marion, a girl brought up in a strict Scottish home. There were all sorts of people on board the ship, and she found she was rubbing shoulders with people she would never have met in her sheltered Edinburgh life.

When they reached Sydney, would they, perhaps, meet convicts who had been transported to Australia? Stories were told of how some convicts had escaped and become bushrangers, living from violence and robbery. As her family embarked on the journey, Marion's emotions probably included mixed fear and curiosity. Her father may well have reminded the family that, 'the Lord shall protect thy going out and thy coming in from this time forth, and even forevermore' (Psalm 121:8 GNT).

One day followed another on board ship, with monotonous regularity. Marion's father probably insisted on the family maintaining its habitual morning and evening devotions, but the time in between sometimes hung heavily on their hands. There was little in the way of housework to be done, and simple meals were soon prepared. The steerage passengers had been divided into groups of 6–12 people who elected one of their number to be responsible for the group's food allocation. Marion's father was presumably their leader, and her mother the cook.

Each day's washing was quickly done with the clothes hung out on make-shift lines on the deck, dancing like a flock of tethered seagulls in the breeze. One day there had been a sudden gale; huge waves had surged over the decks and the whole line of washing had been torn from the line and washed away in the ocean.

More often than not a drunken brawl between passengers brought Marion back to reality, together with her mother's frequent calls to keep an eye on her four younger sisters and brothers. The weather seemed almost as cold as anything she had endured in a northern winter, and she wondered, as they sailed around the Cape of Good Hope and continued across the Indian Ocean, what had happened to the sunny future she had been promised.

'Land ahoy!' The cry went up from the sailors and was soon taken up by the passengers. Many crowded onto the decks, and the adventurous ones even tried to climb up into the riggings for a better view. At first, the land was just a smudge on the horizon. As they drew closer, the ship turned into a wide estuary.

Marion's heart jumped with excitement. At last! The real adventure was about to begin! 'Is this Sydney?' she asked her father. 'No, this is Van Diemen's Land[2]. We will stay here a while until the passengers are taken ashore and other stores unloaded, and then we will continue north to Sydney.'

Looking down the Derwent Estuary towards the open ocean (2015)
(Photo: H Joynt)

---

2   This island came to be called Tasmania in 1856.

Marion looked with interest, as the ship sailed up the estuary, at the many small islands and inlets, the hills and valleys of this new land. The trees were quite different from those in Scotland, having a blue-grey tinge to them, and they covered the cliffs and slopes thickly. Here and there among the trees was a flash of golden blossoms. What could they be? Marion would get to know them as wattles, another lovely feature of this new land. Then Hobart came into view—scores of houses and buildings, some very fine ones, clustered together along the banks of the river.

Smaller boats began to approach the *Thomas*, with folk eager for any news of the Old Country, but Marion was oblivious, absorbed in the new sights and sounds. Then she heard her father calling her to help pack their belongings and gather the children. It was time to disembark.

All was bedlam as passengers with their belongings were herded in turn into the smaller boats to be put ashore. The unloading of passengers and stores continued for hours. Marion and her family finally found a place on a boat and were deposited unceremoniously on land at Hobart Town. It was 11 August, 1833, and they had arrived.

Marion's family did not proceed to Sydney as planned. Why was that? Perhaps it was the unexpectedly mild weather they encountered on their arrival in the new country that changed Marion's father's plans. Or perhaps it was simply a desire to settle down after so long at sea. Whatever the reason, instead of going on to Sydney, he decided to stay in Hobart, soon setting up a drapery and tailoring business there, ministering to the needs of the business community and new settlers.

This decision was cemented within a couple of weeks, when their ship, the *Thomas*, which had not yet sailed on, caught fire in the harbour. The captain made frantic efforts to save the ship, but without avail. There was a good quantity of spirits on board, as well as several casks of gunpowder which blew up accelerating the inferno. The furious flames towering above the ship's masts presented an awesome sight. It soon became clear that the only way to put out the blaze was to sink the ship. When they could get near enough to fasten towlines, boats towed the burning vessel out to Sandy Bay where it was scuttled. Although no lives were lost, a huge quantity of goods, still on board, was destroyed.

Indeed, God's guidance sometimes comes in the most unexpected ways. Although Olive knew little of her great grandmother's life, there were numerous other instances of God's protection and provision for them.

Marion's family in Tasmania

Marion's father soon became a prominent business man in Hobart. He was also an active member of the Independent Church in Hobart which fellow settler Henry Kettle also attended. Meanwhile, Marion was growing into young womanhood in a much more eclectic and varied society than she had left in Edinburgh. It was a society in which industry and innovation were required and often rewarded, and opportunities for those willing to grasp them abounded.

Marion was soon learning from her mother all that was involved in managing a home and family. When her older sister Elizabeth married an accountant in Hobart, Marion was expected to take on additional responsibilities in the family.

In the following three years, it is likely that she learnt from her father how to make her own clothes, and from her mother how to cure ham, make bread, preserve fruit, and even to teach her younger siblings until they were able to be enrolled in a local school.

Marion meets her match

As Marion grew out of childhood she began to be noticed by some of the young settlers. Within four years she was being courted by the handsome Henry Kettle, who was ten years older than she, and who had arrived in Hobart on 7 December, 1832, a year earlier than the Robertsons. He had commenced work in Hobart as a painter and glazier. Marion would certainly never have met him if they had stayed in Edinburgh.

At sixteen, she was considered completely grown-up, and was given her parents' permission to marry Henry on 3 October, 1837. Now she had her own home to run, and she did it with delight. Her mother was not far away if she ever got out of her depth.

Marion moves to the mainland

One settler whom the families frequently met, John Pascoe Fawkner, was a vocal member of Hobart society. He had sailed to Melbourne—the site on Port Phillip deemed a 'most eligible place for a settlement' by New South Wales Governor Philip Gidley King—on the recommendation of another settler, John Batman, and found, as Batman suggested, good pastoral land in the region.

The official foundation of Melbourne by Governor Richard Bourke took place on 19 May 1837, and Fawkner returned to Hobart with glowing tales of the opportunities to be grasped in and around Melbourne. Marion's father went back with him to Melbourne to see the settlement there, which Fawkner believed was going to be streets ahead of the Hobart settlement. After his visit, Marion's father decided to move to the mainland. And so, shortly after Marion's marriage in Hobart to Henry (October 1837), Marion's parents, the Robertsons, moved to Melbourne with their five other children.

The ship carried them up the Yarra River as far as it could, after which point Aboriginal men came wading through the mud to carry them and their possessions ashore. At this stage, Melbourne consisted of little beside a few rough brick buildings, tents and wattle and daub huts. Water was not easily accessible, needing to be carried up from the river, and few fresh vegetables were being grown. [3]

Soon after they arrived, summer was upon them with unendurable heat accompanied by hordes of biting mosquitoes. As yet, there were no sanitary laws and fever was rife throughout the settlement. With the same courage and determination they had shown in leaving Scotland, Mr and Mrs Robertson set about making a home. They purchased a block of land in Collins Street near Elizabeth Street, where William again established his tailoring and drapery business. The younger children he sent to school to Scotch College[4].

Henry and Marion followed Marion's parents to Melbourne early in 1838, and Henry began advertising his services as a painter and glazier.

Marion and Henry lived in what was then a quiet spot in Swanston Street, close to the Flinders Lane corner. It was here, on 14 July, 1838, just nine months after their wedding that seventeen-year old Marion gave birth to their first son, Henry—the second white child born in Melbourne. The government gave him a block of land to recognise the significance of his birth. He would go on to become Olive's grandfather.

While Henry and Marion were getting established in Melbourne, Marion's father, William, had been keen to take up a selection near Mount

---

3 Newspaper report quoted by McGilchrist, op. cit., p. 27, who notes many errors in the report.

4 This was not the school currently called Scotch College which did not open its doors until October 1851. It may have been the Scots Church School which was started in November 1838 using the temporary timber building called Scots Church which had been opened in July 1838.

The Wooling homestead (Picture from *The Illustrated London News*, Melbourne, 11 August 1888, Special Australasian supplement)

Macedon. Although Melbourne was an up and coming young settlement, he took no pleasure in the unhealthy and muddy conditions of the streets there, where it was often so slushy and sticky that anyone needing to pass along them had to be clad in long mud boots or leggings.

He was able to lay claim to a block of about 7,000 acres near the junction of the Barringo and Riddells Creeks at Macedon in 1839. This was almost half the size of the whole parish of Penicuik (18,880 acres) where he had been born! He decided to take possession and commenced the clearing of the property, building a first house, using the timber from his own property which he prepared in his own saw-pit.

Mr and Mrs Robertson moved from Melbourne to Macedon in 1840, and set about turning the house into a comfortable family home which they called 'Wooling' from the Aboriginal term for the area, 'Woolong', meaning 'the meeting of many waters'.

Family joys and woes

Meanwhile, Henry and Marion became staunch members of the Independent Church in Melbourne. Henry was on the welcoming committee for the first minister appointed to that church, the Reverend William Waterfield. In fact, it was Rev Waterfield who baptised Henry and Marion's fifteen-day-old son on 29 July, 1838. He was a frequent visitor to their home, as was John Fawkner, and he saw the little family grow through the addition of another son (James) and a daughter (named Marion, after her mother and grandmother).

But tragedy struck. Henry suffered a stroke and died in July 1842. He was just thirty years old. Marion, at 21, was left a widow with three small children, the eldest being four. How would she survive in this harsh but vibrant new land without a husband to protect and provide for her?

The next few weeks passed in a blur as she arranged for her husband's burial in what became known as the old Melbourne cemetery (now under the carpark of the Queen Victoria Market). As she entertained the many friends who called in to pay their respects, it was likely that she was operating as an automaton, while caring for the children. Her mind seesawed between numb grief and panicky turmoil. What was she to do?

Marion's mother had the best possible solution: 'Come to Wooling and stay with us! There is plenty of space. We can add another room or two on the house for you and the children, and you can help on the farm and around the house as you are able'. Marion's mother had an intensely kind and generous nature. She was often seen riding miles to help a woman in need, whether Aboriginal or white[5]. She would not be less generous to her own daughter. Many babies had their first bath at her hands, so she would gladly help care for her little grandchildren.

Moving out to the bush

So, Marion packed up her things and set out with the children on a bullock dray up the rough track to Macedon. How different this was from the high hopes with which she had left her parents' home in Hobart to marry Henry only five short years earlier. But—this was another chapter in her life, and another adventure.

For the children, the ride on the bullock dray would have been a special treat, and the fresh air and sunshine would put roses in all their cheeks. This time they would not be living in a town with its disease, noise, dangers and mud, but in 'the bush'. There would be lots of space for the children to run around and play in the fresh air, and plenty of good fresh food for them all.

Her father had already stocked his selection with sheep and cattle, and

---

5 Women's Centenary Council, *Centenary Gift Book,* F Fraser and N Palmer (eds.), 1934, Robertson & Mullens, quoted by McGilchrist, op. cit., p. 28.

in the two years since he moved there, his paddocks had produced abundant wheat and oats. The property, being near the junction of Barringo and Riddells Creeks, had a convenient water supply. He also built the first trout acclimatisation ponds in Victoria and imported trout and salmon roe to hatch there and release into the creeks for fishing.

William established a large orchard as well as a sizeable kitchen garden, so food was plentiful. But there was also work to be done by everyone, even the children, and he made sure they all pulled their weight. He had the reputation of driving people hard.

Marion's father had turned out to have a real talent for hard physical work. The block of land he purchased had a plentiful water supply, and the soil was productive. He managed his workers closely. He expected all those around him to work just as hard as he did.

Soon after re-locating to Macedon, William could see the great need for timber to build houses, make bridges, railway lines etc. in the new colony. On his property there was an abundant supply of good timber. He set up a sawmill at Wooling, the first to be established in the Macedon area, run by a large waterwheel. The sawmill provided employment for a considerable number of men, many of whom came to live on the property. Thus, Marion and the children would be joining a little community.

The dray rocked and creaked and groaned as the bullocks strained to pull the high-piled luggage and the little family gradually up and up into the Macedon foothills. Marion had been here occasionally since her parents had moved, and we can imagine that, seeing a remembered tree or outcrop of rocks along the way brought a curious lightening to her spirits. This was going to be 'home' now.

At last, rounding the last bend, Marion would call out to Henry, her four-year-old son: 'Look! There's the avenue of trees leading up to Granny and Grandpa's place, Henry! Can you see it? Behind the house is Mount Macedon—just like the mountains of Scotland where I was born. But first we must drive along this track through the swamp, then we go up the avenue to the house. Oh—and look who's heard us and is coming out to meet us! It's Granny!'

The sight of her mother running out to welcome them undoubtedly released Marion's emotions, and the tears rolled down her face, as the children bounced excitedly beside her.

Four-year-old Henry was soon running around the place, getting to know all the workmen, as well as their families. His brother and sister weren't far behind. It wouldn't take them long to learn the restrictions and the freedoms of living in the Australian bush at Grandpa Robertson's place. They would soon know the places to avoid where snakes might hide, and how to watch out for bull ants or the poisonous redback spiders; they learnt to run to the creek and get into the water in the event of a bushfire. But they also knew where Granny hid her biscuit barrel, and which tree in the orchard had the sweetest apples.

Moving out and moving back to Macedon

Life for Marion continued to have its ups and downs. A year after Henry's death she remarried in 1843. She was now Mrs George Stokes and moved away from 'Wooling' with her children to live at the Bush Inn (about twelve kilometres away), of which hostelry George was the proprietor. This area later became the township of Gisborne where Olive would, so many decades later, live with her parents and siblings.

Marion and George had four children, bringing their little tribe to seven. A school had just been opened in Gisborne, so the children were able to attend.

Then early in 1851, George died in a horse-riding accident, leaving Marion widowed for the second time, this time with seven children under 14 years of age. She had no option but to return again, with her seven small children, to live with her parents and brothers at Wooling.

There she stayed until her own death, seven years later, at the young age of thirty-seven years. And that is where her eldest son Henry Kettle, Olive's grandfather, named after his father, grew up.

Black Thursday, 6 February, 1851

By now young Henry was thirteen—considered almost grown up, and certainly old enough to pull his weight about the place. He had already earned a few pennies minding sheep on occasion for local farmers, since there were few fences. Soon after moving back to Wooling, Marion's brother gave Henry the responsibility of minding his sheep.

Mostly, Henry enjoyed the freedom of rambling over the hillsides with the sheep. It was good to be out in the open air, watching the birds, learning to find his way around the property, and getting to know the sheep in the flock. But he would never forget one dreadful day—6 February 1851—when he was out with the sheep.

This may have been how it happened.

The flock had ranged quite far from the home paddocks and Henry supposed they would need to turn back soon. The air was still, dry and oppressive. The sun blazed down implacably. There was a shimmer over the mountain. The sky was a hard almost steely cloudless blue. The sheep were listless, standing anywhere they could find shade, panting heavily in the heat. Henry stretched out under a tree. How long could they endure this heat? How he longed for the winter.

But what was that discoloration in the sky to the northwest? Were there clouds coming? A few minutes of watching made it clear that this was smoke. He jumped up, scanning the sky and the mountainsides. Fear rose up within him. Would he be trapped in a bushfire?

Within a few short minutes, he could see flames shooting up, and in no time it seemed the whole Macedon Range was ablaze.[6] His stomach bunched up, his mouth was dry and his heart thumped. Which direction were the flames travelling? Would they reach him? What was happening at Wooling? Where should he go?

I look to the mountains. Where will my help come from? My help will come from the Lord who made heaven and earth.

Psalm 121:1 GNT

Henry's mother and his grandparents would have often read this psalm to him.

'O Lord, save us! Save Mum! Save Granny and Grandpa and all the family!'

A hot dry wind swirled around him carrying dry charred leaves and glowing embers. It was followed by loud peals of rolling thunder, and then, the wind changed and huge drops of rain were falling around him.

---

6   The fact that Henry was minding sheep on the Macedon ranges on Black Thursday is mentioned in 'Mr. Henry Kettle, Melbourne's Eldest Son', *The Argus*, Melbourne, 17 November, 1922, p. 10.

> Thank God; the rain had come!
>
> He forgot about his sheep; he must get home to his family. He ran as fast as he could to reach Wooling, soaked and grimed by the falling ash. Everywhere he was met with blackened paddocks, smouldering tree stumps and scenes of devastation.
>
> He rounded the last bend, and miraculously, on that Black Thursday, the Wooling homestead was intact, though much of the run[7] was devastated. Granny and Grandpa and the family had taken to the creek, constantly throwing water over themselves to save themselves from the flames. God had heard and answered his prayers![8]

As Henry grew up, he commenced working on his grandfather's farm or at his sawmill at 'Wooling'. This remained an important industry in the community, and various other families also took up sawmilling. Timber was in plentiful supply and the demand was high as more and more new settlers arrived in the young country, all needing homes to be built.

Two families whose names occur frequently in connection with sawmilling in the Mt Macedon area were the Carnies and Pattersons who emigrated to Australia from Scotland in the 1850s and 1860s. One-year-old Ann Patterson arrived with her parents in 1852 and settled in the Macedon region. Not surprisingly, since both families were attending the Presbyterian church, Ann met Henry Kettle, and, at the age of eighteen, she married him at Cherokee.

Henry and Ann had a large family of ten children—six girls and four boys. Their second child (who was their first son) was called Henry. This Henry Kettle, of the third generation bearing that name in Australia, became Olive's father.

Olive's maternal grandparents, William and Ann Hollis

It wasn't just Olive's father's family who left their home country to go to another place, however. Her mother's family did too.

The story of her maternal grandfather, William Hollis, was heart-breaking. He emigrated in 1853 from Derbyshire in England with his parents

---

7   i.e. The whole farm property where sheep and cattle were run and crops grown.
8   The story of how the 'Wooling' homestead and all the stock survived the fire, as well as the whole family, is told in McGilchrist, op. cit., p. 30.

(William senior, and Ann Hollis) and his sister Ann who was three years older than WIlliam, just over a decade after Marion Robertson and Henry Kettle (the first).

With what high hopes they had boarded that barque in Liverpool. To eleven-year-old William, a fifteen-week voyage on a three-masted sailing ship would have seemed a dream beyond his wildest expectations. This was the family's opportunity to start a new life in a new world where all that was required was hard work, and they had never been afraid of that.

William and Ann were listed as Wesleyans. Devout Wesleyans believed that Christ died for all humanity—and thus everyone is entitled to God's grace. They believed that personal salvation always implies Christian mission and service to the world. The church's emphasis on Scriptural holiness they saw as entailing more than personal piety. Love of God must always be linked with love of neighbours, and a passion for justice and renewal in the life of the world, often manifested in political action[9]. It is likely that William and Ann had prayed long and fervently about this move and trusted that God was leading them out.

The ship they were booked to travel on, the *Derry Castle* was touted as the newest, safest, healthiest ship plying that route from England to Australia. It had a hull sheathed in yellow metal[10], and had a higher than usual ratio of deck space per passenger to reduce the incidence of disease. Yet, just four weeks into their voyage, William's mother succumbed to a chronic abscess and died, leaving William and his sister motherless and their father a widower.[11] Was God indeed leading them out? How could this fit into the divine purposes?

The ship was a government-chartered vessel of assisted migrants, mostly women. The majority of the four hundred or so on board were government migrants, most of them single women from Ireland. William and his family, being English, were in the minority on board.[12]

No doubt Mr Hollis' mind lurched between sombre numbness and an

---

9   The Wesleyan Church, 2018, Indiana USA, *Our Beliefs & Core Values*, viewed 2 November, 2018, www.wesleyan.org/about/our-beliefs.

10 David McDonald, Canberra, Australia, 2000, *The 'Derry Castle'*, viewed 2 November, 2018, www.angelfire.com/ns/bkeddy/HIES/derrycastle1.html.

11 Series: *VPRS 14*; Series Title: *Register of Assisted Immigrants from the United Kindom* (refer to microform copy, VPRS 3502)

12 Andrew Boyle, Preston West, Victoria, *Break o' Day Boyles*, 'Travel to Australia', viewed 2 November, 2018, breakodayboyles.net/Travel_to_Australia.html.

anguished turmoil of questioning as the weeks of the voyage slipped by after his wife's death. Would he emerge from this catastrophe with his faith in God undimmed? And what about his children, Ann and William? How could he be a mother and father to them?

> *The Lord is merciful! He is kind and patient, and his love never fails... Each day that we live, he provides for our needs and gives us the strength of a young eagle.*
>
> Psalm 103:5 CEV

The words of this Psalm would have been familiar to William. He would have heard it read frequently in worship services. Whatever the future held, it was in the hands of his loving and almighty God. So William and his children proceeded to the now greater challenge of migration to a new land without wife and mother.

Why does God allow such things to happen? He is sovereign. Surely, he could have prevented William's mother from succumbing to illness on the voyage—and yet she had died. Through it all, William's father's faith remained firm. It seems they learnt that God was still with them, still guiding them, even though they could not understand all that happened.

Eventually, in May 1853, the Derry Castle arrived in Victoria and the Hollises, together with the other passengers, disembarked. Their new life had begun.

Moving into Bacchus Marsh

Employment was readily available for William's father, and he worked both as a farmer and a carrier over the decades that followed. Then an opportunity came to purchase a flour mill in Bacchus Marsh (just thirty odd kilometres from Gisborne) with a friend, and soon the Hollis family was providing flour for the local community. This broadened into setting up an associated bakery with a second branch nearby in Ballan.

William's father was an active lay preacher in Gisborne and Kyneton, and 'was very quick to remonstrate with the congregation if he considered them to be irreverent or treating church worship lightly or carelessly'[13]. He was a gifted public speaker with strong views about the evils of alcohol.

All the while, young William was being brought up as a strict Wesleyan,

---

13 Smith, P, *Dwellers at the holly, The life and times of William Hollis (1841-1921)*, p. 11.

with their emphasis on personal spirituality, uprightness and holiness, and a concern for service to one's neighbours. Along with all Methodists at that time, his family took a leading role in the temperance movement, seeing alcoholism as at the root of many social ills. Eventually William followed in his father's footsteps as a dedicated and gifted lay preacher.

When his father re-married, eighteen-year-old William began seeking God's provision of a life-partner for himself. Through his service to the local Wesleyans he met Elleanor Jane Hilton, one of the first children to be born in the Crown Colony of Victoria (which was declared on 1 July 1851).

Elleanor was a member of the Kyneton Christian community, and as she grew into young womanhood, her daily fellowship with the Lord shone brightly in her face and her service to the community. William was attracted to such an obviously spiritual young woman and they were married on 28 December, 1870.

Like his father before him, William was a man of strictness and integrity. His children (they had nine) were left in no doubt about what their father believed. He—like many men of his generation—followed the dictum 'Spare the rod and spoil the child'. He believed a father should set clear boundaries for his children and insist on them. It was sometimes up to Elleanor to temper his discipline of the children. On occasion, she might interrupt a caning or whipping of the older boys, saying their punishment was sufficient. She provided a gentler, kinder element in their family life.[14]

William and Elleanor became well known in the community of Bacchus March. William was actively anti-smoking and anti-alcohol, being the first treasurer of the Bacchus March IOR (a teetotal Friendly Society), and often gave public lectures on the subjects, as well as on topics such as 'How we obtained our English Bible'.

Elleanor expressed her faith through practical Christianity and was strongly attracted to the Salvation Army which had just come into Bacchus Marsh. Eventually, she and William and their growing family joined the newly formed Bacchus March Salvation Army Corps, becoming members ('soldiers') in that group.[15]

One of William and Elleanor's children was a daughter, Susannah Hollis, usually known as Susie, born in 1878. At this time, the policeman stationed at Bacchus Marsh was Henry Kettle. Both Henry's and Susie's families were

14 Smith, op. cit., p. 18.
15 Smith, op. cit., pp. 21, 22.

staunch Methodists, but 'when the Salvation Army commenced operations in Bacchus Marsh in 1882, Susie's parents were attracted by the Army's emphasis on practical Christianity'[16] and joined the local Army corps. And there, in Bacchus Marsh, Henry and Susie met and ultimately became engaged. 'Henry and Susie were married in the Wesleyan church at Bacchus Marsh according to the rites of the Salvation Army.'[17]

Soon after, Henry was moved to the other end of Victoria, to become the Policeman at Buchan, and that is where Olive was born. So her great grandparents had travelled in sailing ships halfway round the world for a new life in a new country. Perhaps Theo's course of action wasn't so outlandish after all!

---

16 Smith, op. cit., p. 22.

17 Ancestry.com — Australian Marriage Index 1788-1950, Victoria 1899/8149.
    Smith, op. cit., pp. 22, 43.

Chapter 4

THEO – IN CHINA AT LAST

For Theo, packing in preparation to leave for China, the big question in his mind was—what about Olive? Could he tell her about his growing regard for her? But as he prayed, he believed the Lord was telling him to wait.

It was as though God was saying to him: 'Olive has not yet come to an understanding of her need to hand over control of her life to Me. She is happy to worship and serve at her church. But she has not yet learnt to look to Me to lead her personally in new ways. She would not last long in China if she comes simply to be with you. She needs to come because she knows I am calling her and am able to keep her.'

And so, very reluctantly, Theo held back from mentioning his feelings to Olive.

First impressions

In January 1929, aged just 25 years, he sailed for China, travelling via Borneo, Manila and Kowloon. He just preceded a CIM advance which, in March 1929, led by General Director DE Hoste, called for 200 new workers for China within a two year period.

On this voyage, Theo shared a cabin with two businessmen, neither of whom were believers. They had surprised him whilst praying on his knees several times, and he hoped this had been a 'silent witness' for his Lord.

On board ship Theo joined a Mr and Mrs Curtis, missionaries returning to China for their last term of service. Mr Curtis kindly offered to give some time on the voyage to teaching Theo some Chinese. Theo was glad to take advantage of this opportunity, writing to his sister, Mary, on 22 January 1929,

> *I have been getting along slowly with my study of Chinese.*
> *Now I have finished two lessons from the book. It is not easy but*
> *it's interesting.*

The ship called in at Sandakan[1] on the northeast coast of Borneo. Theo went ashore to explore, becoming appalled at a glimpse into a filthy, dimly lit room which he was told was an opium den. He had heard about the problems associated with the use of opium, and he would encounter it frequently in his missionary service in Yunnan. How his heart ached for people lost in a darkness he could feel.

On their way from Hong Kong to Shanghai, the ship called in at Formosa[2], where they had a three-day wait as cargo was unloaded. For the first time, Theo saw a Chinese temple with many worshipping the numerous gods—walking around to each idol, bowing the head and offering a stick of incense. He longed to share the love and peace of Jesus with each one, but without the language he was mute.

In Shanghai, Theo enjoyed meeting other members of the CIM at the headquarters, as they shared news and fellowship, committing their way to the Lord in prayer. Several days later he sailed on, with other new missionaries to the CIM language school for men in Anqing, in the northern province, Anhui. It was heartening to discover some Australian friends there—a couple of men who had been fellow-students with him at the Melbourne Bible Institute, Rowland Butler and Howard Kitchen. They had arrived in China some time before Theo and had already commenced language study.

Trials and challenges

New workers usually remained in the Training school for several months to get a good grounding in the Chinese language. However, Theo left after

---

1   See Theo's prayer letter dated 10 March, 1929.

2   Now known as Taiwan.

only one month. Presumably this was because his efforts on the voyage out from Australia under the tutelage of Mr Curtis had been so successful. He was a quick and diligent language learner.

His month of intensive language study in the Men's Training Home at Anqing was followed by years of painstaking language study, for which he, like every other CIM missionary, was expected to take personal responsibility. The CIM provided the structured language material for the missionaries and received and marked their language tests at the end of each section.

Theo was designated to work among the Chinese and tribes-people of the mountainous Yunnan Province. There he would continue his personal language study while contributing as he was able in outreach to the local Chinese.

To reach Yunnan, Theo travelled by boat to Haiphong (in French Indo-China[3]), on the coast, then by train from Haiphong to Kunming, the capital of the province of Yunnan. In the fourth-class carriages, there were many Chinese folk travelling to or from market with their purchases of goods, food, poultry and even pigs[4]. Missionaries could not afford the luxury of the first or second-class seats, but Theo probably found a seat in the third-class carriage.

At the end of the first day of the train journey, Theo, together with the other passengers alighted from the train to find accommodation for the night. On this, his first trip on that train, he had to stay in a Chinese inn. The inn itself was clean, but a Chinese 'theatrical show' was in progress outside, at full volume. Theo's ears rang with the enthusiasm of the production.

From Kunming, Theo walked to Wuding, over a hundred kilometres away, where he would be stationed at first. It is hard for people in the twenty-first century to appreciate how little infrastructure there was in China, especially outside the big cities, in the first half of the twentieth century. There was no public transport between Kunming and Wuding, and few vehicles on the very rough road. It took three long days of exhausting walking and climbing up, around, through and over the mountains.

Some Chinese men were hired to carry the luggage, and besides a few Chinese Christian helpers, there was an escort of two soldiers. Travelling

---

3 Now known as Vietnam.
4 See Theo's prayer letter dated 22 July 1929.

on these mountainous roads incurred danger from bandits and the author-ities did not want the notoriety of a foreigner being attacked in their region. Thus, it was quite a procession labouring up and down and over the mountains.

Each night they had to find accommodation in a Chinese inn. In one there had been numerous little bugs taking far too personal an interest in the travellers! At that stage in his China adventures, Theo had not yet become accustomed to the constant company of such creatures.

Another room they stayed in was festooned with opium poppy stalks and seed pods. Already he had come to hate the evils that followed the widespread addiction of the people of China to this drug, and he was ashamed of the role of the West in ensuring this addiction.

Settled in Wuding

In Wuding, Theo was placed with another young CIM worker, Jack Gra-ham, to learn how the CIM work was done in that area while continuing his language study. He wrote,

> In this city and whole district we are the only foreigners. We had an area of perhaps 3000 square miles in which to preach the gospel. For myself I have not enough language to take any part in the work beyond distributing tracts.[5]

As the days went by, he noted in his diary how many hours of language study he had been able to do each day or the characters he had learnt as he walked or rode from place to place. Very often, in the early days, he spent the whole day in language study, either with his Chinese teacher, or alone. At times the local man he had hired to teach him Chinese left, and he would have to try to find another teacher.

From time to time, Jack was called away to another place, leaving Theo on his own in Wuding. How long were those days and nights of loneliness for Theo as he was surrounded by people who could speak no English, who knew nothing of the love of a holy God, and who looked on him as a curious oddity.

In a letter dated 2 June, 1929 to the Melbourne Bible Institute commu-nity, Theo wrote:

---

5   See Theo's prayer letter dated 2 June, 1929.

My heart feels almost bursting at times to tell the story of God's love in Christ. There is one outlet for all pent-up feelings, and that is prayer.

Language study continued as he sought to progress through the CIM's required six language stages, but numerous distractions hindered his progress. Finding a suitable teacher was always a problem, and Theo discovered that he often needed to be his own cook (quickly discovering that meals take time, forethought and attention to prepare).

One of his first bachelor attempts at cooking happened like this. He had been alone at the mission station in Wuding when some surprise visitors arrived. A couple of older missionaries dropped in with their sons enroute to their villages.

Theo had no bread, so he tried his hand at making scones. My, they were hard! On 14 December, 1929 Theo wrote the following to his sister, Mary:

How do you make scones or cook them—so they are thoroughly baked yet not like bricks on the outside?

But the hungry travellers ate the lot.

Lifeline letters

Soon he moved from Wuding to Luquan (a commercial centre near to Wuding) where he endured further times of deep loneliness, for there he was the only Westerner and the only believer in a district of about 150,000 people. When so much of what was said and done around him was incomprehensible to Theo, how he longed for someone to share his concerns and feelings.

Of course, Theo had a band of prayer partners to whom he wrote regularly, asking for their prayer support and encouragement.[6] His sister Mary was the first of these, and he wrote to her most weeks.

Olive too became one of these prayer partners. At her church's Christian Endeavour group, the suggestion was made that for a future meeting, they should each write to a missionary and report back to the group. Theo was the only missionary Olive knew, so she wrote him a very formal letter.

---

6   CIM missionaries were encouraged to enlist the prayerful support of friends and relatives with whom they could share their daily needs and struggles. This group became a vital part of the missionary's spiritual support network, engaging in prayer on their behalf, while the missionary pursued the day-to-day program in China.

Thus began a correspondence that was hugely important to Theo in China. Every time he wrote to Olive, he noted it in his diary. Each time he received a reply—as well as when he did not—he noted it[7]. It was as though these letters were his lifeline, his reminder that the sun was still shining even when he was in the blackest of tunnels.

One day when Theo had called at the Post Office, looking in vain for a letter from Olive, he brought it all to the Lord. Could it be that there was someone else she was becoming attached to? How could he go on if she had chosen someone else?

He felt the Lord's answer challenged him to think about how little he had suffered or endured. Why should his Lord suffer and he be untouched?

---

7   For example, on 15 and 19 January, 30 March, 10 August, 17 November, 1930 and 27 January and 1 and 16 February, 1931 etc.

Luquan (Photo: WT Simpkin collection)

This was a little taste of what the Lord had undergone for him. He wrote this in his diary on 10 August, 1930:

> ...I cannot help but feel that if I'd been home [i.e. with Olive in Australia], our relations would have been far more cordial and intimate. But how I feel so unworthy of a pure woman's love.

So, he plodded on with his language study.

In Yunnan, Theo knew that much of the missionary endeavour was among people of the numerous minority groups (or tribes)[8] in that province. Each one had their own language which was quite distinct from Chinese, and in many cases prior to the advent of the missionaries, had never been written down. Many also spoke Chinese, but this was not their 'language of the heart', and it was hard to convey effectively to them in Chinese the message of a God who loved them personally.

So while continuing to study for each of the Mission's required six sections of Chinese language, Theo was also trying to pick up some Miao, Lisu, Nosu and Laka languages spoken by minority peoples in the CIM field in Wuding County where he was stationed.

These minority peoples were looked down on by the Han Chinese population including the government which provided little if anything in the way of educational opportunities for people in the minority villages. Yet they were so responsive. Theo was eager to take any opportunity that came his way to travel out to these minority villages. When would he be able to really share the old, old story with them?

---

8   Today China acknowledges the presence of 56 ethnic groups within the nation.

Chapter 5

SAFE ON THE MOUNTAINS

G asping, heart pounding, Theo managed a smile.
'Take delight in the Lord, and he will give you the desires of your heart.'

Psalm 37:4 NIV

The words sprang into his mind unannounced.

It was December, 1929. Theo had been in China less than twelve months, but was fast becoming acclimatised to the new sights, sounds, tastes and aromas.

When he had finished his time in the CIM language school in Anqing about eight months earlier, how he had hoped that God would send him to some mountainous area of China where there was little knowledge of the Gospel! He had been delighted to be designated to tribal work in Yunnan and praised God for keeping his promises.

And now here he was in the heart of those mountains, slogging it out as the sweat poured off him, to reach Aguomi, a Laka[1] village, his destination for the day. Perhaps he'd got a bit more than he'd bargained for!

---

1 The Laka are a sub-group of the Yi minority group in Yunnan.

Travelling in Yunnan (Photo: WT Simpkin collection)

Only a few days earlier, Theo's senior missionary[2] Tom Binks had asked Theo if he would like to go up to Aguomi as the church celebrates Harvest Festival and Christmas. Theo's face surely lit up at the invitation. He had been set apart for tribal (now known as 'minorities') work in Yunnan, but was still in the early stages of learning Chinese, and he longed to be fluent enough to share the good news about Jesus with the people he met each day.

At this point, Theo was back in Wuding, a largely Chinese city, from which he could journey out to various minority areas. This was his first invitation to embark on an extended journey into the mountains and the heart of the Yi minority group. He had set out early that morning enthusiastically, like a racehorse out of the starting gate. At last he was going to see first-hand (and perhaps help a little with) what God could, and, please God, would do among the Yi.

By now he was so used to travelling in China that it did not seem strange to be walking or riding a pony or mule over the rough mountain tracks, to reach their destination. His family in Lexton had owned horses for riding as well as for use in taking produce to market, or in his father's road

2 The CIM generally appointed new workers to a region where they would be under the supervision of a more experienced missionary. Mr Tom Binks was the more senior CIM missionary in the Wuding district.

A FOOT WIDE ON THE EDGE OF NOWHERE

construction business. But it had been a good number of years since Theo had ridden regularly. During his study in Maryborough and then Melbourne, and later when teaching, he had travelled by train or bus, or by what he called 'Shanks's pony'[3]! Having reached Yunnan, Theo had had to polish up his riding skills, and could now walk or ride a whole day without suffering too much the next day.

No longer did he remark on eating with chopsticks or sleeping on the earthen or rough wooden floors of the inns or houses where he spent the nights enroute (together with many unwanted little biting companions). It was commonplace to have to take all his luggage—including bedding—as he went. In fact, the men who carried their luggage became a regular part of their trips, together with their local guides[4].

Aguomi was a small Yi village of 40 or 50 families, perched on a relatively flat place on the mountainside. It is about a thousand feet from the top of the mountain, and two or three thousand feet from the river at its foot.

The village of Aguomi (Photo: WT Simpkin collection)

---

3 I.e. Walking.

4 The only way to travel through those mountains was on foot, on a mule or horseback. There would be few inns along the way. Travellers, instead, hoped to persuade a family, in each village they hoped to stop in, to let them hire a room for the night. In that room, they could cook their food, and sleep. All their food, cooking utensils, books, bedding and clothes, even the portable organ, had to be carried. So, hiring men to carry the luggage was essential.

Mountaineering in the dark[5]

To get to any of these Yi villages it was necessary to start by scrambling down one mountain side to the river and then clambering up just as high on the other side, only to begin the process all over again and again.

Theo described this in a letter to his prayer partners[6]:

> *The mountains in this part are terrific, no other word would do to describe them. Not that they are so high—they are no more than 8000 or 9000 feet at the most. But to get from one place to another there is a scramble of about 300 feet down to a river-bed, and then a strenuous climb up the other side.*

For a time the road would carry them in exhilaration along the ridge of a mountain range, yielding a glorious view of billow after billow of high ranges interspersed with these indescribable chasms. Theo often wondered if he would ever get up or down them, let alone lead a pony or mule!

So all day, Theo had been slipping and sliding down one hillside and labouring up the next—down and up, down and up—as the sun rose in the sky, and then sank lower and lower behind the mountains. Eventually the whole party was stumbling along in the dark, with only the aid of a hurricane lantern to enable them to see the person ahead and follow in his footsteps.

They were trudging along a narrow track on the edge of a steep mountain side. The lantern light illuminated the wall of rock on one side and the narrow track they were following. On the other side of the track was only a black and seemingly bottomless abyss.

Theo shivered as, now and again, his foot slipped, dislodging a stone which bounced over the edge. He listened for what seemed ages before he heard the clink as the stone bounced off the first rock many feet below. But at last the small lights and sounds of Aguomi came into view.

On the following morning, daylight enabled them to see where they had been. A tremendous valley lay almost directly below Aguomi. The tracks up and down these mountainsides were perhaps a yard wide at best, but often only about a foot wide, and steep! Below, there might be an almost vertical slope for hundreds of feet; above—an 'unscalable' mountainside.

---

5   This is described in Theo's prayer letter of January 1930, as well as a letter to his sister Mary, dated 13 January, 1930.

6   Theo's letter to prayer partners dated January 1930.

Sometimes the tracks became a kind of staircase cut in solid rock, or over and around rocks, yet the ponies and mules were sure-footed. And, step by exhausting step, they had reached Aguomi safely. The Lord had, indeed, kept them safe on the mountains[7].

Harvests of all kinds in the mountains

That year, 1929, the Harvest Thanksgiving Festival was held on 22 December[8]. It was always a highlight on the church calendar for the people of the isolated mountain villages. This festival was an opportunity for the believers to thank God for the provision of harvests again that year, and to show their gratitude by bringing their gifts (often a generous portion of their own farm's harvest). The gifts would be presented at the Harvest Thanksgiving worship service, to be used as the church leaders decided.

Scores of people travelled long distances from their villages to reach Aguomi, requiring an overnight stay there before returning home. Because of this, an essential part of the celebrations was a festival meal. Tickets were sold which entitled the holder to be present at the feast. The proceeds were used to buy the food for the feast which consisted of three kinds: a mixture of cooked rice and millet (sometimes only millet) which was the staple of the feast; several bowls of well-boiled fat pork soup; and a good supply of green leafy vegetables. Theo and Tom and their guides were all invited to the open-air feast, together with the hundred or so local people who had assembled for the harvest festival.

A vital part of the celebration would be the baptism of new believers—eleven that year—eight men and three women. Before they could be baptised, Mr Tom Binks (the senior missionary in Aguomi) was busy questioning them to ensure that they understood what baptism signified. Meantime Mrs Binks, an excellent singer, was teaching a big group of the people some Yi hymns. She would sing the tune of one line and the people would sing it after her, and so on to the end of the hymn.

Theo had not yet learnt the Yi language, nor the script in which it was written. This phonetic alphabetic script was invented years before by Sam

---

7 'He keeps me safe on the mountains.' (2 Samuel 22:34 *GNT*)

8 Because the different crops grown in the mountains are harvested at different times of the year, many areas will hold several Harvest Thanksgivings during a year. The one in Spring might give thanks for the wheat harvest, and the later one for the rice and maize harvest, for example.

Pollard, a Methodist CIM missionary. Once the phonetic alphabet had been learnt it was then quite easy for novices to read or say some words in Yi without any understanding of the meaning of the words.

This is quite different from Chinese characters which are neither alphabetic nor phonetic. There were, however, a few Chinese-speaking Christians from the Dai minority who wanted to learn some Chinese hymns, so Theo happily went off to teach them.

At last it was time for the main service and all assembled with excited anticipation for the two-hour long gathering. The little church was decorated with branches of trees, possibly camellias (the floral emblem of Yunnan), wintersweet and some early azaleas. The women came dressed in colourful ethnic costumes with blue, white and black headdresses ornamented with beautiful patterns of silver beads.

The believers gave liberally from their harvests. The gifts were administered by the church leaders, and were used to support those set apart by the churches to take the Gospel to nearby villages that had no Christian witness.

There was a great deal of singing, for these tribes-people loved music, and Theo accompanied the singing on the little pedal organ. Tom preached in Chinese and a local believer interpreted into Yi for him. The baptisms and Holy Communion completed this service of worship, praise and thanksgiving.

As Theo continued playing on the organ, many stayed to listen and delight in the music. This was long before the era of radio and recorded music. People made their own simple musical instruments, such as a bamboo flute, or a stringed instrument like the two-stringed erhu, but few had heard a keyboard instrument such as the little organ. This was a real treat.

Early the next morning, the leaders of the churches met together, with Theo and Tom as invited observers. The main discussion topic was how to take the Gospel to the twelve or so villages in the immediate vicinity of Aguomi. Already Theo had been approached by some Dai women who repeatedly urged him to go and visit their village and share the Gospel with their family and friends. As the discussion continued, a consensus was reached that the Aguomi church would take on this responsibility. They would accept the task of taking the Gospel to their nearest neighbours as their harvest thanksgiving.

We do not know precisely what happened next, or how it was that Theo and Tom decided to set out on an evangelistic visit to some villages at the end of the festival meetings. Was it the urgent invitations of the Dai women that sowed the seed in their minds? Or were they so encouraged by the eagerness of the local church members to share what they knew about Jesus, that Theo and Tom felt they too should set out? Had they also been challenged in the festival meetings?

Perhaps it happened like this.

'How can YOU help?' Had someone spoken to him? Startled, Theo looked around. No-one was near. Again the voice spoke into his mind, 'How can YOU help? These people are poor, uneducated, and know little about Me. You have had privileges of knowing the Scriptures from childhood, yourself experiencing the grace and forgiveness of the Lord. What can YOU do?'

Yes, this was exactly what he had come to China to do. Could the entreaties of the Dai women be God's call to him that day? Theo went out on the mountainside, seeking quietness in which to pray and listen for the Lord's answer to his questions. Then he found Tom, his senior missionary, and together they considered the matter. Did Theo have enough Chinese yet to be of help in this evangelistic task? Would there be an interpreter to go with them and translate into the local tribal language? Could they brave the tracks up and down these rugged mountains to reach the villages?

'It's what we came here to do Tom!'

'You're right there Theo! Let's ask the church leaders for their opinion.'

Whatever prompted the decision, we know that as the Harvest Festival gatherings wound up, a happy Theo and Tom found themselves, with the Aguomi church's blessing, preparing for a six-day round-trip evangelistic visit to some of the nearby Yi villages.

Theo recalled the trip, once again discussing the hardships of travel in the region, in a letter (dated January 1930) to his prayer partners.

> But the tracks! Well, as Tom said, they are 'fierce'. We sometimes had to ride or walk along tracks which often narrowed down to a few inches, on the side of a steep incline. The evangelist who accompanied

us had a mule and insisted on riding it.

Once we were riding on one of these tracks; above was an almost vertical wall, below—a steep slope with no foot-hold for hundreds of feet, and the track at its widest was only about a foot wide. Suddenly we came to a turn and had to try and get over a rock in the way—a veritable stumbling block. The old mule did stumble and slip a bit, so when we saw another such a little further, I took the opportunity of slipping off on the up-hill side—much to the amusement of those that saw it! But I preferred to trust my own feet.

With spirits high, he and Tom travelled on, down to the river, and then up over the next mountain. Three or four thousand feet below them they caught a glimpse of the mighty Yangtze river many miles away, snaking its silvery way through the valley. They toiled on and on, finally reaching their first destination late in the afternoon.

As honoured guests, they were invited into the room vacated for them—a very small room. All of its walls and ceiling were hung with the family's harvest, mainly maize cobs by the hundred, so that Theo and Tom could not stand upright. They spread their bedding on mats on the floor, and soon were inundated with visitors.

A maize crop in Yunnan, 2014 (Photo: S Joynt)

Preaching to all and sundry, like St Francis!

The first visitors were the local teenage boys and girls who asked to be taught new hymns. They were passionately fond of singing, these tribes-people, and quickly learnt hymns, and Theo's heart leapt at the request. After dark they held an evangelistic meeting at which Tom preached. The local church-appointed evangelist acted as interpreter for him.

That night about forty or fifty people heard for the first time of the Son of God who loved them enough to die for them. It was a radical idea—that the Creator of the universe did not require their sacrifices to be appeased, as the local gods and evil spirits did. Instead, he knew each of his creatures intimately, and loved them. What a startling message!

Waking early the next morning, and eager to get on with their trip, Theo and Tom set out for the next stop. Down, down, down they went, an almost precipitous drop from the cool mountain air, to the heat and humidity of Jia-Li, a little village on the Yangtze River. Yunnan is in a sub-tropical zone. Because so much of it is well above sea-level, it is sometimes thought of as having a temperate climate. At the bottom of the valleys however, where the altitude is low, it can be intensely hot and humid.

Here, as in some other villages, there had been a great mass movement, twenty years before, as people burnt their idols and turned to the Living God. A chapel and a school had been built. But there had been no missionaries and no local pastors to teach them, and their enthusiasm had faded. They had relapsed into their old pagan ways. How important it was for there to be trained local leaders to teach and pastor such new believers. The thought must have made an impression on Theo's mind: 'Is this how I could best contribute to the local church, training such leaders?'.

After being warmly welcomed, Theo and Tom started—as so often they did—by vaccinating many babies (probably against smallpox which devastated many villages in Yunnan). Smallpox and diphtheria were not very common in Australia, and community immunisation was not introduced there until 1932. However, when CIM missionaries travelled to China where smallpox and diphtheria were more common, they were expected to be vaccinated before leaving Australia. Once in China, where there was not yet any community program of immunisation in place, the missionaries were taught how to administer the vaccine to others. This was a relatively economical and simple way they could show practically the love of Christ to the villagers in these remote areas—by providing protection for their children against epidemics.

Some more tuneful sounds followed as many came asking to learn new hymns. At night a service was held and the good news about Jesus preached, Theo and Tom taking turns, with another service held the following morning, being Sunday.

At Jia-Li, the chapel had fallen into ruins, so the services were held in the courtyard of the house where Theo and Tom stayed. Most Yi houses had a similar courtyard. A doorway led in from the road; the yard itself served as a stable where goats, cattle, donkeys, pigs, dogs and fowl were kept. At all the services they had a very eclectic congregation, comprising about 50 people, 30 or 40 goats, dogs, and an old sow with a litter of piglets![9]

The courtyard had buildings on every side—some being two storeys high—and one of these was the room where they slept. Although it was 'midwinter' in Yunnan, the weather was probably as hot down beside the Yangtze as it would have been in Australia at the height of summer.

After breakfast, they set off eagerly for their third village, about two thousand feet higher. They had been told that this village was re-xin—spiritually 'warm-hearted', so they climbed with great anticipation, despite protesting muscles and aching joints. When the village was about a mile off, they forgot their weariness and aches as they were met by about fifty young people who had come out to escort them in. What a welcome!

They commenced the service in the room made available to them, but were driven out by a swarm of bees, one of which took an intense antipathy to Tom and stung him. They continued the service outside, under a large spreading tree, and even there another bee got up Tom's trouser leg while he was getting warmed up to his preaching, but he pressed on undaunted.

As usual, there were a dozen or more children to be vaccinated, and ten people to be baptised. Pastors came to these villages only infrequently. So, any who had previously shown their interest in the Gospel by registering as 'enquirers' and had proved the sincerity of their faith in the intervening months, were glad of the missionaries' visit to seek baptism, so their membership in the church could be finalised. Another result of this visit was that eleven more enrolled as 'enquirers'.

Later on, six or eight of the Christians offered to go for varying periods,

---

9 Mentioned in Theo's letter to his sister Mary, dated 13 January 1930.

from a week to a month, to preach in other non-Christian villages. Few of these tribes Christians would have been in positions of paid employment. Theirs was a subsistence economy, where the whole family helped as able on the small family farm, and the crops were used to feed the family, with any excess sold at market. Between these offers, and the offerings of grain (which could be sold or used to support the families and so, free up family members for itinerant evangelism), six months' labour was provided by these young Christians to get the gospel to their own unsaved people.

And singing! They just didn't want to stop. Right up until 11 pm or so, and again at daybreak, Theo and Tom were urged to teach them more songs. In the days long before the arrival of radio to this area, opportunities to learn new songs were limited. Even in Australia, radios did not become commonplace in most homes in the capital cities, until the 1940s. In China, it was not until after the Communist regime had been established that it began to be possible for people in remote areas of Yunnan to access radio. Every time these music-loving people heard a new song they wanted to pick it up.

However, after a meal—habitually of millet and pork, rice and pork, or occasionally peanuts, for a change—and a last hearty sing together, they were off to the fourth and then the fifth village. In each case there were babies to be vaccinated, hymns taught, the Gospel preached. Each time, the local believers met to discuss how they could share the good news about Jesus with their friends and neighbouring villages.

New Year's Eve and Chinese New Year Celebrations

Finally, just before sundown on the last day of the year, Theo and Tom were able to get away to a lonely place for a quiet talk and prayer together. How good it had been to be able to preach the Gospel; how heart-warming to teach the Yi people new songs of praise! Theo's heart glowed as he remembered the joy in the bright faces and their intense interest as they listened. Could he help to ensure there would be sufficient numbers of trained local leaders for these new believers?

New Year's Day was occupied by the return 'walk' to Aguomi. On the way they ate peanuts by the pound. This is the region where they are produced by the ton, and at every village they were given baskets full, usually roasted and ready to eat, and they filled their pockets with them.

On the last day they were about full up. Indeed, Tom tried pinning his pocket up to keep his hand out, as peanuts in large quantities had dire effects on their metabolism, but to no avail. The pockets had all been emptied before midday.

Again there was the long pull to the top, then the steep slope to the river, a mile or two along the river bed and then up, up, up. That last climb back up to Aguomi, after walking for about 22 miles was almost a killer, but, oh, it had been worth it! Their hearts sang as they gave thanks to God for giving them the privilege of being the bearers of good news to these people in Yunnan.

Chapter 6

LETTERS FROM CHINA

Theo longed that Olive would join him in this privileged ministry. Would that ever happen?

Initially, his prayers had been heavily motivated by his longing to be able to declare his love for her. As time went on, he knew that God was calling him to put his feelings to one side and seek the very best—God's purposes and blessing—for Olive.

Early on in their correspondence, Olive wrote only two or three times a year. As Theo replied, adding more details about his life and work, and asking for specific prayer, so her letters began to arrive more frequently.

Sometimes he would share about how God was teaching him to trust Him more, or about his need to put the Lord first in every area of his life. She would reply, sharing her own experience of trusting and obeying the Lord. How happy Theo was when he learnt that she had for many years been giving one tenth of all she had to the Lord's work[1]!

There was so much he did not know about Olive and her life of faith. On 8 September, 1931, Theo wrote in his diary:

> I have been praying three things for Olive now, for quite some time:-
> (i) That she may have yielded her life wholly to the Lord,

---

1   Theo's diary entry for 13 June, 1931.

(ii) That she may have entered into 'victory' and 'rest'.
(iii) That she may have had a <u>definite</u> <u>call</u> to China.
In her letter written June 1, there had been none of them. Several
times I have been inclined to feel anxious & impatient and have
had to just take them & leave them with the Lord, and I feel He will
answer them for His Great Name's Sake.

More new experiences for Theo

After their trip out to the villages, Tom remained in Aguomi where he and his wife were stationed, while Theo returned to Wuding. He was joined soon after by Tom Mulholland, a new CIM missionary from Northern Ireland who became Theo's very firm friend[2].

In order to be free to make good progress with their language study, they hired a cook. However, as Chinese New Year approached (late January 1930) the cook asked to be allowed to take a holiday. And that is how Theo and Tom Mulholland came to be eating their meals at a Chinese 'restaurant' on the main street of Wuding. Theo and Tom were soon invited to have their meals in the private dwelling at the rear. This gave Theo and Tom an intimate glimpse into local Chinese customs and worship. It made a marked impression on Theo. This is how he described it:

As one enters the door one sees on the door two hideous pictures
of men pasted. These are the 'door gods'. (Sometimes they are good
looking men—but as a rule they are fierce looking, and armed either
with big knives or sticks). These are to keep out the evil spirits! Every
night and every morning sticks of burning incense are placed in a
small cavity near these gods. On the wall directly facing one are
pasted a good many Chinese scrolls, the most important being the
'Tien dee' (heaven and earth) scroll. This is a red scroll inscribed to
the unknown powers of heaven and earth. Below this there is placed
a small table on which are placed three little lamps burning oil, and
three bowls for incense. Ever since New Year we have seen people
light these things, morning and evening before meals, and quite
regardless of our presence. It was a good witness for their religion.

---

2 Theo's letters and diaries did not always indicate clearly whether the 'Tom' he wrote about was Tom Binks, his senior missionary, or Tom Mulholland, his younger fellow-missionary. I have made my best judgment in each case on the basis of context.

We are glad to be able to offer thanks to our heavenly Father always before we take food: they were very impressed and at first surprised to see us. I always do so in Chinese that they may see our witness for our Lord.

The room has no chimney and there is no fireplace as we have them at home. There is an iron dish on which a fire is lighted—sometimes made of charcoal, but usually of wood. As a rule we had to wait a good while, for the food is not always ready when we arrive.

At New Year the old door gods are replaced by new ones; plenty of crackers are fired off to scare evil spirits away and to welcome the 'gods'; then incense is burned near the door. In a similar way the new rolls are put up, and the people bow and worship before them.

Food and money are offered to the gods and also to the spirits of departed relatives. The money is only make-believe money. This is burned in various places, and by some means becomes of value to the departed spirits on the other side, as well as heaping up merit for the one who does the service! On New Year's Eve we (Tom Mulholland and I) went down as usual to our host's place and sat down to wait. Out in the yard there was placed a table with the bowls of food on it. As we waited the man came in and lit the incense before the Tien dee scroll. Next he burned a handful of the paper money below it, then he and his wife in turn knelt before it about three times saying some prayer that we could not follow. A little later he went out to the table in the yard and burned more paper under it. He took up each bowl in turn, waved it as though in offering to some unseen being muttered a prayer and put it back on the table. Then he put it on a table in the room.

Perhaps you can imagine how we feel to see these dear, sincere people worshipping some unknown vanity. Other thoughts besides a great heart yearning too were coming to our minds, for Paul's warning to the Corinthians about eating food offered to idols came very forcibly to each of us. We felt constrained to rise and go home where we got a meal for ourselves as well as we could...

A day or so ago our host came round to see us, bringing with him a friend. They came right in without knocking so we had to entertain them. After a little talk we gave them some bowls of tea.

'Who are your venerable teachers?' 'Our venerable teachers are Mr Lo and Mr Cheng.' Then as usual with Chinese, the next question was 'How much do you pay them a month?' 'Oh, we give them a few tens of dollars a month' (noncommittal, you see). So they go on asking all sorts of questions as things come to their minds. Then they begin looking all around the rooms (you see they got into my private room—we try to keep all visitors to the guest room). Photos, Primus, some clothes and boot brushes are all inspected, as well as clothes and nearly everything else. At last they sit down again. Questions and flattery ended. Then it is my turn. I get a few tracts and ask 'Can you gentlemen read?' 'Oh, we know just a few characters' (very modest) so I give them a tract or two and try with my very poor vocabulary to tell them of God's love and the way of salvation through Christ. After a time they depart and we are free once more to go on with study.

Dear friends, as you read these lines, will you please pray for us that the Holy Spirit may fill our hearts and give us power in all such times? We are often out preaching on the streets, but one feels then that we cannot speak well enough to hold much interest. But when souls come right to us, for whatever reason, we have a better opportunity, and one can be sure they will follow what is being said. We know that it is the Spirit who quickeneth: please pray that our feeble halting words may be backed up by the power of God and that He will give us the joy of seeing the light of life streaming into these hearts.[3]

The believing faithful

Through all the challenges, Theo was encouraged by the faithful who clung to Christ as a beloved treasure in spite of persecution by those who did not share their faith. Many of these he mentioned in his regular prayer letters to friends and family at home, and Olive was one who was now hearing about his struggles and joys—and including them in her own prayers.

One young Christian girl Theo heard about had been married into a

---

3 Theo's prayer letter dated January 1930.

non-Christian home. Her mother-in-law died, and she was expected to take part in the customary practices at the funeral. For example, all the sons, daughters and daughters-in-law were to bow down and the coffin was to be carried over their backs—a pagan superstition. She refused, bravely standing out against all her relatives and guests. She was courageous for the sake of Christ.

Her relatives were enraged. They bound her up, tied her hands with ropes, hung big mud-bricks from her feet and plaits, and then hung her by her hands on a tree. Soon she lost consciousness. After an hour or so they let her down. Alarmed at her state, they took her to the CIM for treatment. Her hands were paralysed, and three weeks of treatment did little good. She had nowhere else to go and was sent home to her parents.[4]

Another Christian girl was married into a non-Christian home. They did not respect the Lord's Day, and continued their worship of devils. She was forced to work with them on the Lord's Day and could not go to worship. She came to the missionary and asked: 'Do you think the Lord Jesus would mind if I sang my hymns and prayed to Him, and then went out to work on His Day with the others?' Fitting in with family work practices was just another difficulty faced by new believers.

In another district several families turned to the Lord. They burnt all their idolatrous paraphernalia. They bought books and put up gospel posters in their homes. Then persecution began. The landlord came and with terrible threats forced them to tear down the scrolls. These and the books were all sent back to the missionary. The old landlord feared to go any further—but each believer was fined $20; two were thrown into prison; and the missionary also was accused at the Wuding Yamen (magistrate's court).[5]

It was not easy being a Christian in such an environment.

In flames and flood

In August every year, there was a festival in which each household burnt paper money, or, to be more exact, brown paper cut into the shape and size of paper money. This was supposed to deceive the gods and spirits into thinking the family was sacrificing money. This money was supposed to get to the next world as real money for the use of the ancestors. It was a way

---

4   This is recorded at the end of Theo's 1930 diary.

5   All of this is recorded at the end of Theo's 1930 diary.

Beseeching the gods to send rain
(Photos: WT Simpkin collection)

Throwing water
over the boys

of marking filial respect for ancestors—something supremely important in the Chinese culture.

Another ceremony Theo had seen at Luquan was the annual 'Seeking rain' festival, especially significant to those of the Dai tribal group. Much of Yunnan depends on the summer rains, and if they do not come, there will be famine for many. To try to prevent such famine, the south gates of the city were closed up for many days, and there was a proclamation to sweep the streets. A special dragon procession was held, and a group of young men were roped together with green boughs, while others threw water over them. Many homes pasted up signs outside their doors, promising grateful thanks to the Dragon King if he sent much rain this year. Today this has become largely an occasion for getting together and having fun with water, but for many in Theo's time, it was taken very seriously.

While many temples were in a bad state, there remained plenty around Wuding—like the big city temple Theo saw being repaired[6]. He sighed as he watched a young man making idols out of mud, and then making devils (also out of mud) to protect the 'gods'. How could he share the good news of an All-powerful God who needed no protection, and who loved them?

Dangers travelling in the Yunnan mountains

Theo was under no illusions about the dangers associated with his life in the mountains of south-western China—the condition of roads and tracks

6 Mentioned in an undated page of a letter from Theo, probably from 1930.

often devastated by storms and floods, the lurking presence of wolves[7], and the menace of robbers, were but a few of these. As Olive read Theo's letters telling of these hazards, she must have offered up many a quick prayer for his safety and the safety of the other missionaries.

Travel itself was hazardous over the steep mountains of Yunnan. When they set out on a preaching trip, they never knew what conditions the roads would be in. Often, Theo had rounded a mountainside to discover the expected footbridge across the gorge had been washed away in a recent (or not-so-recent) storm[8]. Without the bridge, he would need to scramble down the steep rocky hillside to the riverbed and then laboriously climb up the opposite side back to the path.

His heart still beat erratically each time he remembered an occasion on the way back to Luquan from Sapushan. He had felt impelled to dismount from the pony to pray and re-consecrate himself to the Lord for the work of Bible teaching. After Theo dismounted, the pony stumbled down a steep rock, fell on his neck and turned almost a complete somersault. Theo and the pony, amazingly, were safe.[9]

Robbers

Robbers[10] were a continual menace in a country with little in the way of social welfare and no expectation of full employment. Yunnan, with its mountains and valleys, provided many suitable places for thieves and brigands to hide and rendezvous. Following the successful revolution against the Qing dynasty early in the twentieth century, China had fallen under the control of many local warlords. In many cases, the local warlord's army consisted of local scoundrels, deserters from the Imperial army, or brigands. The city governors claimed to have the situation under control, which was not necessarily matched by reality. (One would lose face by openly admitting that one was not powerful enough to keep one's residents safe.) Scores of robbers were known to hide out in the mountains between Kunming and Wuding.

At first, Theo thought that it was a bit unnecessary to have an armed

---

7   Mentioned in Theo's letter to his sister, Mary, dated 2 July, 1929.

8   See diary entry for 8 May, 1930.

9   See diary entry for 18 July, 1930.

10 Robbers were often mentioned in Theo's letters, such as his letter to his sister, Mary, dated 25 July, 1929.

escort, as advised by the governor as well as the consul. However, he took the Mission leaders' advice. Even the soldiers were often afraid of the robbers who had been known to attack and kill members of an armed escort.

Since then, Theo had heard many stories from fellow-missionaries in the more remote villages about the times they had had to flee from robbers, sometimes losing all their meagre possessions to the assailants. In this they were sharing the experience of the local people, including their servants, who were often grateful for escaping with their lives.

At one place where Theo was working (Makai), he had been obliged to rent a house outside the city walls. Several times robbers attacked and killed people outside the city, and the magistrate twice sent messages to Theo to instruct him to move inside the city. But Theo had been unable to find a house to rent inside and had to remain where he was.

Once when he was preaching in the Makai chapel, two men suddenly rushed past toward the Yamen (official's residence). His congregation got up to see what had happened. Five robbers with four guns had just attacked and robbed a silversmith, a few hundred yards away, outside the city. They did not dare come into the city on this occasion, and Theo was kept safe.

On one occasion when Theo was travelling to Yuanmou with CIM money to rent a house there, he wrote in his diary,

> *December 13 [1932] I am taking over $2000.00 of Mission money, but following Mr. Nicholls' advice I'm asking the Lord for an escort of angels, instead of the Magistrate for an escort of soldiers.*

And the following day's entry included:

> *We heard that several armed robbers had been operating on the road a few days before, but we arrived safely, praise the Lord.*

Two years later, Theo wrote the following in his prayer letter, dated 18 October, 1934:

> *On 2 August I left [Wuding] for [Taogu] to help Mr Mulholland in a Short Term Bible School. The journey is long and tiring and contains one or two long steep climbs, but as the weather was fine I managed to get in in two days, though the [carriers] did not arrive until the next morning. At the school we had a time of blessing in spite of the fact that a murder had preceded the gathering, and there was a good deal of lawlessness about.*

Friends, pray for [Taogu] and the work and missionaries there. Robber scares and threats of violence are frequent, and the nervous strain to missionaries there is often severe.

Lawlessness

Early in Theo's time at Luquan, he had been diligently studying the language when he heard a commotion out in the street. When he went out to investigate, he was told that some soldiers had been gambling. One had passed a fake note, and a fight broke out in which one man was killed.[11]

On another occasion, he heard about two American Seventh Day Adventist missionary ladies[12] who were murdered in their beds while their husbands were away, and their children in the house, though unharmed. It was chilling news. It was suggested that the perpetrators may have been recently dismissed servants.

Through all this, Theo was learning to trust the Lord and to prove the Lord's faithfulness to him.

Boys will be boys

Chinese schoolboys —like boys the world over—always had an eye to making mischief. Often they would pass the chapel laughing and joking about going in to 'listen to Jesus'. How Theo longed that they would!

Once at Luquan, a group of such mischief-makers discovered a novel way to disrupt Theo's meetings.

Since there was no electricity in Luquan, the lighting was provided by a kerosene pressure lamp. The boys arrived as the meeting was getting under way with pockets full of big beetles. The beetles were liberated at the door, and flew straight to the big white light of the lamp where the preacher was standing. It was difficult to hold the listeners' attention through this distraction.

Eventually, after several nights of this, Theo decided to move upstairs

---

11 See Theo's diary entry on 3 March 1930, and a subsequent letter to MBI dated 8 March 1930.

12 Theo's letter to his sister, Mary, dated 15 May, 1931.
This is also mentioned in an article in the *Burlington Daily Times* (Burlington, North Carolina) 17 March, 1931, Tue, Page 7.
Ancestry, *Newspapers: Miller and White slaying, 1931*, 'Two Women Missionaries are Murdered in China', clipped by Archives 806, n.d., viewed 2 November 2018, www.newspapers.com/clip/18444187/miller_and_white_slaying_1931/.

for the meeting, and the boys—lacking the courage of their convictions—did not follow him up, so their beetles failed of their objective and the boys gave up[13].

The lure of opium

One of the biggest problems Theo encountered everywhere in Yunnan was the widespread addiction of the people to smoking opium. Opium had been used medicinally in China from the seventh century, but it was the practice of mixing opium with tobacco for smoking, introduced in the seventeenth century, that caused problems.

During the eighteenth century various Chinese authorities endeavoured to prohibit the importing of opium. However, England's dependence on the opium trade for maintaining its powerful commercial position resulted in Britain fighting two wars along the China coast, forcing it to remain open to unrestricted opium imports. The continually increasing local demand for opium led to widespread local production, much of it in the rugged south-western province of Yunnan. Although the British parliament did pass a motion to end India's opium exports to China, the damage had been done. Huge numbers of Chinese people were addicted—both men and women—and the opium trade fell into the hands of local criminal groups.

Theo's letters told how widely he saw opium grown and used throughout the province. Laws had been passed against smoking opium, but with little effect.

Theo and his fellow-missionary, Jack Graham, had been invited[14] to a local Chinese wedding (being the only foreigners in the town, the invitation would be seen as paying honour to the foreigners as well as bringing VIPs to the occasion). At this wedding, the father of the bride invited Theo and Jack to join him smoking opium while they waited for the wedding feast. The opium was most noticeable, but what was more remarkable was that the man who had invited them was an important local government official, and a law had been passed some time ago against opium![15]

---

13 See Theo's prayer letter dated 18 June, 1932.

14 Mentioned in an undated fragment of a letter from Theo, probably from 1930.

15 Anderson, P 2007, *Spectrum: From Right to Left in the World of Ideas,* Verso, p. 378, writing about the 1930s in Yunnan, claims that 'Yunnan had the largest opium crop in China', and that the Governor of Yunnan at that time, General Lung Yun, was known to be 'a heavy opium-smoker'.

Frequently Theo would encounter people looking dazed and disoriented from smoking. When they invited him to join them, he would encourage them to try to break the habit. Sometimes they would ask for medicine to help them kick the habit, but seldom made any serious attempt to break the addiction.

Still, not all who were addicted to opium remained that way. The animistic religion of the Miao and Nosu tribal groups was peopled with a multitude of spirits, many of which were believed to be evil. The lives of these tribespeople were often governed by fear of the evil spirits, and the suffering they might cause if offended. The story of a God who loved them enough to die for them was a powerful message, and many turned to Christ away from their fear-motivated animism. As one sign of their change of heart, they gave up opium.

This led to its own problems since opium was a great source of revenue for local authorities (despite having been officially banned by law). If people grew it, they would be taxed for doing so. If they did not grow it, they were forced to pay a 'lazy tax'. In this context, the Christians raised the question at Bible School, 'What should our attitude be under persecution? Should we be patient, or may we become impatient and take the case to court?'[16]

Many times, Theo was called to try to help someone who had apparently overdosed on opium, either on purpose, or accidentally.

Opium taking was the most common choice for those wishing to commit suicide or draw attention to themselves, especially for young women, some as young as fourteen or fifteen. Theo had often been called out to try to help one or another such. In one month he was called out six times, three in one day.

All he could advise was to give the person something such as warm salty water as an emetic, to make them vomit. If they had not sought help early enough, Theo's best attempts were unavailing.

Seeking healing

In this, his first period of missionary service in China, Theo was often called on to try to provide first aid for real or imagined complaints to sick people, who sought his totally untrained help. These village communities

---

16 Since laws had been passed against opium, there was hope that, in a court of law, a magistrate might uphold the law and protect those refusing to grow opium.

had no trained doctors or nurses, and the local witch doctors lacked any medical knowledge or understanding of how diseases were contracted, and provided little help for the sick. At least Theo's comprehension of basic hygiene and his ability to provide medicines to alleviate fever and pain was better than nothing.

One of the first who came to him was a Chinese woman whose jaw was out of joint. With the aid of a 'doctor's book' (an important part of a new missionary's equipment in those days) and prayer, Theo managed to pop it back in. The same thing happened with another woman a couple of years later. (He was told it was quite a frequent occurrence for that woman, who often quarrelled with her husband.)

On another occasion, he happened to hear about a baby who had been drowned. He hurried out and spent twenty minutes trying to resuscitate the baby, but without success. The young mother's anguish moved him deeply. Chinese bystanders, noting his concern, remarked on how '...we Chinese folk didn't have pity on her'. To many of them, life was relatively cheap. What was another infant's death?

Then there was the postman who persuaded Theo to accompany him to help a sick relative. Theo found that the woman had a huge goitre on her neck—nearly the same size as her head. Clearly it was a case for expert surgery, not something an amateur could attempt, even with the aid of the 'Doctor's Book'. There was nothing Theo could do but advise them to take her to the hospital, several days' journey away. But hospitals in a big city were too foreign a concept to many of these largely uneducated rural people, who preferred to stay in their familiar environment.

An unlikely story was told about one young woman who was supposed to have got a leech in her throat while drinking at a stream. The locals explained that this leech was cunning and though, at times, it could be seen, it could never be caught. The treatment for the woman was to shave the hair off the crown of her head, smear some honey on the crown of her head and let her sit in the hot sun for a time. The leech would then certainly come out. Theo considered both the supposed complaint and the treatment unscientific, but the people concerned (who were believers) were quite serious and looked upon him as being very ignorant for doubting.

There were some missionaries with medical training, but in Yunnan they were few in number. One, Miss Daisy Kemp, was a nurse in high demand among both the local and the missionary community. Theo remembered one occasion when he was escorting Miss Kemp on the mountainous road to Taogu to nurse a fellow missionary who was very ill. On the second night of their trip, as they mingled with some village folk, they saw a group of children playing in the road.

Suddenly one child began to scream loudly. He had been playing with a razor when another boy bumped him. He fell and ripped his hand open. Miss Kemp immediately began to bathe and bind it up—while the mother stood by and cursed the child. She said, 'I've cursed you till you're deaf and still you are no better'. (Perhaps the mother felt that she would lose face in the presence of the foreigner for not caring for her son sufficiently and allowing this accident to occur.)[17]

On one such trip, Miss Kemp herself tripped over some rocks on the steep mountain track. She grabbed at trees and rocks, desperately trying to save herself. In the ensuing clamour, as the servants reached out to grasp her arms, her medical bag with all its instruments and medicines fell over the precipice, losing all the contents. She was left with only her knowledge and nursing skills to help her patients, but she was safe. How easily she could have been with her medical bag at the bottom of the cliff.[18]

As Theo's years of service in China passed, there were many times when he or one or other of his fellow missionaries succumbed to various illnesses.

On one occasion his close friend and fellow-worker, Tom Mulholland, become seriously ill while at Taogu[19], with no-one to care for him. Tom's senior missionary (Mr Metcalf) had travelled to Kunming with his son to have a broken arm set, so Tom was on his own. He was able to send a messenger over the mountains to tell Theo who left without delay to make the two-day journey to take care of him.

On the way up, Theo stopped for lunch at a poor Christian Miao family's house. While talking to the owner of the house, he noticed a movement in a bundle of rags at his feet. When he asked about it, the father pulled back the covering to show a poor baby covered from head to foot with small-pox pustules. The situation was too far gone for Theo to be able to supply help. There was nothing he could do but pray with the family and offer his comfort.

He continued to Taogu, finding Tom in the grip of a malarial intermittent

---

17 See Theo's prayer letter dated 27 August, 1932.

18 See Theo's letter to his sister, Mary, dated 27 April, 1934.

19 See Theo's letter, dated 20 June, 1933, to Mr. Stark.

fever. Theo was able to take charge of the cooking and general care for a couple of weeks until Tom was strong again.

When illness attacked the missionaries' children, the parents' faith was sorely taxed. Dysentery was something that laid many Chinese low, and missionary children were not immune.

Very early in Theo's time in Yunnan[20], Betty, the five-year old daughter of Mr and Mrs Nicholls from Australia, came down with dysentery several times. The family together with their fellow-missionaries prayed earnestly for the little lass. Would her parents need to take her to Kunming where antibiotics were available? But that journey would itself be fraught with danger. They had a very anxious few weeks before she was restored to health. Medical help was many arduous days' journey away for workers in the mountains of Yunnan.

All these concerns, and many others, Theo shared with Olive when he wrote, but how he wished he could share them in person!

---

20 See Theo's letter to his sister, Mary, dated 25 July, 1929.

Chapter 7

PRAYERS FROM THE HEART

Meanwhile, back in Australia...

Theo's prayer requests were made known not only to the Christian Endeavour group but also to the branch of the Young Women's Missionary Movement at the Thornbury church. Olive became a regular supporter of the church's overseas missionaries, hearing about lives being transformed through the Gospel in Pacific island nations such as Tonga, Samoa and Fiji. She was also able to contribute, from Theo's letters to her, by telling about the people of China who were hearing the Gospel for the first time.

As Olive's father's health failed, her mother began to depend on her more and more for support. Her older sister, Gertrude, was married and had two small children, one of whom was very sick, so she was unable to help her parents much. And Olive's younger sister and brother, Marjorie and Murray, were still at college and school, respectively. Olive's older brother, Howard, was away, studying in preparation to become a Methodist home missioner.

It was up to Olive to help keep the household running and deal with school requirements and paying the bills. Her position with the chartered accountant's office was secure, so she was also able to contribute a little financially. Much of the responsibility for the family, including baking for school lunches, and darning and mending for her siblings, fell on Olive.[1]

Throughout this stressful and emotional time Olive began to look forward to the sympathetic and caring letters she received from Theo. He knew her family well, and seemed to know just the best kind of encouragement to give Olive. He undoubtedly reminded her that she had the inexhaustible resources of the Almighty God to draw on and assured her of his daily prayers for her.

In return she would make intelligent comments on the dilemmas and problems he experienced as he commenced language study in China, and on his spiritual challenges when he moved out to live among the Chinese. As she shared his news with the YWMM group, the need for prayer and financial support for missionaries like Theo became obvious.

Olive hears God's call

The YWMM ran camps at Easter and during the summer, to share the challenge of taking the Gospel of Jesus to those who had not heard of him. Olive was enlisted as a leader. It was at one of these camps, that she was challenged to give the Lord Jesus full control over her life.

'But what difference will that make? I still have responsibilities to my family' she thought.

At first, her family situation meant that Olive did not give the matter very serious thought. There was no way she could go anywhere. Her mother needed her.[2] She was probably too old to try to start learning another language anyway[3]. But as the months passed, the sense grew stronger that God did not just ask for her weekends, or her occasional devotion, but her whole self, her whole future. Theo's letters contributed to this growing realisation.

In her own words, Olive said,

> After joining the YWMM I was led to see that I personally had a debt to pay to the heathen, and the growing conviction that God was calling me to the foreign field would not be stifled[4].

---

1   Olive later wrote about this time in a letter to Theo's older sister, Mary, dated 31 May, 1932.
2   Referred to in Theo's letter to his sister, Mary, dated 17 May, 1932.
3   Theo notes, in a letter to his sister, Mary, dated 11 November 1931, that Olive had written to him, suggesting that she might be too old to learn another language.
4   As written in Olive's application for service with the China Inland Mission, file held in the

There was something more that God was asking of her. He could, indeed *would*, provide for her and her family if he called her into his service.

As she began to share these concerns with Theo, he wrote back something like this: 'God must come first in all our decisions. Yes, it may be that any thought you may have to serve Him overseas will have to go. You need to learn to be willing to give up your heart's desires to the Lord. Trust the Lord with your future and your family. Believe that His way is best'.

Counting the cost

Some time later, Theo wrote again to Olive, recording the following in his diary on 31 May, 1931:

> *I was very much impelled to write about the necessity of counting the cost in coming to China as a missionary. So I wrote about it in detail. Though she is everything in the world to me, I would not for worlds have her come under any delusion as to what it may mean.*

> *Some months ago, I promised the Lord I would not write a 'love-letter' to her till he gave me the assurance that He had called her and is sending her out. Her last letter has given me assurance that He is dealing with her.*

> *'Delight thyself in the Lord and He shall give thee the desires of thy heart'. I do pray that I may be able to faithfully keep my side of this promise...*

> *One thing that has come home very forcibly to me is this:–That the Lord is willing to answer our prayers—but are we content with asking only little joys and blessings? So I have been led to ask the fullest blessing and clearest revelation of His will and grace and power to be given to Olive. Then if her coming is wholly of Him, our joy will be complete.*

Little did Olive know how much it cost Theo to write that letter to her—and how her reply made his heart beat faster. For she wrote telling Theo that she had been having great heart searching before the Lord. She felt there was a deeper blessing that she hadn't received and wanted to know what it was.[5]

Melbourne School of Theology library.

5   In a letter dated 11 July, 1931, Theo told his sister, Mary, about what Olive had written.

Perhaps, after all, his prayers for her were being answered. Sleep was a long time coming that night.

When Theo wrote to his sister, Mary, telling her about Olive's questionings, and asking her to write to Olive too, he added:

> ...she has been exercised about the 'call' to the Foreign Field. China has been much on her heart & mind. But _how_ to be _certain_ what is the Lord's will has been the thing that troubles her. Then she has felt that one must be willing to go _anywhere_ and do _anything_ that the Lord wants. I'm glad she has been having some "searchings of heart" and that there are difficulties, for only thus can her faith be exercised & strengthened. Her father is ill with heart trouble, not expected to live. Her eldest (married) sister is laid up with rheumatism. So you see she has a little trouble.

Olive's father's heart, weakened from years of stress, did not recover. Eventually, on 7 November, 1931, after months of anxiety and much pain, Mr Kettle passed into the presence of his Lord. Olive was left as the main provider for her family and support for her widowed mother.

By this time, Olive had become aware of Theo's deep regard for her—though no words had been spoken or written—and was aware of an answering affection for him growing in her own heart[6]. But what hope was there that anything could come of it? As she sat darning her brother's socks, or busied herself baking a batch of cakes for the family, she could see no way out. Perhaps this was the life that God had called her to—perhaps this was to be her service to the Lord. She imagined Theo telling her to trust the Lord and seek to do His will first, and then the way ahead would become clear. 'Lord, help me to know You, to love and obey You, to trust You to do what is best in my life.'

But what if the Lord was asking her to give up Theo? Would she be willing to remain at home while the one she was coming to love was so many thousands of miles away? To stay at home now would be by far the hardest thing required of her[7]. But the assurance of the Lord's goodness filled her heart, and she was able to rest in this knowledge and wait patiently for God's will to be made plain to her.

---

6 See Olive's letter to Mary dated 22 December, 1932.

7 In a letter dated 14 January 1932, Theo told his sister, Mary, that Olive had written this in a previous letter to him.

Some months later, Theo received a letter that set his heart singing again! Olive had been to the Keswick Convention at Upwey, and, at the big missionary meeting, she felt that the Lord was speaking directly to her. She had stood, with about forty other young people, to signify her willingness to serve the Lord overseas if the Lord willed it. [8]

She wrote, 'Now only to wait until He opens the way'. It was incredibly hard for Theo not to immediately put pen to paper with his proposal of marriage to Olive, but still he felt an insistent voice telling him the time was not yet. On 17 May, 1932, he wrote the following to his sister:

Bless the Lord for what he has done and is doing for her spiritually! Although her way is not yet clear, and although she has not the full assurance that the Lord wants her in China yet, she feels very deeply the need and does want to go for Him. However, she has still to support her mother. And as long as these two things remain (her need of full assurance, and the provision for her mother) I have refrained from telling her that I want her—lest that should make her hurry out before the Lord has planned.

Olive had to think about the next step. Where was it that God wanted her to go? Her interests now were strongly tied to China, having heard so much about that country from Theo. It now featured in her prayers regularly. Was this where she should go? Would her life become entwined more closely with Theo's? Yet he had said nothing specific in his letters to suggest that his feelings for her were leading on to marriage. And who could support her mother? Even so, finding and doing God's will was what had to be paramount.

So Olive made plans to go to speak with Mr Lack[9], the CIM Assistant Home Director for Australia, regarding the possibility of her proceeding to China. He was most discouraging. Perhaps he thought that she was too old to be able to learn the language successfully. Olive wrote to Theo, telling him about her conversation with Mr Lack. Still, Theo prayed on, as did Olive.

Although she had read the Bible regularly alone and with her family, Olive had done no serious Bible study. She knew she needed training if

---

8   See Theo's letter to his sister, Mary, dated 27 February, 1932.

9   Theo refers to this in his letter to his sister, Mary, dated 29 October, 1932, and in his diary entry for 30 December, 1932.

she were to be able to teach others. To begin with, she started attending evening classes at the Melbourne Bible Institute (MBI). She had heard enthusiastic accounts from Theo of his time in MBI under the leadership of Rev CH Nash. She too found these evening lectures most enjoyable.

Write that letter now!

In the meantime, she was unaware of the struggles Theo was undergoing regarding telling her of his feelings for her.

Many times, his spirits had been weighed down, wondering if his hopes would ever have a chance of being realised. One such time was when he had travelled to Kunming for a local conference of the CIM missionaries.

His heart glowed with the joy of being with others who shared his love for the Chinese people as well as his love of the Lord. It had been so stimulating to hear about God's blessing on the work in various places. How encouraging it was to be with people interested in his concerns about his work; how challenging to listen to the messages brought by the Mission leaders. Especially did he enjoy opportunities to sing the Lord's praises with others who also loved music.

Some of the younger missionaries at the conference were sharing their excitement and news of forthcoming weddings. As Theo listened to the conversations, he was weighed down with a pall of loneliness.

On 9 October, 1932, he wrote to his sister, Mary:

> Sometimes I felt a bit lonely & downcast. One day last week even. It was Thursday. The nicest of the young ladies – Miss Ament (she is really most sweet & attractive, & a fine spiritually minded girl) – told us all she had just accepted an engagement from a young man in North China (in the CIM of course).

> Then in the afternoon we went to a double German wedding. It was most solemn, reverent & beautiful, and indeed a most happy ceremony.

> After that I escorted Miss Wilson (Isa) out along the Wuting Road a bit to meet Tom [Mulholland, who later married Isa] who was bringing Miss Kemp back to the Capital.

> Somehow or other that night after all had separated I felt a bit lonely & how I _wished_ I could just have a talk with Olive for a while.

But don't misunderstand me; <u>really</u> I wouldn't have it otherwise under the circumstances. The Lord is doing such great things for her. In her last letter she was telling of visiting all the homes in the street, giving out tracts & invitations to the church service—an evangelistic meeting!! Well, Praise the Lord; at one time I thought that to be outside the realm of possibility. But while I waited He's brought it about.

Theo's diary contained many entries agonising over whether the time was right to write THE letter to Olive.

A year earlier, on 25 October, 1931, he had written in his diary:

Mr. Chang of Sichuan brought an elderly man to enrol as enquirer. Afterwards I felt I couldn't write to Olive: I felt I must spend the hours in prayer & meditation.

A year later, while at Taogu, this was his diary entry on 13 November:

The evening I spent mainly in prayer that I might know the Lord's will about Olive. In His goodness and mercy He led me to Prov. 16:7, and I felt once more that I couldn't write to tell her of my love unless <u>He</u> gave me rest from my enemies—the lusts, & passions, & evil desires, & sins that have so often saddened & defiled. As I prayed the conviction deepened that He would do this for me <u>now</u>, so I felt more restful about writing <u>the</u> letter to Olive.

At last, the following day he wrote his declaration of love and proposal of marriage to Olive, whom he had not seen for four years. It was 14 November, 1932, a date that would ever after be a red-letter-day for Theo. This is how he described it in his diary:

<u>The Day:</u> Was up fairly early, & spent much time in prayer about Olive & about <u>the</u> letter to be written to her.

I didn't go down to breakfast, but wrote the letter to Olive that I've longed to write these <u>four</u> years. Nearly every time I wrote in that time there has always been this great desire to tell her of my love, but only now have I felt that God's blessing would be upon it. Never before have I felt that it was His will to write, but this morning I was able to write with much joy & blessing in my own soul. How ashamed I feel of all my doubts & fears & anxieties of the past—now that God has so far opened the way that I could offer her my love. Blessed be His Holy Name for ever.

It must have been hard for Theo to wait in patience, knowing it would be over a month before he could expect to hear Olive's answer.

In the meantime, as Olive prayed, her conviction became firm, that it was indeed China to which she was being called. She wrote to tell Theo this.[10] Her letter to Theo, telling him this, crossed that very important letter he had just written to her, telling her of his great love for her and asking her to marry him. To Theo, Olive's conviction that God wanted her in China was a God-given confirmation that he had done the right thing in proposing to her.

And about the same time, Olive started making enquiries about enrolling to study at the Melbourne Bible Institute. She realised more than ever that she needed more Bible teaching than she would get in just the MBI night classes. So, Olive applied to the Melbourne Bible Institute to study and equip her to teach new believers.

The morning before she received THE letter from Theo in December, Olive had heard that her younger sister had failed in some of her university subjects and would need to repeat her year. Would that mean Olive would have to stay at home yet another year, providing for her family?

She prayed that if it were God's will for her to proceed to China now, the letter from Theo, that she had been ardently awaiting for months, would arrive *that very day*.

It did.

The postman brought it by a late mail delivery that day, 22 December, 1932, and Olive received it when she arrived home from work, taking this as God's confirmation that he wanted her to move forward to service in China. In her heart, she said 'Yes!' knowing that God's timing, as always was perfect. This precise timing of the letter convinced Olive that this relationship was God's plan for her and Theo, and that He would provide for her mother. [11]

Theo chuckled as he remembered his own certainty that her answer would be 'Yes'. So sure had he been, that on December 23, more than a month before he received her answer to his proposal (remember, letters

---

10 By November 1932, Olive had told Theo in a letter he referred to in his diary, that she felt 'that God does want me in China' (diary entry 25 November 1932).

11 This is recounted in Theo's letter to his sister, Mary, dated 12 February, 1933. We do not know how her mother was provided for, but it may have been through an aged or widow's pension and/or a police widow's pension.

took weeks, if not months, to reach their destination), he wrote to the CIM Director Mr Kitchen, to inform him that he and Olive were engaged. 'So that while she was on her knees thanking God for my love', thought Theo, 'I was writing to Dr Kitchen about it! Surely He is a God who works for them that wait for Him'.[12]

Back to school for Olive

In order to study at MBI, Olive would have to resign her position with the chartered accountant. The decision was made. She submitted her resignation at work and sent in her application. It was accepted and in 1933 she commenced study.

Olive had known that she got on well with her workmates, and that her boss trusted her. She was quite surprised at the warmth of his appreciation expressed in his letter of reluctant acceptance of her resignation.

Early the following year, while studying at MBI, she applied to join the China Inland Mission for service in China.[13]

Olive at MBI
(WT Simpkin collection)

---

12   Referred to in Theo's prayer letter dated 10 April, 1933.

13   See Olive's Application for service with the CIM, file held in the Melbourne School of Theology library.

ALAN J HUTCHISON, F.C.A. (Aust)   Telephone number F1994
CHARTERED ACCOUNTANT (AUST)
STOCK EXCHANGE BUILDING
426 LITTLE COLLINS STREET
Melbourne, C1

25 February 1933

Miss Olive Kettle,
'Sherwood,'
41 Williams Road,
Windsor, S1.

Dear Miss Kettle,

Many thanks for your letter advising me, as promised, of your address and telephone number; should the occasion arise I certainly shall seek your assistance.

I am glad to know that the time you spent in my office was a happy experience for you. As far as I am concerned I can assure you that our long association (nearly 14 years) was a very pleasant one, and I sincerely regret your departure. I may also say that several clients, who have called, have expressed sorrow when they heard you had left the office.

When quite a young girl, you came as stenographer and typiste, and proved yourself immediately very efficient; however, being a neat and quick writer, and apparently having a natural aptitude for figures it was not long before you were of very material assistance in the accountancy work of the office; for years past I have considered you capable of taking complete charge of any set of books.

During the whole period, not only have you proved capable and absolutely trustworthy, but always you have taken a keen and intelligent interest in everything you were asked to undertake. In fact, I can unhesitatingly say that in all my experience I have not found your equal.

Now that we have come to the parting of the ways I thank you for your good wishes, which I heartily reciprocate.

Mrs Hutchison was surprised, but delighted, to receive your telephone ring before you left the office. We admire you for the decision you have made, and realise that you have voluntarily accepted a life of sacred devotion to duty. At all times we shall be glad to hear of your welfare and happiness.

With all good wishes for the future,

Yours sincerely

Alan Hutchison.

Full speed ahead

Things moved quickly. Although the CIM Assistant Home Director for Australia, Mr Lack, had been very discouraging about the likelihood of Olive becoming proficient enough in Chinese, because of her age, yet she was accepted by the Australian Council of the Mission on 20 June 1933. Less than three months later, on 11 September 1933, just after her thirtieth birthday, she sailed for China with a small group of other new and returning missionaries from Australia and New Zealand. She was not only sailing to a new country, for a new life, but also to set up a new home and family.

The next step was confirmed in Shanghai where initial interviews with the CIM Directors took place.

From Shanghai they proceeded to the language centres (or 'Training Homes' as they were known): the women went to Yangzhou in Jiangsu province for some months intensive introduction to Chinese language and culture, as well as to the principles by which the CIM worked. The men went to Anqing in Anhui province for a similar program.

Meanwhile, Theo was over two thousand kilometres away in Yunnan. It would be another six months or so before Olive would see the young man to whom she had become engaged by post.

The Australasian party when they reached Shanghai.
Back row: Eric Norgate, Arthur Kennedy and Bob Ament.
Front row: Cath Galpin, Vera Young and Olive.

Olive welcomed to
Shanghai with flowers
(Photos: WT Simpkin collection)

Olive and Vera Young at Yanghzhou
(Photo: WT Simpkin collection)

At Yangzhou, the new female missionaries learnt how to wear Chinese dress and use chopsticks and how to interpret mannerisms and social customs. They began to be acclimatised to a very different climate and weather pattern. For the first time, Olive found herself in a city covered with a blanket of snow at Christmas time.

Strong bonds with her fellow-students were forged during those heavy months, as all struggled to hear and pronounce the different Chinese tones, so as not to inadvertently cause misunderstandings. Olive was delighted that one of the other new missionaries was Vera Young, a young lady she had got to know while at MBI. Now here they were together again in China, studying the Chinese language. They became very firm friends, and Olive was disappointed when Vera was designated to work in Sichuan, a province to the north of Yunnan. Olive showed good progress, passing her first section language exam. She was designated to work in Yunnan, and initially to be based at Wuding.

In later years, Olive would be able to look back and see how so many of her early life's experiences had been preparing her for the service that would follow. She could not have imagined, however, all the adventures that still lay ahead.

A FOOT WIDE ON THE EDGE OF NOWHERE

Chapter 8

LOVE IS IN THE AIR

Theo awoke early. It was May 1934. The sun was already well up in Wuding, and warm breezes ruffled his hair. He'd had no need of an alarm today. His heart was singing, and it beat a happy and steady rhythm as he washed and dressed. Today was THE day.[1]

Today he was to set out from Wuding to meet Olive at last. She had completed her preliminary study at the language school where she had been learning Chinese for the past few months, and Theo was to bring her back to Yunnan together with the other lady missionaries designated for work in this province. It had been good knowing she was in China—so much closer than Australia. But he had still not seen her for five and a half long years.

Soon, though, he would. Yes, today the sun was shining. Today it was not hard to trust in the love of a good and kind God. Today he would be able to sing with sincerity the hymn so popular in CIM circles:

> How good is the God we adore–
> our faithful, unchangeable friend,
> whose love is as great as his power,
> and knows neither measure nor end.[111]

---

1 The details of this day and the following journey to Haiphong and back are found in Theo's prayer letter dated 26 May 1934, and Theo and Olive's joint Prayer letter dated 29 May 1934.

There was a spring in Theo's step as he ran down the stairs for a quick breakfast. It seemed a waste of time to eat when his whole being shouted at him to hurry, hurry, hurry!

He ran into the yard to check that his pony was saddled ready for the ride down from Wuding to Kunming, the capital of the province of Yunnan, where he would catch the train to Haiphong to meet the boat carrying the new workers. They were travelling by boat from Shanghai to Hong Kong, and then from Hong Kong to Haiphong. Theo was to meet them there and they would proceed to Yunnan by train.

Theo's excitement was infectious, and his pony broke free and cantered out of the yard to fight with the neighbours' horses. Twice he had to chase it, catch it and bring it back. Only then, panting and breathless, could he get his luggage loaded up, and commence the long ride down the mountains to Kunming.

Once he arrived in Kunming, Theo spent a few days making sure that all the requisite documentation (including visas and travel passes for all the party, since they would be passing through French Indo-China) was in order, for the journey down to the coast at Haiphong and then back with the new missionaries. Soon he was on board the train, steaming out of the Kunming railway station and on its way along the narrow-gauge line southward through Yunnan, and then French Indo-China to Haiphong.

The train line climbed up a thousand feet from the Kunming plain, and then down over seven thousand feet through mountains, along precipitous gorges covered with luxuriant subtropical vegetation. On the higher levels, there were hillsides still covered with the wild azaleas and rhododendrons[3] whose vivid beauty had almost stopped his heart when he had first seen them. How he would enjoy showing them to Olive! He was sure she would be enthralled as he had been.

And tunnels... there were more than a hundred and fifty of them to go through, as well as numerous, frighteningly high bridges to traverse, leaping across seemingly bottomless gorges.

At times, the train line snaked along the edge of a deep gorge on its long journey from Kunming to Haiphong. The train seemed to be clinging precariously to the cliff edge, with a steep drop below the line to a river-bed, hundreds of feet below.

---

2   Hymn written by Joseph Hart 1759.

3   See Theo's report on the Tribal Workers' Conference at Salaowu in April, 1932.

At the end of the first day of the train journey, Theo, together with the other passengers alighted from the train to find accommodation for the night.

On the second day, the train followed the course of a small river for a hundred miles or so through some magnificent gorges. By evening, the train had descended about 6000 feet. They were leaving the gorges behind now, though the land was still hilly.

Are we there yet?

The train rattled on through the last long day of travel, now passing from the hills to a beautiful plain where scores of people were working, preparing rice fields. The rice harvest was a good few months away, but Theo's thoughts turned to the Lord's harvest. He had been praying the Lord of the harvest to send out labourers into this particular harvest field for years now—one particular 'labourer' in fact. And now she was already in China, and soon would be here with Theo.

At last the three-day train journey from Kunming to Haiphong was over. Theo's impatience was mounting. Olive's boat was due in the next day, so he began counting the hours until he would again see the woman he loved. They had both been tested in so many ways, but now, it seemed the Lord was giving them all they had asked for. He hurried down to the office of the shipping company to find out where and when the ship would dock. He was dismayed to be told his waiting was not over. The boat had been held up and would not arrive for several more days.[4]

It was hard for Theo not to give way to anger and impatience. Hadn't he waited patiently for five-and-a-half years? Why must he wait again? Immediately he felt rebuked for his impatience. Hadn't he been telling Olive to trust the Lord's timing? He used the extra time to check and re-check that all arrangements were secure for the party of new missionaries to travel up to Yunnan.

At last, it was the day the ship was to arrive in Haiphong. In a fever of impatience, Theo was down at the wharf early, watching the boat dock. It seemed to take forever, and his eager eyes continually scanned the crowded decks among the passengers for the figure he was sure he would recognise. Was that Olive? Yes, indeed, there she was, on the deck, leaning on the railing, searching the crowds of faces on the wharf below for the one

---

4   See Theo and Olive's prayer letter dated 29 May 1934.

Olive on the deck of the ship
(Photo: WT Simpkin collection)

she longed to see. Their eyes met. Theo's legs surely nearly gave way beneath him, as his heart turned over. Thank You, Lord!

There was still another delay to endure as they waited for the French police on board the ship to check Olive's passport.

At last, Theo was free to hurry up the gangway to where Olive was waiting for him on the deck. What words, what actions could they find to express the long years of hoping, waiting and praying? Theo suggested that they might find a little privacy in a cabin and Olive led the way. With the door shut behind her, she hesitated, diffidently moving across to adjust the curtains to ensure they would not be observed. Theo could wait no longer and took her in his arms. And after a long embrace, they fell to their knees to give thanks to the Lord whose mercy endures forever.[5]

The return journey to Kunming (in Yunnan) seemed so much quicker than the downward trip, and Theo found himself looking forward eagerly to the tunnels. Olive may have been a little shy when she first met Theo on the boat. After all, she had only known him on paper for the last five-and-a-half years. But now that the ice was broken, she made good use of all the tunnels![6] They had no knowledge of all that the future would hold, but those five-and-a-half years had given them confidence that God is indeed to be trusted.

---

5   Theo and Olive describe this day in their prayer letter dated 29 May, 1934, as well as in letters to Theo's sister, Mary, dated 14 and 30 September, 1934.

6   See the letters dated 29 May, 14 and 30 September, 1934.

Chapter 9

THE LONG WAIT WAS OVER

At last, Olive and Theo were in the same province of China, Yunnan, and in the same city, Kunming. But there were still about five months to go before they could set up a home together. Both Theo and Olive wanted to get at least one more language section passed before the Big Day. They realised there would be more distractions to interrupt their language study sessions after they were married, and the more language they could master early on, the better.

Also, there were so many arrangements and preparations to be made. Sadly, no family members would be able to be present at their wedding. International travel was still relatively uncommon in those days. Before air travel had become commonplace, going to China meant a three or four week journey each way by ship, and few people could afford either the time or the expense of such a trip—especially since they were, no doubt, already giving sacrificially to the CIM for the support of all its missionaries. However, Olive's mother would help by sending Olive's veil, stockings and gloves,[1] and all of the relatives would, no doubt, have posted wedding presents to Yunnan.

---

1   See Olive's letter to Theo's sister, Mary, dated 30 September, 1934. Probably Olive took her wedding dress with her to China when she went in 1933.

Olive and Theo in Kunming, about
five months before the wedding
(Photo: WT Simpkin collection)

Theo ready for rain
on the road to Luquan
(Photo: WT Simpkin collection)

Olive was to live at Wuding, a provincial town about three days' journey from the Yunnan provincial capital, Kunming, until the wedding when they would return together to Wuding to settle down. In the meantime, Theo would stay at Luquan (about an hour on horseback from Wuding) apart from frequent visits to Wuding 'for no reason at all'! Theo got to know the road from Luquan to Wuding very well over the next five months.

Travelling like the locals

All Olive's household goods, including their wedding presents from family and friends at home in Australia, had to be transported up the mountains from Kunming, being carried by Chinese hired men. There was no public transport to Wuding and the other mountain villages, and very few motor vehicles at all. The only way for luggage to get from Kunming to Wuding and the villages was by 'man-power'. There were always men seeking to be employed this way. This would be Olive's first experience of everyday

Chinese village life and travel, which would be so different from the ship and train trips she had experienced so far. She was looking forward to it eagerly.

She would be accompanied by the Binks family as well as by Theo. Mr Binks was Theo's senior missionary, and the Binks family were returning from Kunming via Wuding to the remote village of Aguomi where they lived and worked. They too had a lot of luggage to be carried up and over the mountains to their village.

They all needed to take their own beds and bedding, besides food and clothing for the trip up the mountain. The road from Kunming passed through Wuding, which was the last town of any size before the long climb up to Aguomi. Luquan was on the way from Kunming to Wuding, but Theo wanted to be sure that Olive arrived safely.

Much of Olive's luggage had to be re-packed into baskets so each weighed no more than about 40 lbs. One man would carry two of these baskets slung from a pole over his shoulders. Three of her big boxes were left as they were. Three men carried the biggest one between them, two men carried the second box, and the third one (a tin trunk) was carried all the way by one man on his back.

Men were also hired to carry the women and the children. Mrs Binks and Olive were each allocated a *huagan* (a Chinese style sedan chair). Two of the Binks children were carried in baskets on a man's back while the other two were in a kind of *huagan* chair made especially for children. Some Chinese families also travelled this way for long trips if they had no horse or mule. Mr Binks and Theo both had ponies. There were 31 carriers altogether and making all the arrangements seemed interminable, but eventually the procession started. The street in front of the CIM home in Kunming was only a little

Someone being carried in a *huagan*
(Photo: WT Simpkin collection)

narrow street about seven or eight feet wide and it was crowded with inter-ested onlookers to see them off.

The *huagans* are very comfortable things to sit in, but the motion as the men walked along was too like the rocking of a boat 'on the briny', and less than half an hour into the journey, Olive and her breakfast had parted company[2]. Theo soon caught up with her and suggested she ride the spare pony. And wasn't she glad of that little pony! Although it had been about 12 or 15 years since Olive had last been regularly on horseback, as a girl she had often ridden over the hills of Gisborne. Although the unaccustomed riding was a bit tiring, she thoroughly enjoyed it. However, she had to get back into the *huagan* now and then when the pony was not free.

Throughout the trip they were seldom all together at one time—it was impossible to keep everybody going at the same pace. Mrs. Binks had three men to carry her, but she had to walk quite a lot of the way, as they flatly refused to carry her over certain stretches of country. An armed escort of only two soldiers had been provided, indicating that the road was consid-ered quite safe at that time. The soldiers were exceptionally pleasant men and were continually running aside to pick flowers and give them to the children.[3]

It was a typical warm June day in Yunnan, a day in which sunshine and showers chased one another across the sky, with the promise of summer heat not far away. The occasional showers made the roads rather muddy and slippery. On they went all day, trudging and trotting up and slipping down the mountains—winding round others, and occasionally coming to a little village, where they were immediately surrounded by children and grown-ups, crowding round to see these strange-looking people with all their luggage. The Binks twins were usually the centre of not very welcome attraction. The locals had never seen foreign twins before!

They all stopped to eat their sandwiches (prepared for them before they left, by a fellow-missionary in Kunming) at one of these villages, sheltering in a little tea house when the rain came down. As the day began to cool, they arrived at another village, which they decided to make their stopping point for the night. Mrs Binks, the children and Olive waited out on the street while Mr. Binks and Theo went to look for a room, and again, while they waited, the twins were surrounded by children. Because foreigners

---

2   See Olive's letter to the Simpkin relatives, dated 16 June, 1934.

3   All the details of this trip are as described in Olive's letter of 16 June, 1934.

The first rest stop. Olive is holding the ponies, far right.
(Photo: WT Simpkin collection)

were so rarely seen in those parts of China, this curiosity was something the missionary parents had come to expect and accept. Not always, however, was this attention welcomed by the children.

Soon Theo came back, and they followed him through an open doorway, into a room with just an earthen floor and mud brick walls which were none too clean. In one corner of the room was a fireplace and the 'good woman' of the inn was busy getting the meal ready. On one side of this room was the pigsty containing three good-sized pigs. Next to the pig sty was the stairway up to their room—a loft where they would sleep for the night. It contained two Chinese beds—merely boards with straw matting on them. Underneath the beds was the inn's stock of chaff while at one end of the room was a stack of wood.

However, there was plenty of space, and they soon had their own mosquito nets hung up ready for the night, with their camp stretchers made up, each covered with a *pugai* (a thin portable mattress) and rugs. They made a meal of tomato soup, veal and eggs (all of which they had brought with them) and boiled a little kettle for tea on the primus. All these proceedings were watched by a constant stream of people on the stairs, peeping up to watch the foreigners. Eventually all was quiet, and except for a grunt or two now and then from the pigs immediately below, all slept well. And so, Olive experienced her first night in a Chinese inn.

To the gates of Wuding

They were astir early next morning—about 5 am and cooked porridge on the spirit stove. Mr Binks had rice and vegetables supplied by the inn, but the rest of the party stuck to their western-style porridge, and soon they were on their way again.

The day was hot and trying. Although there were not so many mountains to climb this day, at one stage their path wound round a very high mountain. On one side there was a gurgling stream while on the other the mountain rose sheer up above them.

They had a pleasant surprise as they walked through one village to see a foreign lady in front of a shop. She immediately came over to speak to them, and insisted that they come to her place for a rest and early lunch. She was Miss Cook of the Presbyterian Missionary Union mission in Fumin.

The cleanliness of that little home was a delight to Olive (and a reassurance that, as she set up home, she would be able to maintain a clean—while not luxurious—dwelling). Miss Cook and Miss Stokes, her fellow worker, were kindness itself. They did all they could to make the travellers comfortable and to speed them on their way.

Around five o'clock, they arrived at a place called Chae-peh. Mr Binks and Theo again went ahead to find an inn. This inn was much bigger, and was built in the traditional Chinese style around the four sides of a central courtyard. Their room comprised only four walls, a floor, a ceiling and two holes for windows, so carrying their own beds and bedding was essential. By morning Olive had experienced the unwelcome attention of some uninvited but ubiquitous little 'guests' that had decided to share the beds. Although she did not see them, she felt the effects of their bites, and both Theo and Mr Binks caught a bug in their beds.

The third day saw them up even earlier, before the heat of the day—ready to set out, after a quick breakfast, on the last stage of their journey. Theo had woken that day with a sore throat and headache, and had decided to take a turn in Olive's *huagan* while she rode the pony. There was a lot of rough climbing to be done this day, and no doubt the porters were very tired from carrying their heavy loads. At any rate they dropped the *huagan* passengers so often that the passengers got out, choosing to go on by foot instead.

Finally, they saw the gates of Wuding town where they ran smack into a pagan festival. The gates were closed for a ceremony 'beseeching the gods to send rain'. Theo had told Olive about this festival in letters, but this was the first time she had personally encountered it. It must have been a sobering reminder of the reason behind her presence in China that day. However, they found another way in to the town of Wuding, the place that would be Olive's 'home' for the next few years.

Hidden glories

In succeeding months there was a deep note of joy and thankfulness in Theo's letters home. How good the Lord was!

Just three months after the trip to Haiphong to bring Olive up to Yunnan, Theo went to Taogu to help Tom Mulholland run a Short Term Bible School there. One afternoon he went for a walk. This is how he described it:

One afternoon I went for a walk round the corner of a hill which overlooks a series of vast gorges and mountain ranges. How I wish I could show you that scene.

Looking towards the east one could see [Aguomi] perched on a shelf halfway up a mountainside on the further side of the gorges—26 miles away. Beyond there, range after range of hills rose up and all bathed in the rays of the setting sun. The shadow of the mountains behind [Taogu] filled the valley and a line of sunlight seemed to run just below the [Aguomi] chapel which was just visible in the distance as a white speck.

A rainstorm was passing across just then and the end of the rainbow seem to rest almost vertically on the chapel! What a glorious range of colours! And what a reminder of our Father's mercy and grace, and of His eternal promises which are ever being sounded out from those chapels...

At the close of the [Taogu] Bible school I went across to [Aguomi] to help with another school there. Here the numbers were less, and the work was a little harder as the students understood Chinese less. However we had an average attendance of about 12, and I feel sure that the effort was well worthwhile.

The trip back to [Wuding] was not very pleasant as I met with some heavy rain and plenty of mud. For the first day of the journey I had either misty rain or thick fog to travel through.

At one point we went along a mountain track overhanging a valley. One could hear a stream pouring over a waterfall, but could see nothing because of the veil of fog. The men stopped to rest before descending the slope, and I tried to peep beyond to the beauty of a scene that I knew must be there.

Suddenly, as by an unseen hand, the veil was drawn back and I saw, for an instant, the river rushing over some huge high rocks. The spray rising from the bottom looked like steam. The waterfall, a wooded background, and some lovely green rice fields and grassy slopes are all taken in in an instant—and then the curtain of mist was drawn as before.

Half an hour later I was standing up in a steady shower to eat a little lunch—there was no shelter to be had—and that experience has remained with me ever since as an illustration of the vision our Lord sometimes grants to us of himself and the glory just hidden from our view.[4]

Olive's new home in Wuding

Will and Elise Browning, another Australian missionary couple, had taken responsibility for the work in Wuding until Theo and Olive were able to take it on, and Olive lived with them until the wedding. After the wedding, she and Theo would lead the work in Wuding while the Brownings moved on to the new place to which they had been designated. Olive's room was the one that bachelor Theo had used when in Wuding, and, with alacrity, Olive set about to unpack and make it more homelike.

She kept the pictures which Theo had put on the walls, as well as a table and bookcase. Theo had made her a wardrobe, in front of which she hung a blue cretonne cover. There was a wooden table for a washstand, and she made a dressing table by pasting white paper inside three kerosene cases, blue paper outside, with a matching blue cretonne cover in front. Two blue mats helped to cover the board floor.

A window looked out over a neighbour's vegetable garden, and in the distance was a huge mountain. Under the window was Olive's tin trunk, covered with a rug and cushion and at each side of it, two chairs completed the picture of her 'blue room'.

---

4   From Theo's prayer letter dated 18 October, 1934.

One day, Olive went for a walk up the beautiful tree-covered mountain—Shishan (Lion Mountain)—behind Wuding, following the path to a temple with a number of huge idols around the walls. There were chicken feathers on the steps, and Olive learnt that it was likely that someone with sickness in the family had come to the temple to try to obtain help from the gods for their family member. Presently several men, women and boys arrived, bringing two chickens, bundles of wood, an axe and cooking pots. Very soon they had a fire going, and dispatched the chickens, sprinkling the blood and some of the feathers for the gods, and then sharing the feast of the cooked chicken. Olive's heart ached at the helplessness of these people who not only had no recourse to modern medicine, but who also did not know of the loving Saviour who cared for them enough to die for them. She wrote, in her long letter[5] to the family:

> You will pray for us won't you, as we try to tell them of a Saviour who loves and cares for them, and who died to save them, and even lives to intercede for them.

Olive soon began to discover what her work and home life would be like in a Chinese town. She was quickly back into the swing of language study, working her way through the language books prescribed by the Mission, as well as having regular one-on-one sessions with a Chinese language teacher. At Yangzhou, the language taught was a standard Chinese. Here in Yunnan, Olive was learning that the tones to be used were often quite different from the ones she had learnt. So there was a deal of un-learning as well as re-learning to be done.

She also attended the various meetings held by the Brownings each week in the local chapel—Sunday services, gospel meetings, prayer meetings and women's meetings.

Olive was particularly interested in the latter. Elise would tell some Bible stories, with the aid of picture rolls, on four successive Wednesdays. Then on the fifth, she would invite the women present to get up and re-tell the stories to each other. Olive hoped to be able to take a more active part eventually in these women's and children's meetings.

To give her more time for both language study and the work, they had servants to do some of the housework—something she found strange at first. But if she were to be able quickly to take an active part in the

---

5   Also from her letter dated 16 June, 1934.

ministry, she would have to become far more proficient in the language. Employing men and women to help them with household chores as well as the language was considered the best use of their very finite resources. It also gave the missionaries good opportunities to develop close friendships with these Chinese people who, in effect, became part of their family. Very often, it would be these who were among the first to register an interest in the Gospel.

Fresh fruit and vegetables were in good supply at local markets, and 'mutton' (goat, not sheep) was always available. Surprisingly to Olive, chicken was too expensive for general consumption. There was no fresh milk, but milk powder was readily available and could be made up as required. All butter was tinned and often developed a rather rancid taste. Theo had mentioned the possibility of buying a cow to give them fresh milk and butter regularly, and Olive looked forward to the task of supervising the milking, separating and churning the cream into butter.

They were able to make their own peanut butter since peanuts were grown everywhere in Yunnan. With the current availability of fruit, Olive decided to make some jam, as well as preserve some fruit. She soon discovered how careful she needed to be, since both the jam and preserves very quickly fermented if the sterilising and sealing process was not done properly in that warm humid climate. Despite all their best efforts, they had to throw out a lot of the fruit and jam that went fizzy—making the pantry smell like a brewery.

Since Olive was not impressed at the quality of the locally cured bacon, she wrote to her mother and to Theo's mother asking for any recipes they had for curing bacon[6]. She was prepared to try her hand at anything in this her new life.

As she studied and waited for this new life with Theo, Olive found her eyes straying often, with delight and thankfulness, to the ring she wore on the fourth finger of her left hand. Since Chinese people at that stage did not wear engagement rings, Theo had no way of purchasing one for Olive. Instead, he sent her the money to buy herself one in Melbourne! Of course, neither Theo nor Olive could afford a very expensive ring, but it's value had nothing to do with the size of the gem, nor the quality of the gold, and all to do with the depth of love and commitment it signified.

---

6   See Olive's letter dated 11 August, 1934, to her mother and Theo's Lexton relatives.

A Miao family and two young Miao ladies (Photos: WT Simpkin collection)

Ethnic minorities in Yunnan

The province of Yunnan is home to a great many ethnic minorities (known as 'tribes' by Theo and Olive). Indeed, in Wuding, almost half the population was from these minorities.

The wearing of wedding or engagement rings was not common in China, but among the Miao tribes-people, it was easy to distinguish single girls of a marriageable age from married women by their hairstyles. Single women wore their hair in two tapering 'cones' at the back or sides of their heads until they were married and had a child, when they changed to wearing a single 'cone' from above the forehead.

Beginning life together

All foreign marriages had to be performed officially at the British consulate in the provincial capital, Kunming, but Theo and Olive also wanted a Christian ceremony for the solemnising of their new relationship. That ceremony

Olive's bouquet featured
tuber roses

(Photo: WT Simpkin collection)

would be performed by Mr Will Allen, the oldest missionary in Yunnan, and would take place in Kunming, the capital of Yunnan. As for best man and bridesmaid— that would depend on who, of the missionaries they knew, would be able to be in the capital at that time. In the end, Arnold Snow (who was living in Kunming) was Theo's best man and his wife Betty was Olive's bridesmaid.

In the missionary community in Kunming, it was customary to invite as guests to each wedding practically all the other missionaries who happened to be in Kunming at the time. The British Consul usually attended as well. Because the CIM did not organise tennis parties or other social engagements as some other missions did, it was felt to be a duty to invite outside guests to CIM weddings, and, on occasion, to attend weddings of missionaries from other missions. This meant that the guests were a very multicultural group, including British, Americans, Germans, Chinese, and others too.

Theo and Olive knew there would be a larger group to cater for at their wedding than might have been expected for people so far from home. It would compensate, in a small way, for their own families' inability to attend. However, usually the 'wedding feast' was nothing elaborate—just sandwiches, cakes, buns and tea, served on the lawns, and on this occasion, it is likely that Olive's mother would have helped to pay for the food.

The honeymoon

They had hoped to spend their honeymoon in some rooms at one of the temples in the mountains above the Dianchi Lake, Kunming. A couple of years earlier, Theo had enjoyed an outing across this lake with a group of other missionaries, while he was temporarily in Kunming. They rowed across the lake where they had a picnic lunch. The more energetic ones then decided to climb the mountain, eventually reaching a large temple with huge idols, twenty or thirty feet high. They continued climbing until they reached the ancient Taihua Temple. There they discovered that this temple had rooms set apart for guests to rent.

In fact, two German missionaries, whose wedding they had attended a week or so before, were there on their honeymoon. Theo and his group surprised the newlyweds with a visit and were treated to a cup of coffee before they scrambled back down to re-join their own party. So perhaps it was this previous chance encounter that suggested the location for Theo's own honeymoon.

It is a beautiful and very peaceful place, built about 800 years ago in the Yuan dynasty, and is surrounded by many lovely flowering trees and shrubs. Outside the Temple is a 600-year-old ginkgo tree.

No letters have survived from their honeymoon, so we do not know where it took place. However, there is a possibility that this may have been where Theo and Olive commenced their married life.

The lovers' tree

Previously, while at Salaowu, Theo had passed what he called a 'lovers' tree'. Actually, they were two trees planted one at each side of a gateway and so trained that they had grown together, not merely intertwining but uniting so that it was difficult to distinguish to which trees the limbs belonged.

These 'trained trees' are still commonly seen in Yunnan.

When a husband and wife quarrelled, they would cut a bit of the bark or a chip from the tree, boil it and drink the water. This was

'Trained trees' growing together in a street in Dali, Yunnan, 2012
(Photo: R Joynt)

supposed to cure domestic troubles, and bring husband and wife into a happy and harmonious relationship.[7]

As they started their life together, Theo and Olive sought a different route. Theo did not want their marriage to be founded on secrecy and ignorance. He trusted Olive as he trusted no other person, and so, in shame he shared with her the many times he had failed his Lord. How many times, temptation had come, to harbour wrong thoughts, to speak out of anger or pride, to act impetuously, in ways that did nothing to glorify God!

He longed for some 'magic bullet' that would enable him to conquer personal evil in his own life[8]. Despite all his deepest longings and prayers, he knew he would never be free from temptation and sin until the day he met his Lord, face to face, in the new creation.

Together, Theo and Olive acknowledged their sinfulness, and promised, in their new life together, to encourage one another regularly to confess failures, repent and start again.

There were, no doubt, many things for Theo and Olive to see and do on this lovely mountain, to enjoy and to talk about in those treasured first days together.

---

7   See Theo's prayer letter dated 26 May, 1934.

8   Theo's diaries record numerous times when he 'fell into sin' (unspecified). E.g. 1 and 16 July, 17 Nov., 9 Dec., 1930.

A FOOT WIDE ON THE EDGE OF NOWHERE

Chapter 10

DANGER AT THE GATES

Fear almost immobilised him. Theo's heart was thumping so hard in the darkness he was afraid it would attract the attention of the Communist soldiers who were intent on destroying any resistance in the city. His stomach was bunched tight, his mouth dry and his hands sweating as he lay on the wet ground in the cool spring night. Overhead the stars shone down oblivious of the drama being played out below. The stones, twigs and grass stuck through his shirt, but he did not feel them. All his attention was focused on listening, and watching. Shots rang out unceasingly—but were they getting closer, or receding? What would the morning bring? Or would there even be a morning? Was he to be ushered into the heavenly kingdom by a Communist soldier's bullet without ever seeing or holding in his arms his firstborn child? Oh Lord, save us!

Only that day, in May 1935, just six months after their wedding, Theo had spoken to the Wuding magistrate who assured him that any rumour of the advance through Wuding by the Communist army was false. He had all the power necessary to keep Theo and the other missionaries safe, he vowed. He would take responsibility for protecting them. But to Theo, his words sounded hollow. Earlier that day another letter had come to them from the Mission leaders in the capital, Kunming, urging them to leave without delay. What were they to do?[1]

Over the past month rumours of the advance towards them of the Red army were rife. Theo took little interest in the details of the political situation in China except as it affected his ministry in Yunnan. In 1919 the Nationalist Party (Guomindang) was formed by Sun Yat-sen. The Communists worked within the Guomindang during the early and middle 1920's (1922–27).

After Sun Yat-sen's death, there was a leadership struggle and Chiang Kai-shek emerged as the leader. After consolidating his leadership he organised an expedition to defeat the many warlords who controlled areas of the north. When he moved to Shanghai the communist-dominated labour unions staged an uprising against the Guomindang, and from this point on the Guomindang commenced a purge of communists in their ranks. As part of this, Chiang Kai-Shek launched a huge attack against the communists in south-east China[2].

Within a year the Communists had lost half the area they had controlled, and sixty thousand of their troops had been killed. It was then the Communists decided to change tactics to a full-scale retreat to the north. This came to be called the Long March, and part of the army was now passing through Yunnan.[3]

Although retreating, the Communist groups were prepared to fight any opposition from the Nationalist soldiers they encountered. They also plundered the areas they passed through, taking food and anything else they needed.

The death of Betty and John Stam

Contributing to the general atmosphere of stress was some disquieting news they had received some months earlier. A tragedy had unfolded in another province of China, Anhui, just a short while after Theo and Olive's wedding in Kunming.

---

1 The details of this event were described in a long letter to MBI friends, dated 9 May 1935, and an article entitled 'Pursued...yet not forsaken'(possibly for *China's Millions*), dated August 1935, written by Theo.

2 Encyclopaedia Britannica, 2018, *Chiang Kai-Shek Chinese Statesman*, viewed 2 November 2018, www.britannica.com/biography/Chiang-Kai-shek.

3 See map on page 18 above.

A FOOT WIDE ON THE EDGE OF NOWHERE

The whole CIM family had been shaken to the core by the news of the martyrdom of a young couple of American CIM missionaries, John and Betty Stam[4], at the hands of some communist bandits. All Westerners, Americans especially, were viewed as 'enemies of the people', and the Nationalist soldiers had enough to do fighting for their own existence, besides trying to protect unwanted foreigners in inaccessible places throughout the land.

Rumours of possible attacks by communist bandits, or bandits who found the Communist movement a convenient one in which to hide, were rife. No-one could sort the fact from the fiction. Later one of the Mission's leaders wrote:

The stories were contradictory and confusing, the rumors wild and unconfirmable. No one knew the truth. In the end the authorities were caught off guard.[5]

The story of the Stams' brave service for the Lord, and their ultimate sacrifice, as well as the amazing rescue unharmed of their orphaned three-month old daughter, served to strengthen the commitment of the rest of the CIM family.

Olive and Theo had counted the cost of serving the Lord in China. They believed that they could give nothing less than their whole-hearted service to the One Who had freely given His life for them. But it did not do to dwell on it. For their own wellbeing, they needed to focus on the positives rather than the dangers in their situation. In addition, they did not wish to add to their families' anxieties by sharing too many details with them. They believed that they would be spared as long as it was the Lord's will for them to continue in China. However, the experience of the Stams coloured their reaction in their own situation now in Yunnan.

Evacuate to Kunming, but when?

Mr Graham, a senior CIM leader, had warned the Yunnan missionaries in early April, that they should be ready to evacuate to the capital, Kunming, where they would be safer. In fact, one of these Yunnan missionaries,

---

4   This story is told in Mrs Howard Taylor's book, *The Triumph of John and Betty Stam,* China Inland Mission, 1935.
     See also Dunn, G 1984, *The Martyrdom of John and Betty Stam,* first published in *East Asia's Millions,* November/December 1984, as 'For the Stams No Deliverance', OMF International, viewed 2 November 2018, omf.org/us/the-martyrdom-of-john-and-betty-stam/.

5   Dunn, G, loc. cit.

Mrs Browning, who with her husband was stationed at an outlying village, Salaowu, had been ordered by the British Consul to evacuate to Kunming immediately. It is not known why this happened. Had her family in Australia asked the Consul to intervene to ensure her safety, since she was expecting her first child soon? Whatever the reason, she was about to set out for Kunming escorted by the CIM nurse, Miss Kemp. At this stage, however, it was not decided that any other missionaries should join them.

However, just after Mrs Browning and Miss Kemp arrived in Wuding (Friday 26 April 1935) from their mountain village of Salaowu, enroute to Kunming, a special runner arrived from the Mission leaders in Kunming, ordering the missionaries to evacuate without delay. This was the only way messages could get through to the mountain villages—by a runner. Days could pass between sending and receiving the message, depending on how quickly the runner could go.

On the strength of that order, Theo and Olive agreed that Olive should accompany Mrs Browning and Miss Kemp on the three-day trip to Kunming. Since Wuding was the centre for CIM work in this county, Theo felt unable to leave while there were still other missionaries out in villages further away in the mountains. He would know whether or not the messages had got through to those furthest places.

Theo and Olive had not yet shared with the other missionaries their secret hopes and expectations that within the next six or seven months, their home would be blessed by the addition of a new little life.

As Theo and Olive farewelled each other, they wondered if they would ever see one another again. Had the Lord overcome so many obstacles to bring them together only for them to have the cup of happiness dashed away just after they had tasted it? And what of this new little life just fluttering into existence? Would they ever share the joy of parenthood together or hold their own child in their arms?

Theo believed he should not leave Wuding while there were still missionaries in the outlying villages of Sapushan, Salaowu, Aguomi and Taogu. So, while Olive set off on the three day journey to Kunming with Miss Kemp and Mrs Browning, Theo immediately sent a copy of the recent CIM order to each of the outlying mission stations.

It is hard for us in this day of instant messaging and mobile communication to appreciate the difficulties and dangers associated with living and working in such remote areas. There was no telephone. In many cases the only road was a narrow track or shelf cut into the rocky hillside. To get a message through entailed sending someone to walk, climb or run for several days, up and down over the mountains, carrying the message. Then they would wait for a reply to be written which would be taken back over the same mountains and gorges.

Four days later, on Tuesday, 30 April, Mr Binks had sent a message back from Aguomi to Theo, saying Mrs Binks was ill and could not be moved. The Porteouses in Salaowu suggested they might hide out in the hills nearby, where there were Christian families who could help them. On receiving the letter from Theo, the Mulhollands (Tom and Isa) and Arnold Snow left Taogu, arriving in Wuding on the 30 April. At the same time, Olive, Miss Kemp and the Brownings arrived safely in the capital, Kunming.

Later that evening back in Wuding, Theo was called to the Yamen by

Map showing relative positions of villages around Wuding

the magistrate who was seeking help for his son who was dying from the effects of opium compounded with excessive wine drinking. But Theo had been called too late, and the young man died. Theo took the opportunity to speak to the magistrate about his need to repent and believe the Gospel.

They discussed the Communist situation, and again the magistrate assured him there was no danger. He assured Theo there was no need for anyone to leave the next day, Wednesday, 1 May.

As Wednesday dawned, Theo received another letter from Kunming, telling them to leave at once. Theo hurried up to Sapushan to ask Mr Nicholls for advice about how to help Mrs Binks. When he arrived back in Wuding in the afternoon, he received a further letter from Mr Graham urging him to leave without delay.

As they were making preparations to leave at sunset, a messenger arrived telling them the Reds were near Luquan—only an hour away from Wuding. Theo called again on the magistrate who refused to believe the story and again promised his protection.

The missionary group in Wuding—Theo, the Mulhollands and Arnold Snow—gathered together to pray. What should they do? Should they leave now or wait until daylight? Should they trust the magistrate and the Nationalist soldiers in the town to protect them? Yet it was known that many Nationalist soldiers were afraid of the Communists. Would the Communists stay overnight at Luquan?

Under fire

Just then a shot rang out at the East Gate, and soon after, firing began in earnest. The decision had been made for them.

Hastily locking the front gates of their compound in the vain hope it might afford some protection for their property, they made their escape in the darkness through a small gate at the back of the property. The ponies were saddled but had to be left behind, together with Mrs Mulholland's *huagan* and all their other possessions. Arnold Snow had been intending to leave next morning for Aguomi taking money to bring Mrs Binks and the children in to Wuding, but it was out of the question to attempt to go now. By this time the firing was at its height, with bullets whistling overhead.

They made their way across a little wheat field inside the city towards the South Gate, creeping along the ground most of the way. Near the South Gate they heard the Communist sentry challenge someone else attempting to escape, so they knew that road also was blocked. Every road seemed blocked.

And so it was that they were lying as low as they could on the wet ground, praying for some sense of the Lord's presence and guiding hand. How could they find a way out?

As Theo prayed, the words of the Lord Jesus came vividly and forcibly into his mind—'Do not let your hearts be troubled. You believe in God; believe also in me' (John 14:1 NIV).

Had not the Lord led him through all the ups and downs of the past six years or so, bringing him into Yunnan to serve the Lord and the people of Yunnan? Had the Lord ever failed him? As he dwelt on the Lord's faithfulness his rioting heart quietened, and his mind cleared.

He saw the city wall looming up before them and suddenly knew that was the way they should take. He led the others up onto the top of the wide ancient city wall. (Some of these old city walls were several metres wide, and over the years dirt had gathered on them, and weeds grown up.) There they hid among some brambles for about half an hour. While there, they could hear what was being shouted below them. Apparently, the whole city had been overrun by the 'Reds', the Yamen taken, and, as they learnt afterwards, the magistrate and his family killed.

The 'Reds' carried torches, lanterns and Petromax[6] lamps, and were seeking out any who would oppose them.

Just then the two local soldiers guarding the South Gate left their post and fled along the top of the city wall, almost treading on the missionaries in their eagerness to escape. They jumped down a broken part of the wall and disappeared outside the city.

This is how Theo later (in a letter to the MBI community dated 9 May, 1935) described the rest of that evening.

> It now seemed that the Lord had opened a way of escape before our very eyes. So we followed, creeping and crawling all the time. We went about 200 yards to the motor road, which runs down from the South gate. Again, the way seemed blocked, as the Reds at the South gate and lower down the road were flashing torches up and down and stopping everyone.
>
> Praying that the Lord would close their eyes and that for the glory of

---

6 Pressurised kerosene or paraffin lamps, using an incandescent mantle.

the Lord Jesus, He would lead us out, we waited for an opportun-
ity to cross the motor road. As we waited someone tried to pass the
South gate and the 'Red' guards immediately stopped them, and
during the argument we hastily scuttled across the road in the
darkness, into the fields at the other side.

All night long we crawled and scrambled through fields and ditches
and brambles, but not along any road until we were about ten li
[about 5 kilometres] from the city. We did not dare follow any road
because the 'Reds' had pickets set to stop any refugees escaping...

By daybreak on Thursday, they had gone about ten kilometres. They made for some Miao villages in the mountains. By the afternoon, they had safely negotiated the mountains, reaching Daqing, a Miao village about 30 kilometres from Wuding, and well over 9000 feet in altitude. At last they were among Christians who cared for them, generously providing them with food and bedding.

The following day, Friday, 3 May, they were able to borrow a pony so Mrs Mulholland (who was in the early stage of her first pregnancy) could ride, while the menfolk walked. Two Miao Christians led them by small paths over still higher mountains to another village where they stayed the night.

They could not keep the pony for the journey on Saturday, so all had to walk to Fumin. This was largely a long descent from about 10,000 feet to about 5,000 feet. In Fumin, Theo and the other missionaries were very relieved to find Nationalist troops there, and to hear they had gone on to Wuding in pursuit of the Communists. The missionaries were accommodated overnight at the PMU Mission in Fumin, and Theo remembered with gratitude the kindness of the two women missionaries who had ministered to him and Olive when Olive first travelled up from Kunming to Wuding almost a year earlier. It seemed like another existence.

On finally reaching Kunming, what joy there was as Olive and Theo were re-united! How wonderfully the Lord had delivered them from danger and provided a way of escape!

Love letters

It was some time before the Chinese authorities or the British Consul would give permission for the missionaries to return to the villages, and as they expected, all their possessions (including all Olive and Theo's wedding presents etc.) were gone—looted by the Reds or the Nationalist soldiers, or any local opportunist.

Some time later, when visiting a poor home in Wuding, Theo discovered that some of their love letters had been used by the poor man to paper over the cracks in his flimsy bamboo walls, keeping the cold winds out and his home warm.

Theo and Olive smiled to think that those letters, written in the heat of passion, were now helping to retain some heat for this poor Chinese man.

Chapter 11

MORE TO LOVE... AND LOSE

Theo's heart was full now, as he rejoiced in the way God had worked in Olive's heart and circumstances, to bring her out to China and to share his life.

What a difference it made—not just having a much better cook, but also having someone to share his concerns and burden for the people they lived among, someone to pray with. It had taken some adjustment to get used to being one of a couple instead of a bachelor. In planning his day, Theo had two people to take into consideration now. However, because Olive too was in the habit of starting her day in prayer, Theo had been able to continue his practice of rising early for prayer and meditating on Scripture at the start of each day.

Being married also added new pressures. While he was alone, Theo's decisions about things like how to respond to rumours of robbers, or Communist soldiers in the area, affected only his own safety. Now he had a wife whose life he valued far above his own, as well as the prospect of their first child, for they were eagerly looking forward now to the expected birth in November or December 1935.

The birth of their firstborn

There was no hospital and no doctor nearby to help. To make matters worse, there had recently been a bad robber scare in Wuding. A small band of about twenty robbers had been driven by the Luquan soldiers into Wuding territory and forty Wuding soldiers were sent out after them. There were about a hundred soldiers stationed in the city—quite enough to guard it. A few of the robbers were caught and executed without delay, and later others were caught and their heads hung up to adorn Wuding's city gates.[1]

The missionary nurses were needed to attend Olive at the birth. So, Theo had no option but to leave Olive alone in Wuding while he travelled to Kunming to escort the missionary nurses back up to Wuding. In addition, there was a large consignment of stores[2] to bring back for the various missionary families in the mountains. A military escort had been supplied, to keep watch over all the loads being transported back up the mountain, but Theo could not entrust the care of the women missionaries to them.

'Can't we go a bit faster than this?' the nurses asked uneasily, as they plodded along the track. 'At this rate, any robbers could easily catch us!'

At one point on a lonely stretch of the road, they saw a couple of armed robbers. One of the Miao carriers threw down his bundle and ran for his life when he saw them. It turned out he needn't have, as for some reason, the robbers slunk off into the bushes as the missionaries passed by. Another carrier later picked up the bundle of bedding and proceeded with it safely.

Olive was glad to welcome them to the Wuding mission home. As far as she knew, the birth was not due for about three weeks, so she expected there was plenty of time for final preparations.

A few days later, after checking Olive's health, Nurse Kemp decided to go up to Sapushan for a few days of rest and language study before the birth. But her hopes of some respite were foiled, for Theo had to send a boy off to Sapushan at 3 pm, asking her to return quickly. The baby was on the way well ahead of schedule!

There were no complications, and at 10.50 pm on that day, 24 November

---

1 See Theo and Olive's letter to their mothers dated 27 November 1935.

2 Foodstuffs could be purchased in season in local markets, but anything beyond the most basic household equipment had to be purchased and transported up into the mountains from the provincial capital, Kunming. They ran the risk of being stolen by robbers on the way. In addition, whenever the missionaries travelled to the capital, or to the villages, they had to carry all their bedding and food with them, besides their own personal luggage.

1935, Theo and Olive welcomed the birth of their beautiful first-born. Wasn't his Daddy proud of his little 6½ lb son! He had what Theo used to call Olive's 'perpetually surprised expression', with arched eyebrows, and his Dad's nose and blue eyes. [3]

They named him 'David Martin': 'David' after King David who was described by God as 'a man after my own heart' (Acts 13:22 NIV), and 'Martin' after Theo's mother, Elizabeth Martin. Her birth in 1866 had not been so dissimilar from his son's birth, thought Theo—without any hospital or doctor attending, and far from her mother's homeland of England.

Olive with her firstborn son
(Photo: WT Simpkin)

Similarly there would have been few, if any, gifts at Elizabeth's birth. It would have been months before any relative knew about the birth, and her mother would have had to make all her own provision for the new baby, as Olive had to for David's birth.

The gifts Theo's little family received from local Chinese friends, on the birth of their son, would have seemed strange to friends in Australia.

Most of the villagers had never before seen a foreign baby, and were surprised to see him so fair and clean! All brought gifts; altogether they were given 160 eggs, three hens, rice, dried beans and sunflower seeds. All were gratefully received.[4]

Subsequently, there were often broken nights, making it harder for Theo and Olive to wake early for a quiet time (and even if they did wake early, it was likely that their prayer time would be interrupted by David's insistent crying for a nappy change and feed). Still, they wouldn't be without their wee son for all the tea in China.

---

3 See Theo and Olive's letter to their mothers dated 27 November, 1935.

4 See Olive's letter to her mother, dated 23 December, 1935.

More anxious times

Following the harrowing evacuation of Wuding in May 1935, Theo had not been sleeping well. At times he would wake with a start, thinking he had heard gunshots and shouting. There were memories that could make him break out in a cold sweat and start his heart racing. Then there were new rumours that Yunnan would once again be invaded by Communist soldiers, and difficult decisions had to be made as to whether it was safe to remain. On 16 March, 1936, Theo wrote to his sister, Mary,

> We are living a real pilgrim life here these days—waiting the order to quit if needs be. The Consul assures us we are in no danger from the 'Reds'—but to wait and see—so we hold on! If they can break through the line of soldiers they may bolt through these parts on their way to [Sichuan]. Otherwise we are quite alright. However we are praying earnestly that the Lord will not let them come again through our part. At Sapushan they (the Nichols) have hidden a lot of their valuables...in the ceiling and nailed the boards up again. We had a lot of things up in our ceiling but now have taken them down again.

Something more of the uncertainty about their situation, with the attendant difficulties of knowing how to proceed with their missionary work can be seen in this excerpt from Theo and Olive's prayer letter dated 18 June, 1936.

> Early in February, Theo had the privilege of going to [Taogu] to help in the short term Bible school, Olive and David stayed home with Miss Barberini for company. Over 40 students enrolled for Bible study before the end of the week, and times of blessing were expected. However, Theo was not permitted to stay. Rumours were many that the Reds were again going to invade Yunnan and that they were already quite near to [Wuding], so Theo felt it his duty to return home to [Wuding]. For a few weeks, then, all was quiet but later the Reds became active again, and our friends [i.e. other missionaries] from the tribes stations came in and went on to the capital. It was our privilege to entertain them on their way through.
>
> During a lull in the midst of all these rumours a few trips were taken to villages where there are Christians and happy times were spent preaching and teaching to the people. On one trip all four of us went

and stayed a night in a Chinese home. David was a great attraction and of course a source of wonder as many of the people had never seen a foreign baby before and were surprised to see him so fair and clean!!

In March the rumours about the Reds became alarming at times and the magistrate at [Luquan] ordered Albert Allen and Gilbert Moore to leave and go to the capital at once. However, the British Consul over the phone said that [Wuding] was quite safe and there was no need for us to move yet.

On Sunday, the 22nd, the nervous strain became so great that it was decided that all except Theo should leave next morning for [Kunming], together with the ladies and children from Sapushan. However, that night [Wuding] was in a panic, and some people said that the Reds were near at hand, and would attack the city before daylight; others were carrying loads of their possessions to hiding places of safety; one even came and told us that [Luquan] had already been captured and that the Reds might reach [Wuding] soon. He advised us to pick up a few things in our hands and spend the night on the mountainside. We were kept from doing this, and after prayer our hearts were kept in peace.

After hiding things in the ceiling and under the floor all of us left next morning for [Kunming]. This was David's first long trip and he enjoyed it very much, especially when Daddy took him for a short while each day on the front of the saddle with him.

Yet even there in the capital of the province, they were not free from rumour. At 11 pm that Good Friday night they and the other CIMers who had evacuated to Kunming were woken with the news that the Reds were right on the outskirts of the city, and they should prepare to leave.

Within ten minutes they were up and dressed, throwing a few articles (mainly for David) into a case and making their way with the others along the dark, deserted streets of Kunming to the railway station. They spent a rather hectic and anxious night mostly walking up and down the platform or sitting about waiting for the signal to board one of the trains waiting at the platform with steam up. David could not get to sleep until about 3 am, after Theo and Olive found him a quiet spot to lie down.

Theo and Olive with other missionaries
travelling to Kunming for safety
(Photo: WT Simpkin collection)

Theo with baby David on
horseback[5]
(Photo: WT Simpkin collection)

There were about two or three hundred foreigners on the station that night, waiting for the signal to board the train, and be evacuated. But as day dawned, they were allowed to return to their homes. The Red Armies had swerved north into Sichuan, avoiding confrontation in Yunnan.

The CIM missionaries who evacuated to Kunming about Easter time, 1936
(Photo: WT Simpkin collection)

---

5   Theo understood the immense value of pictures for conveying the story of their missionary work. He was a keen photographer, and learnt to develop and print his own photos. A camera would have been one of the first items he chose to purchase, probably in Kunming, after the loss of their possessions in May 1935. Some of the more useful ones he had made into large glass lantern slides for use in Australia with a 'magic lantern' projector, in deputation. These he coloured himself, by hand. This is one such photo.

Mr RA Bosshardt and Mr Arnolis Hayman

However, as the CIM family in Kunming gave thanks for their own safety, they continued to plead with God for the release of Mr Bosshardt, a fellow missionary who was believed to be at that time held by the Reds in Yunnan.

CIM missionaries Mr RA Bosshardt[6] of Switzerland and Mr Arnolis Hayman of New Zealand had been captured by Communist soldiers from their mission station in Guizhou province. When the huge ransom demanded by their captors for their release was refused (the CIM refused to put its other members at risk by acceding to ransom demands), the men were compelled to join the Sixth Army on its gruelling trek, the Long March. On one occasion they managed to escape but were betrayed by local farmers, and were retaken.

Although they were sentenced to death, the death sentence was never carried out. Who knows why? Perhaps it was because they had shared so many privations with the soldiers on this journey, and the soldiers were impressed by their bearing and honourable behaviour. Whatever the reason, the missionary family saw God's restraining hand in this, and rejoiced at their release.

Theo and Olive wrote in their prayer letter dated 18 June, 1936:

Mr Bosshardt as he was met near Kunming, April 1936.
(Photos: WT Simpkin collection)

6   Bosshardt, RA 1936, *The Restraining Hand: Captivity for Christ in China*, Hodder & Stoughton, London.
See also Moran, MG 2015, *Someone to be with Roxie*, Lulu, 2 pp. 69–77.

On Easter Saturday, as you probably know, Mr Bosshardt was released. And on Easter Monday we had the joy of welcoming him to the capital, and Theo took some photos.

Mr Bosshardt had walked 2500 long miles during his 18-month captivity.

That immediate danger was over, and the missionaries returned to their stations. For Olive, Theo and David, that meant returning to Wuding, but that scare passed only to give way to another.

Illness in the mountains of Yunnan

On his first birthday, David developed severe tonsillitis.

Theo and Olive had seen too many of the local and foreign children and adults succumb to illnesses such as this—illnesses which, in Australia, were seldom fatal. But antibiotics were almost unknown except in the biggest cities in China.

What could they do to save the life of their darling son?

If only they could get some sulphanilamide, but the nearest was three days' journey away, in Kunming. Theo called a loved and trusted servant, begging him to make the trip to bring back the precious medicine. Being a local Chinese man, he would be less at risk on the road than a Westerner. Besides which, he was very likely stronger and better able to run the distance. Theo bargained with the servant to pay him much more than the usual rate if he could get back in half the usual time.

The latter indeed earnt his extra reward, for he returned quickly with the life-saving medicine, and David's life was saved.

Other kinds of growth

There had been a number of Short-Term Bible Schools held in Salaowu and in other centres over the years. Theo had often been asked to go to teach the tribes-people who attended. But the feeling had been growing that a permanent Bible School should be set up for the leaders of the tribal churches. The outcome was a unanimous request, sent off immediately to Mr. Fraser, then Superintendent of this work in Yunnan, 'Please establish a Bible School at Salaowu without delay'. And so, about the middle of the year (1937) a hopeful beginning was made at Salaowu with about 30 students, and Theo and Olive went to help.

Theo's first encounters with those students had been eye-opening. How little they had known of the Lord! How meagre had been their understanding of the means by which their salvation had been purchased and how they should respond to Jesus' costly love! During the course of the Bible School, as their understanding and knowledge grew, there was a parallel growth in their awareness of their sinfulness.

After special services at which a fellow missionary, Dan Smith, spoke, many of the students were brought to their knees in deep sorrow over unconfessed sin. Some who had no definite experience of regeneration were truly born again, and a new spirit was evident in the classes. At the end-of-the-year service several made a full consecration of themselves to the Lord. How encouraging it had been to see the Holy Spirit at work in these uneducated mountain tribal people.

Yet, despite the thrill of being able to teach the Bible to these believers from the various minority groups, as Theo had long desired, the task was proving to be physically and mentally exhausting. Even teaching one class a day had become a burden almost more than he could cope with, to say nothing of the general oversight and management of the Bible School. In a letter to his sister, Mary, dated 27 October, 1937, Theo wrote the following:

> At the Bible School I find it rather a burden to take even one class of the day in addition to the general oversight and management. I don't really get headaches only a tired brain.

The Salaowu Tribes Bible School in 1937.
Theo is in the second row from the front, the third from the left, and two places to the right is Olive, holding David. (Photo: WT Simpkin collection)

His one sure recourse was to take it all to the Lord in prayer.

Theo couldn't help wondering what would become of all those keen students, were he and Olive to go on furlough.

One place where Theo could usually find some respite and relief was in his garden. Now that Wuding was his family's home base, Theo had dug both a vegetable garden and a flower garden. His letters home to his sister Mary would report on the vegetables currently setting fruit in his garden, such as tomatoes, French beans, runner beans, pumpkins, melons and lettuce. Another day he might list the flowers out in his garden, such as pansies, a dozen or more different shades of snapdragons, four kinds of sweet peas, a few pink carnations, stocks and geraniums. Clearly, the garden gave him much pleasure and relaxation.[7]

Something Olive could do to help support and sustain Theo with his onerous responsibilities was by cooking him nourishing meals. She soon found out the kinds of food he appreciated most, and was pleased when their cows were producing milk[8], so they had fresh milk for their breakfast.

A last trip among the tribes

By December 1937 it had been decided that Theo and Olive would go on furlough during 1938. As they thought about it and prayed together, Theo became convinced that he should first accompany Tom Mulholland on a last itineration trip west of Yuanmou, looking for Lisu tribes-people to preach to. They had started by looking for tribes-people in the Chinese towns, but they seemed too timid to want to be singled out for attention, so Tom and Theo decided to strike out into the mountains, searching for tribal villages, leaving Olive and Isa to hold the fort in Wuding.

The first place reached was a village of about seventy families, situated on a bitterly cold and bleak plain, well over 7000 feet high.

Their arrival caused quite a stir. Why were these foreigners coming to *their* village?

After they had found somewhere to stay and eaten a meal of local food a crowd of about thirty gathered to hear what they had to say. The message was listened to with evident interest, and they stayed there several days. In a letter dated 15 January 1938 to his older sister, Sarah, he wrote:

---

7   See, for example, Theo's letters to his sister, Mary, dated 10 May and 11 June, 1936.

8   See Theo's letter to his sister, Mary, dated 10 February, 1936.

As I write here at this horse inn several pigs have been running about at the open doorway of the room, and a few dogs have just chased them away. A [Chinese man] has just been mending a wooden tub, another group of Chinese is eating breakfast round a table in the sunlight out in the yard. Our own men are just having their meal— steamed rice, a kind of cabbage or spinach boiled, and pork.

In the yard a man is sitting by his pony, feeding it with beans. Here goes a little girl with a rope and wooden bucket to get water from the well near the stable door. A father has just given his son a good belting—for something, or nothing perhaps but cheek!

On the other side of the yard are two women grinding beans to make bean curd...

The main business we have—the real and only business—is to preach among the heathen the unsearchable riches of Christ. It is a wonderful work to be Ambassadors for Christ. Yet it is very tiring, and very difficult; poor souls are hardly won. Do pray for us, that God will fill us with His Spirit and strengthen us with might in the inner man for this work.

Theo knew that the few he and Tom had reached on this trip were a drop in the bucket compared to the many thousands in the Yunnan mountains who had never heard of the love of God. Who would tell them?

In the meantime, back at Wuding, Olive was kept busy with preparations for going on furlough. She wanted to make marmalade for whichever missionary would be in Wuding when the Simpkins left. She also had sorting and packing to do, besides making clothes for herself and for David for the boat trip home.

Amidst all this, she responded as she was able to the many calls for help that came to her door. Here is an excerpt from one of her letters home to her mother and Theo's mother, dated 29 January, 1938.

Last Monday I went three miles out to a village on the [Aguomi] road to be with Ella Graham while she attended a poor woman who could not deliver her baby. Ella had been to her on a Sunday, but could do nothing, so sent for one of us to see if we could help. The baby had been dead already for four days—the woman had had her labour, the waters broken, and then apparently the way had been blocked and the baby choked in some way so that it died. I got to the place at noon on Monday, found Ella awaiting and after talking it over with each other when we argued like this: 'Well, we don't know much about the business, but we have books and certainly more knowledge of the subject than the friends of the patient. If we leave her as she is, she will certainly die, and whether we can do anything for her remains to be seen, but we certainly can do no harm, and we may be able to save her. If her life is saved, then we may be able to save her soul'. So we got to work—she needed a good wash first, and we needed cloths over our noses! We worked on her for half a day but could make no impression.

As a last resort we wondered if Isa would be able to do any more than we had done, so we came home, and Isa said she would go early next morning, though she feared she would not be able to do more than we did. It was of course a case for a surgeon—he would have had the baby away in no time, but there's none available, we felt we could not let the poor woman die without doing all in our power to relieve her. Isa and Ella were there for another half day (I stayed home with the children this time), but finally they had to leave her. By this time the baby had been dead six days! Can you imagine how she was still living—I can't, but it was true.

Isa offered to give her a [huagan] and have her taken across to Irene [Barberini]at Lotze, but her husband was not willing—there were many superstitions in the way—one that if she died on the road her spirit might not be able to find its way and, if it did the door god would not let it in. Another was that no carrier would carry a woman in her condition, so all we could do was to tell her of the One who loved her, and Isa especially had a long talk to her and we pray that she may have found the Lord before she passed on.

Just after Isa got back from her visit to this woman, we were sitting over a cup of tea when someone came in and asked us if we could sell him any milk. On enquiry we found he had a young baby of four months, but his mother had no milk for her. As he lived two or three days journey away it was useless to give him a wee drop of milk so we asked him if he did not have any goats. He had over 100 he said and 30 of them had young kids so would have plenty of milk. We *told him to give the baby goats' milk, but he feared if he did that the kids would die for want of milk We asked him whose life was more important—the baby's or the kids!*

These two paragraphs will give you an idea of how little life out here is valued—the husband did not care whether his wife got better or not, and the father thought more of his goats than his baby girl. Poor people, but precious in His sight, are they not?

Leaving God's work in His hands

Theo's head still ached and his brain felt tired just at the thought of the past few weeks of packing and travelling. They had passed in a frantic blur.

For years he had been under increasing stress with a level of responsibility for the work in the Wuding region, beside the continuing strain of perils at the hands of local bandits and the unpredictable incursions of the Red Armies.

And now, after completing his trip through the mountains with Tom, he and Olive and David had packed up and travelled down the mountains to board the SS *Tanda*, on their way home to Australia for their first furlough.

Olive was not a good traveller. Theo used to suggest she could get sick in the bathtub. It had taken a week or so for her to get used to the ship's roll and be able to keep a meal down. Thankfully, Theo almost never suffered from sea-sickness and was able to look after David until the weather was calmer.

Theo closed his eyes and lay back in the deck chair. It was early evening, and a cool breeze was ruffling his hair. The sea was calm and the sun was very low in the sky. The tension lessened as he breathed a big sigh. Olive was in their cabin with David, reading him a bedtime story before tucking him in for the night.

But who would continue the work at Salaowu, Makai and Wuding? How would the other missionaries cope under the added work load of a depleted missionary force? Many missionaries from the Yunnan field had been compelled to return home, suffering from nervous exhaustion. Indeed, when Theo and Olive were taking their furlough, they were joining seven other couples leaving their field in Yunnan alone.

Theo had steadfastly denied any need for a holiday, possibly seeing it as acknowledging some weakness, though more likely because of the overwhelming need in the villages, and the small numbers of workers there. In fact, in his CIM medical report covering the period 1939-1946, Theo wrote, regarding his custom as to a yearly holiday:

> We haven't had any. Yunnan has a cool equable climate, and no need to go to a hill resort as we live in the hills. Bible School vacations were spent doing itinerant Bible teaching etc.[9]

However, now that nine years had passed since he first arrived in China, he was glad to be on his way home with his wife and young son.

The difficulties of travel in China, and the length of time it took to reach the homeland, together with the great expense, meant that the CIM at this stage did not promise to give workers furloughs[10], though generally they were taken after seven years of service unless required earlier for health reasons. Theo went to China early in 1929, and Olive late in 1933. Since Olive had been in China fewer years than Theo, their combined term of service now added up to fourteen years. This explains why Theo had been in China for so long before his first furlough.

There were few people on deck, most passengers gathering instead in the saloon for the evening's entertainment. The beauty of the setting sun and the tranquil sea would have been balm to Theo's spirit. Day followed day on board the ship and as his responsibilities were very few, Theo's exhaustion would have begun to abate, the tight bands around his head loosening.

At last the ship berthed in Sydney. The family took the train to Melbourne where their journey ended on 25 March, 1938.

Another new chapter was beginning. Theo had a wife and child to introduce to his family. Olive had a husband and son to introduce to hers. And both would have the challenge of speaking to groups in English, something they had not done for years.

---

9   A copy of this report is held in the Melbourne School of Theology library.

10 See Theo's letter to his sister, Mary, dated 14 April, 1932, where he explains this.

Chapter 12

AUSTRALIAN INTERLUDE

The late 1930s were momentous days on the world stage. Aeroplane travel was fast improving. Howard Hughes set a new transcontinental flight record, and soon after, he set a record round the world flight in 91 hours. Franklin Roosevelt was inaugurated for a second term as the US President, and Hitler formally declared the German withdrawal from the Treaty of Versailles. During the same year (1937) the German airship *Hindenburg* exploded; King George VI and his wife, Queen Elizabeth[1], were crowned at Westminster Abbey in London shortly before Neville Chamberlain became the Prime Minister of the United Kingdom; and Amelia Earhart's aeroplane was lost at sea.

In China, 1937 started with the brutal murder of the adopted daughter of the retired British Consul in Beijing. This murder became the focus of fascinated discussion for months in China until it was displaced by news of the Japanese invasion of China, launched on 7 July 1937 near the Marco Polo Bridge in a Beijing suburb. In the subsequent weeks, further attacks were launched by the Japanese, capturing Beijing, Tianjin and other cities. As the year went on there were disturbing reports of terrible atrocities

---

1 The elder daughter of Queen Elizabeth and King George VI, also named Elizabeth, went on to become Queen Elizabeth II when King George died. Her mother was then known as the Queen Mother.

such as killing, raping, looting and burning in cities, towns and villages through which the Japanese soldiers passed. Later estimates of the number of civilians and prisoners of war killed during the first six weeks of the Japanese occupation were over 200,000.

While all these events were taking place, Theo, Olive and young David were being reminded how unlike their village life in China it was to live in Australia. The sights and sounds and smells were vastly different. To begin with, Australia seemed so clean. There were properly formed and paved roads and working drains and sewerage systems in the cities and suburbs, and simply dropping rubbish in the streets was widely frowned on.

They had been used to seeing mountainsides covered with wild azaleas and rhododendrons out in flower. In Australia, the trees were mostly sparser, and had the blue-grey tinge of the eucalypts.

As winter drew on, Theo's spirits lifted as gleams of cream and gold appeared in the bush as the family made their way up towards his relatives in Maryborough. It was wattle season again.

And the birds... he had forgotten how much he loved the warbling of the Australian magpies on a warm lazy day, or the currawongs up in the tall gumtrees. The infectious laugh of a group of kookaburras, declaring this to be their territory would have brought a smile to his face. And the inquisitive little blue wrens, hopping around the grass and shrubs in the garden, or the flashes of crimson, blue, green and gold of the rosellas and lorikeets, swooping into flowering shrubs to feed on nectar, fruit, berries, leaves and flower buds, would have touched a chord in his memory.

Cultural adjustment

Arriving in Australia after an absence of over nine years for Theo, and five for Olive—had seemed, at first, like being in a different world. It was very strange to hear English spoken everywhere, and they kept wondering where all the people had gone. Australia seemed so empty in comparison to China's millions. When doing the shopping, Olive probably had to stop herself from bargaining with the shopkeeper as she routinely did in China.

It was several months before Theo felt able to take in much of the local situation.

The existence of 'culture shock'[2] when people travel to another place

---

2   Irwin, R (University of Oxford) 'Culture shock: negotiating feelings in the field', *Anthropology Matters*, Volume 9, No. 1, 2007, viewed 2 November 2018,

with a different culture, and 'reverse culture shock' when they return to their homeland, is well documented now. The idea of 'culture shock' was popularised by the anthropologist, Kalervo Oberg, in 1954. In 1938, however, it was an unacknowledged concept.

Theo's familiar, automatic social responses had had to change when he'd first travelled to China. Now he found those reflexes had been recalibrated, and he needed to relearn them all again. It was all he could do to remember the names of Olive's relatives and friends, many of whom he had never met before going to China. Also, they were always living in someone else's home, adapting to doing things someone else's way and trying to meet someone else's expectations.

Their home base was in Carnegie where they lived with Olive's mother, Mrs Kettle. As the year lengthened, it became clear that Mrs Kettle would have her elderly mother, Grandmother Hollis, coming to stay with her the following year. The house would not be big enough for them all, so Mrs Kettle's younger brother, 'Uncle Paddy', came to add a two-roomed sleep-out[3] to the house. Helping as Uncle Paddy's labourer was just what Theo needed—something practical to do, with someone else making the decisions and telling him what to do.

He was glad to do any odd jobs around the house and garden too, finding relaxation in the simple manual tasks that did not require much brain power. He had always enjoyed gardening, often asking his sister to send him seeds of various vegetables, fruit and flowers, so they could have food for body and soul wherever they were living in China. Now he was eager to dig a small vegetable garden for Mrs Kettle so he could plant vegetables for her for winter and the coming spring.

A need for rest

At first, Theo and Olive's days seemed to be taken up with attending numerous engagements—reporting to the Mission's Home Council, meeting prayer partners, and going to endless medical appointments.

Theo's medical report from the Mission recommended that he should be freed from taking deputation meetings for a good period[4] until he was

---

www.anthropologymatters.com/index.php/anth_matters/article/view/64/123.

3   A small bungalow or closed-in veranda, in this case, attached to the house.

4   See Theo's CIM medical report on arrival for furlough in 1938. A copy is held in the Melbourne School of Theology library.

sleeping better, free of carbuncles and boils, and no longer showing signs of nervous exhaustion.

Olive, too, had her share of medical appointments. How disappointed she had been that after the birth of David, month after month went by, stretching into nearly three years, without there being any sign of a brother or sister for David. Dr Roberta Donaldson, the gynaecologist whom Olive consulted in Melbourne, assured her that, with rest, she was very likely to have another child before returning to China.

A precious reunion

Theo made plans to go into western Victoria, to Lexton, Maryborough and some surrounding towns, to catch up with his side of the family. What a reunion it was with his little old mother. The tears flowed, as he recalled how his father had died five years after he went to China. It grieved him that he had been unable to do anything in person to support his mother at that time[5].

Catching up with his sisters and brothers and their families, as well, would have further invigorated him, for family had always been important to Theo.

Especially significant was his meeting with his older sister, Mary, who had been his confidante and prayer partner throughout his time in China. Before Olive had come to share everything with him, Theo's correspondence with Mary had been of immense importance to him—an outlet for all his anxieties, his hopes and fears, and a source of helpful opinions and advice.

The stories to tell

During this time, Olive was Theo's anchor. Being, as she thought, a 'plain Jane and no nonsense', she believed in keeping 'calm, cool and collected'. While Theo struggled to find the energy to develop new ways for engaging people with his stories of the Miao, Lisu and Nosu tribes-people, she peeled the vegetables, washed the clothes, and kept the home running smoothly.

Finally, six months after their arrival back in Australia, Theo felt able to start accepting speaking engagements. He once again began to enjoy telling people about his dear Christian brothers and sisters in Yunnan.

---

5   See Theo's letters to his sister, Mary, dated 18 August, 1933, 13 September, 1933 and 17 October, 1933.

On one of these occasions, Olive's mother had been present. After the meeting, she was heard to say, 'I wish I had more children I could send to China to meet this need'.[6] It is interesting to note that of her four surviving children, one (Howard Kettle) became a Methodist minister, one (Marjorie Kettle) married a Methodist minister (William Hunkin), and one (Olive Kettle) became a missionary in China.

A local paper, *The Sunshine Advocate* of 7 October, 1938 carried this advertisement:

Baptist Church

A special Young People's Service will be held at the church on Sunday next at 7 p.m. There will be a boys' and girls' club parade. The speaker will be Mr. W. Theo. Simpkin, a missionary on furlough from China. Mr. Simpkin, who has spent over 9 years in China, has a great story to tell of travel, adventure, danger, and deliverance; of the needs of the people, and how Christ alone can meet that need. He will also give a lantern lecture on the work of the China Inland Mission on Friday night, October 14, at 8 o'clock.

Long before the days of television, computers, Powerpoint, or videos, Theo had had many of his photos made into large glass 'lantern slides' which he coloured by hand. These images could then be projected onto a screen using an electric lantern projector to add visual content to his talks.

People craned their necks to see over or around the heads of those in front, as they listened, rapt, to the stories told in these novel 'lantern lectures'. They crowded round the book tables afterwards, poring over what Theo had set out — stories from exotic places, and captivating little carved curios of rickshaws, temples, miniature shoes (for those whose feet had been bound), as well as books and magazines from the CIM for sale.

Olive never saw herself as a public speaker and was happy that her contribution was in sharing her experiences with various women's groups, such as the YWMM and WAOM (Young Women's Missionary Movement and Women's Auxiliary of Overseas Missions, both Methodist church organisations), Ladies' Guild and Home League.

Whether it was a Prayer Meeting attended by only half a dozen, or a lecture given to hundreds, Theo and Olive took advantage of many

---

6   This is mentioned by Theo in a letter he wrote to his mother and his sister, Mary, dated 26 October, 1938.

Some of Theo's lantern slides (Photos: WT Simpkin collection)

opportunities to enlist the prayer and personal support of Australian believers for the work in China. At this time, CIM Policy expressly ruled out any public solicitation of finance. Missionaries were to live by faith, making their needs known only in prayer to God, who would move people to give. However, it was acceptable to encourage people to pray, seeking God's guidance on how they should be involved in the work of the Mission.

And there was clearly need for reinforcement of the ranks in China.

Since they arrived back in Australia, Theo and Olive had heard of the

death of a fellow Australian worker, Mr Eaton, after complications aris-
ing from a gallstones operation, and also of their Yunnan Superintendent,
Mr JO Fraser, who died from malaria, in September 1938. And Mrs Binks
had gone to a hospital in Hong Kong for treatment. Who knew when she
would be able to be back in the work in Aguomi?

Theo was itching to get back into harness—even as he realised they were
not ready yet to return. He still had the occasional boil or carbuncle appearing, and Olive was now, to their delight, pregnant. The Mission decided
they should wait until after the birth—but the need of China weighed on
him, and the relative comfort and ease of the Australian church grieved
him. He began to think about planning a different sort of road trip from
those he had done in China.

A different sort of road trip

He pulled out some Australian road maps, poring over them for hours,
thinking about the best route to take to share his stories of God's work in
Yunnan. In which of these places—most of which he had never visited—
might the Lord have someone chosen to hear Theo's message and answer
God's call to serve him in China?

Prayerfully he began to draw up an itinerary for himself, covering large
areas of both Victoria and New South Wales. He planned to travel from
Melbourne via Sydney as far north as Tamworth, and then back again,
speaking anywhere he could elicit an invitation.

He was used to the itinerant lifestyle from his work in Yunnan. (The big
difference was that here, rather than having to hire a porter to carry his
luggage, and walking or riding a pony on his journey, he would have a car
and mostly good roads to get from place to place.) He would take a camp
stretcher to sleep on, a primus to boil a kettle for a cup of tea, and books
and pamphlets to sell.

Having gained the Mission's approval of his plan, he started writing to
pastors, ministers and CIM prayer partners in many churches in the towns
along the route. Some of the ministers were already sympathetic to the
work of overseas missions, while others had shown no interest.

It was a round trip visiting over thirty towns, including (in order of
visiting them) Warby Spring (near Wangaratta), Chiltern, Rutherglen,
Wodonga, Albury, Wyalong, Wagga, Junee, Cootamundra, Goulburn, Bow-
ral, Sydney, Gladesville, Narrabeen, Gosford, Mayfield, West Maitland,

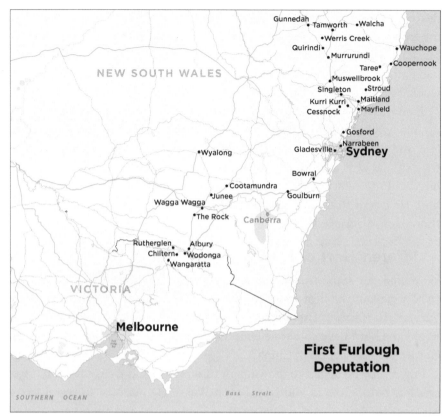

Map of Victoria and New South Wales, showing towns Theo visited on this trip

Kurri Kurri, Cessnock, Singleton, Muswellbrook, Murrurundi, Quirindi, Werris Creek, Gunnedah, Tamworth, Walcha, Wauchope, Coopernook, Taree, Stroud, Sydney, Goulburn, The Rock, Albury, Wodonga, Chiltern, and Wangaratta.

In many of these, he spoke at multiple venues. Schools, prayer meetings, young people's meetings, church services—Theo was happy to tell his story wherever they would welcome him.

The Goulburn Evening Post dated 3 March, 1939 carried this advertisement:

> LECTURE ON CHINA
> *Those who are interested in the latest happenings in China should hear what Mr. W. Theo Simpkin, of the China Inland Mission has to tell in pictures and story. Mr. Simpkin has spent over nine years in*

this vast land, and has a great story to tell of travel adventures and the need of the people. He will give his lecture on Thursday. March 9. at 8 p.m. in the Goldsmith Street Methodist Hall.

Within the space of six or seven weeks, from 23 January until 17 March, he spoke, led a Bible Study or gave his lantern lecture more than sixty times. Just as when he was in China, he continued his habit of writing regularly to his mother and sister (and, of course, Olive), telling them about his travel, and the people and places he had seen, as well as the responses to his various meetings.

In a letter to his mother from Wagga Wagga, dated 27 January, 1939, Theo wrote:

On Wednesday I went to Wodonga and met [Mr H]. He wishes to be remembered to you all. He still thinks of the apples out at 'Burn-bank'! The parsonage was very small so he said I had to go to a boarding house. We went to three, but all were full so finally I slept at the parsonage on my own camp bed on the veranda…The lantern lecture was not well attended, only thirty, mainly young folk being present. Still one trusts good seed was sown in their hearts and lives.

Several weeks later, when he had reached Quirindi, New South Wales, he wrote to his mother and his sister, Mary:

At night I preached at the Methodist service. Over 120 were present, and then we went into the Sunday school hall for the lantern lecture. Well over 200 people were there for that. They seemed to listen with great attention and interest. At the close, two young ladies (teachers training in the Teachers' College) came to have a talk to me and to enquire about getting training for the Lord's work.

Some welcomes had been warmer than others, but in each case Theo told his story, trusting in the Lord to take his words and make them fruitful.

No April fool

Theo was very happy to return to his family who had missed him while he was away. He arrived just in time. His daughter, Dorothy Hollis ('Hollis'— Olive's mother's maiden name), was born in the comfort of the Bethesda Salvation Army hospital early on 2 April 1939. The family declared ever after that she had delayed her appearance to avoid being an 'April fool'!

Olive and David with baby Dorothy
(Photo: WT Simpkin collection)

Young David, who was now three-and-a-half years old, was very proud of his baby sister, and of his new status as a big brother. Theo and Olive were equally besotted with their wee daughter. Visits to a baby health centre were quite a novelty for Olive—there had been nothing like that for her in Wuding after David's birth—and she was pleased to be reassured that Dorothy was thriving.

Longing to return

Despite rumours of war, the fledgling church in China still needed teachers and evangelists.

'Surely it's time for us to return', thought Theo. 'When we arrive, we can do our part in taking the Gospel into Lolo territory.' For some time, Theo and Olive had had a burden on their hearts for the Lolo and other minority (tribal) groups in Yunnan, whose lives were bound by fear of evil spirits.

Following the heavy load of meetings and the disruption to their lives of the new baby, they went away for a brief holiday before they would embark on all the preparations for the return to China. They were loaned a small house in Rosebud, a Victorian bayside holiday resort. The house was just a few hundred metres from the beach on a rise, so that, from the veranda, they could see Port Phillip Bay.

Beside the house was a very high wooded hill, topped by a lookout, known as Arthur's Seat. One day during their holiday they drove back to Dromana, going via Arthur's Seat. The views over the Bay and Melbourne in the distance were magnificent, but Olive was not impressed by the fifteen or so hairpin bends they had to negotiate to get up and down again.[7] It had much the same effect on her as being in a ship going out through the Heads at Sydney. That was one part of returning to China she did not anticipate with pleasure.

The next few months passed in a whirl of shopping, medical checks,

---

7   See Theo's letter to his sister, Mary written from Rosebud on 15 May, 1939.

vaccinations, meetings, farewells—and heartache. Theo's mother was not well, and he doubted that he would see her again this side of 'Glory'. He was comforted to know that his sisters—especially Mary—would be beside her to support her when the time came.

From a nation at war

Theo and Olive had expected to board the ship SS *Nankin* leaving Melbourne on 2 August. Instead, they found themselves in Sydney on 12 September, waiting to board a different ship. Meanwhile, the family members split up, being billeted at various places where a bed could be found. David was with his Grandma Kettle at her sister's place, Olive and Dorothy were with some friends in Dulwich Hill, and Theo was at the CIM Home in Stanmore.

The change in plans was probably due to Great Britain's declaration of war on Germany following Germany's invasion of Poland. Consequently, on 3 September, 1939, Australia's Prime Minister Robert Menzies informed the nation that Australia was also at war.[8]

It was from a nation at war, then, that the family boarded the SS *Nellore* from Sydney—enroute to another nation, under siege from Japan. A small group of new male missionaries joined them on this trip, and they looked forward to happy times of fellowship together.

It was quite a forlorn embarkation however. Navy precautions allowed no-one on the boat or on the wharf to see them off, and Navy requirements were that the ship should travel 'blackout' at all times.

The War would have all sorts of unexpected impacts on their next term of missionary service.

---

8   This was announced on every national and commercial radio station in Australia. The Australian War Memorial, 2017, *Prime Minister Robert G. Menzies: wartime broadcast*, viewed 2 November 2018, www.awm.gov.au/articles/encyclopedia/prime_ministers/menzies.

Chapter 13

A SURPRISING VENTURE

On board ship

'Theo! Quick! Fetch me a basin—I'm going to be sick again.'
'Me too, Daddy.'

The young family was on board the SS *Nellore* enroute from Australia to China. It was September 1939. Baby Dorothy was the only family member apparently oblivious to the ship's rolling and plunging. Even Theo was unable to manage a meal at first, but after the first night he was up and about as usual.

'If only we could have the portholes open and let some fresh air in', sighed Olive. 'Just let me change the baby's nappy and give her to you to feed. Then I can turn the light out and open the porthole for you', said Theo.

Having bathed, changed and dressed the baby, and handed her over to Olive to feed, Theo gave David a book and a toy to play with, while he went out to the ship's laundry to wash the dirty nappies. Long before the advent of disposable nappies, this was an inescapable task. He was not alone doing that job. Another Australian passenger, whose Chinese wife was too seasick to get up, was also washing their baby's nappies.

During the war, 'blackout' regulations meant all portholes had to be kept tight closed while any lights were on, and even then the only lights allowed in the cabins were the very weak pale blue nightlights.

Ships always seemed to have a smell of stale paint about them, and the cabins were suffocatingly stuffy. My oh my, it was hot! The ship's unpredictable movement was exacerbated by their inability to see out, or to have fresh air in their cabin. Occasionally, once they were all in bed and lights out, Theo would open the porthole, and turn on the electric fan to get some fresh air.

One night, their cabin was so hot and stuffy, they decided to try sleeping on deck. Olive reclined in a deck chair, David in a couple of chairs placed together, Dorothy in her pram, and Theo on a bench with some rugs and coats to cushion it. [1]

What a delight to lie down to sleep under the clear sky and twinkling stars.

Unfortunately, the bench and chairs became rather hard after a few hours, and they made no mention of trying that again.

The only way to reach China was by sea. (Photo: WT Simpkin collection)

---

1 See Theo's letters to his mother dated 14 and 21 September, 1939.

No ocean cruise

After a few days they sailed into calmer weather and began to be able to enjoy their voyage.

Olive and Theo and family were accompanying some new young CIM missionaries from New Zealand and Australia, who were travelling to China for the first time. Arthur Gunn from New Zealand had been the only one quite unaffected by the rough seas, and he had kept up his reading and preliminary language study while the others—Hector Hogarth from New Zealand, and Harry Gould, Frank White and Geoff Malins from Australia—were confined to their berths. There were several other missionaries on board: Miss Betty James, a new LMS (London Missionary Society) missionary, and a returning Brethren missionary, Mr Vines. But now, all were up and about and settling into a shipboard routine.

Right from the start of their voyage from Australia to China on 13 September 1939, there was a happy atmosphere of sharing and fellowship among this group—whether members of the CIM or not.

For each one, the three weeks voyage to China would be an important time of preparation for the mammoth task ahead, an interlude for spiritual retreat and refreshing.

Theo saw it as something else as well—an opportunity to get the new missionaries started on learning the Chinese language. How helpful it had been when he was first travelling to China to have some private tutorials in Chinese culture and language from Mr Curtis, a fellow-passenger and a returning missionary. He decided to offer the same to the new workers on the SS *Nellore*.

Shipboard experiences[2]

Once they were through the rough weather, their shipboard life developed a routine. The day started for the Simpkins as soon as baby Dorothy awoke. Following breakfast, the missionaries met for a half hour of Bible study and prayer.

Theo then took the new workers for a session of Introductory Chinese language and culture. During this class, the cabin attendant or steward usually brought them iced lime juice or ice cream.

A few games of quoits or deck golf followed for those who did not

---

2   See Theo's letters to his mother dated 28 September and 2 October, 1939, and a prayer letter dated 20 October, 1939.

On board the SS Nellore
Back row: L-R Frank White, Geoff Malins, Arthur Gunn, Reg Vines
Centre: L-R Hec Hogarth, Miss James, Harry Gould
Front: L-R Theo and David, Dorothy and Olive
(Photo: WT Simpkin collection)

want to swim in the pool. Three-and-a-half-year-old David loved jumping into the pool. He did not always remember to check that there was someone to catch him. He soon learnt his lesson though, after once or twice getting more of a ducking than he reckoned on before his father, or another swimmer reached him to lift him up, coughing and spluttering!

Dinnertime was at 12.30pm, after which all retired to their cabins or deckchairs for a siesta or study and letter-writing time. Another swim or game before tea-time was often followed by a Christian worship service or fellowship time. On Sundays they would hold a worship service in either the first or second-class saloons for any who wanted to attend. A few passengers and some of the ship's officers joined in.

A real treat for young David was going down to the dining room where there was a menu for each day's meals from which he could choose his meal. He couldn't read, of course, but loved the idea of making his own choice.

Asked one day what he would have, David insisted on taking the card and pointing out what he desired. He caused a great deal of amusement when his finger pointed to 'the Captain' at the top of the menu card.

The first port of call was Rabaul, in Papua New Guinea, where many passengers left the ship, including a tall strong police inspector, in charge of a miner—a 'guest' of his Majesty. This miner had absconded with a lot of gold from someone else's mine. He and the gold had travelled back on the ship to Rabaul where he would be lodged in the King's 'guesthouse' for such men.

Thereafter there were only six Europeans and six Chinese passengers, apart from the nine missionaries. One man was heard grumbling that wherever he went on the ship he was likely to come across missionaries singing hymns or having a prayer meeting.

The next stop was Manila in the Philippines. For two days and nights the ship was unloading cargo non-stop. Theo wrote to his mother on 2 October 1939:

Tens of thousands of bags of flour; thousands of boxes of milk, cheese, butter, jam etc; and thousands of carcasses of frozen meat had been unloaded—mainly by machinery. About 2000 tonnes of cargo has gone off, and now a few tons of hemp are going on for Japan. But noise!! It's deafening at times...

Respite in Hong Kong[3]

From there they sailed on to Hong Kong, expecting to receive word from the CIM Directors about their ultimate destination. Would they be able to go straight to Yunnan from Hong Kong? They were longing to be able to commence work with the Lolo minority people (sometimes called Nosu, now collectively called Yi). Or would they stay on the ship until it reached Shanghai, where the CIM Headquarters were?

As it turned out, the ship spent two days at the Kowloon wharf unloading more cargo, and then went into dry dock for five days. All the passengers were put up at the shipping company's expense at the 'Peninsula Hotel'—one of Hong Kong's finest—until the ship was ready to be boarded again. Meanwhile, the Simpkins received word from headquarters that they were all to stay with the ship and proceed to Shanghai where they would be given their instructions.

'I guess we will be travelling inland to Yunnan from Shanghai, then', thought Theo.

Their luxury stay came to an end, however, and they rejoined the ship as warning lights in the harbour signalled an expected typhoon.

They headed straight into the middle of it and endured two days of intense seasickness.[4] Even some of the crew were prostrate, and one of the five new CIMers from Australia and New Zealand earned the nickname 'the corpse' from his fellows for his evident misery[5].

One day when Olive was especially sick, Theo encouraged her with the

---

3 Letter from Theo to his mother dated 8 October, 1939.

4 See Theo's prayer letter dated 20 October, 1939.

5 Andrews, M 2012, *My China Mystery,* Even Before Publishing, Australia, p. 4.

words from Revelation 21:1 (KJV) regarding the new heavens and new earth: '...and there was no more sea'! [6]

Even that journey came to an end, however, and they finally berthed in Shanghai. It was so good to be on terra firma at last.

The war with the Japanese was very evident in Shanghai. Since the early 1930s there had been a continued succession of small conflicts between China and Japan, each one seeing China losing territory bit by bit. The Chinese troops fought doggedly but they were unable to repel the Japanese with their superior air, naval and armoured fighting power. Shanghai had fallen in 1937, and the remains of the Chinese army retreated to try to defend the capital at Nanjing.

By the time the Simpkins and their party arrived in Shanghai, Japanese soldiers could be seen in the streets with guns at the ready, and the signs of war were plain in the ruin of so many factories and industrial complexes.

Still, it was good to be in Shanghai at last. The drive from the wharf to the Mission headquarters was a very slow one—even slower than usual that day because the city was flooded. Theo described it in a letter on 20 October 1939:

> Shanghai greeted us with a flood, and the car which brought us to this home splashed through inches of water all the way from the wharf. The streets were rivers. We hear that the river has not been dredged since the war in China began, so it is well silted up and during heavy rains quickly overflows its banks. Shanghai has never before experienced such floods. The compound here was under water for two or three days, so we were not able to get out during that time.

An unanticipated challenge

A new CIM General Director was at the helm, and he had a surprising proposal for Theo and Olive. This was the gist of it:

> 'Travel and living conditions in China are very uncertain just now. It would not be wise for the CIM men's language school to be run as usual at Anqing in Anhui. So we have been looking for a safer alternative. In fact, Japanese incursions into China mean that nowhere near the coast would be safe. We cannot send our new missionaries into areas occupied by the Japanese Army. After much prayer, the

---

6   See Theo's letter to his sister, Mary, dated 4 February, 1940.

directors feel that Yunnan is the only place for the men's language centre to be situated this year.

We are asking you, Theo and Olive, to take the new male workers from Canada, the UK, New Zealand and Australia to Dali and run the training home for them there.[7] You are seasoned missionaries and have good language skills.

Theo, you are a trained teacher and will be able to find good language teachers for the new workers as well as teach and encourage them in their language study; and Olive, your many years of experience in an accountant's office in Melbourne will serve you well in all the records you will have to keep, besides cooking and housekeeping for the new workers.

We are asking you to talk together about this proposal, pray over it, and let us know whether you believe this is God's call for you at the moment.'

Olive and Theo were stunned. Their heads were spinning. This was indeed a new challenge for them to consider, though it would put on hold any ideas of work among the Lolo, for the present, at least.

They understood from their own experience, how important those first few months in China would be for the new workers. Missionaries were of little use at all until they had a good grasp of both language and culture, and they needed good teachers and encouraging support as they struggled to gain the language. Would Olive and Theo be equal to the task? After all, they were still relatively new missionaries. This would be just their second term of service with the CIM in China.

From their experience in Wuding, they expected it could well be difficult to get servants in Dali, and servants they would need, to help provide for such a large family. Also, they would have to be able to source all their produce from nearby, since stores from the coast were prohibitively expensive. Since the Dali mission home had never been used before for such a purpose, it would probably require considerable modification. It could be

---

7   *China's Millions*, dated 1 January, 1940, p. 5, notes that whereas the Australian, New Zealand, British and Canadian new workers would go to Dali, the American new workers would be accommodated somewhere in North China. According to *China's Millions* this was so that they would '...be more readily available when required in that area...'

difficult getting such a large international party through all the customs and immigration offices along the way.

As they prayed together about this, it soon became clear to them that this was indeed God's call. They wrote home[8], sharing the news and their confidence of God's leading:

> ...we cannot get stores from Shanghai by post as formerly. No parcels or books can be sent by post now. Yet, with all the problems, 'God is still on the throne, and He will remember His own. Though trials may press us, and burdens distress us, He never will leave us alone'. And 'our sufficiency is of God', who will bring us through 'more than conquerors'...

> ...'He is able'. We are full of praise and thanksgiving for all that the Lord has already done for us and know He will not fail us in this new venture for His sake.

Two hectic weeks flew by in Shanghai as they made their preparations. They had to meet with the new workers as well to advise them about what they should purchase while in Shanghai. The five who had travelled out on the SS *Nellore* with them from Australia were now joined by seven others: another Australian, Ted Holmes, who was returning to station work in Dali, three Britishers—Bill Pape, David Johnson and Steve Knights, and three Canadians—Don Cunningham and brothers Frank and Doug Muir.

Theo and Olive had to speak with those who had previously run the language schools, to learn all that would be expected of them. The Mission Treasurer, Mr Embery, went through all the processes that were required to keep the financial records up-to-date and accurate. Another meeting about the actual language teaching was with Mr Matthews who had prepared the new dictionary and language primer and was the CIM language examiner. The CIM General Director, Mr Gibb, and the previous General Director, Mr DE Hoste, also spent time with them, discussing their role, and praying with them about the coming task.

Because of the continuing conflict with Japan, they would be unable to travel from Shanghai to Yunnan overland. Instead, they would have to go around the coast by boat to Hong Kong, and then on to Haiphong in French Indo-China (now Vietnam). From there, the only way to get to Dali

---

8 Letter to Theo's mother dated 29 October, 1939.

would be first, to go through the mountains by train, taking them inland to Kunming, the capital of Yunnan province. From Kunming, they would be able to hire motor lorries to carry the missionaries and all the luggage and stores up the newly finished Burma Road to Dali. At least they would not have to walk and hire men to carry all the luggage.

Several visits were made to the British and French consulates to organise visas. A 'food-box' had to be prepared to take with them as well, to feed the large party throughout their month-long journey to Dali. No longer would they have meals provided for them on boat or train.

New workers (L to R): Frank White, Arthur Gunn, Geoff Malins, Harry Gould and Hector Hogarth
(Photo: WT Simpkin collection)

How grateful they were for the young men—the 'Uncles'—whom their children had got to know and love on the voyage out from Australia, who now cheerfully took on baby-sitting roles.

> At Shanghai we bought several boxes of stores (tea, cocoa, coffee, milk powder, butter etc etc ...) for the home at [Dali]. These largely are now 'embargo' goods because of the war: we had to get a special consular permit to enable us to bring them into the country[9].[10]

Proceeding through pain

The short weeks sped by and soon they were all back on board ship—this time the SS *Esang*—retracing their voyage as far as Hong Kong, from where they would sail on to Haiphong, followed by the three day train

---

9 Because of the route by which they must travel to Yunnan, they would cross from China to French Indo-China and then back to China. The permit would allow them to bring the embargoed goods across the border from French Indo-China into China.

10 From Theo's letter to his sister, Mary, dated 19 November, 1939.

trip to Kunming. The breaks in the Yunnan railway line resulting from recent flooding had just been repaired, and they were among the first to get through directly without delay, but the journey was still fraught with challenges, as Theo's letter indicated:

> We had quite a tiring trip from Shanghai—three days on a steamer to Hong Kong; four days there (organising visas); two days to Haiphong in the same boat. The Lord graciously gave us calm seas while on the boat...[11]

> At Haiphong all the goods and our personal luggage—totalling 99 boxes or suitcases or trunks—was passed through the customs free of charge. I got all onto the train safely and paid the freight on the excess baggage—totalling about £95 (Australian).

> These things all arrived at Kunming about three days after we did, so all day Monday (November 13) was spent in getting all this stuff through the customs. About £10 customs duty had to be paid. Since then I've felt rather conscience smitten that some things were passed through which should have been dutiable so I sent a cheque for five pound to pay the balance. I felt that unto the Lord I had to do this to be honest: 'Render to every man their due—custom to whom custom is due' etc.[12]

While in Kunming, Theo received a telegram[13] informing him of the death of his mother. Receiving such news at the height of their busyness and disruption in Kunming added another strain. He had no time to grieve.

Communication with Australia was so unreliable—and took so long. Theo knew he would have to wait weeks, if not months, to hear the details about his dear mother's final days. And the loving and newsy letters he had written to her in the past few weeks would never be read by her.

He was so glad his sister Mary had been with his mother in those last days. And how grateful he was for Olive's support, steadying and comforting him—reminding him again that 'Underneath are the everlasting arms' (Deut. 33:27 KJV).

> We were at Kunming only for a few days, but they were hectic days

---

11 Theo's letter to his sister, Mary, dated 19 November, 1939.

12 From Theo's letter to his sister, Mary, dated 19 November, 1939.

13 Mentioned in Theo's letter to his sister, Mary, dated 19 November, 1939.

indeed. *The mission home was so full of missionaries that we couldn't be entertained there. Instead we had to stay at the 'flats' (some rooms that are very barely furnished)—over the Street Chapel. There we had to cook for ourselves and for the eleven men...There was scarcely any equipment, no servants, practically no pots, pans or dishes, no stove...so we were put to some difficulty to cook. Servants were unobtainable and foreign stores almost unprocurable!*

...We had a safe, though very tiring journey down from Kunming to Dali. The men got on one bus: we went on another with some luggage and a third bus had to be hired to take all the rest of the luggage. The first day was very wet but the second two days were dry and fine. Our bus was bogged once, and we had to dig it out. The baggage bus was bogged in the middle of the road at a landslide, and we had to jack it up, then pack stones under the wheel and get it out before we could go on. However, at last we arrived safely at Dali. Praise the Lord[14].

Buses usually drove no further than Xiaguan[15], the large market town at the southern end of Lake Erhai, and private transport had to be arranged for the remaining ten miles to Dali. It had been agreed that the baggage bus and the one carrying Theo, Olive and the children, would continue on to Dali. The new workers, however, were glad to stretch their legs after the hours of bumping along in the bus. They chose to get out and walk[16]. It was a glorious, crisp autumn afternoon as they set out on the last lap of this journey.

Surrounded by beauty

Dali, one of the most famous cities in Western China, sits on a large extremely fertile plateau at an elevation of about 2,000 metres, between the majestic Cang Mountain Range to the west and the large beautiful freshwater Erhai Lake to the east. The road leading to Dali was a broad,

---

14 From Theo's letter to his sister, Mary, dated 19-22 November 1939. Now an excellent highway links Kunming to Dali, and the whole trip can be done easily in less than five hours.

15 Today, industrial activity in the area has been confined to the Xiaguan region, with Dali preserved as largely a tourist destination, showcasing much of the area's rich historical and cultural heritage.

16 Noted in a letter from Frank White, quoted in Andrews, op. cit., p. 10.

paved road, leading past fields of ripening harvest between the lake on their right and the mountains on the left.

The mountains were all snow-capped when the party of new workers arrived, and there were glorious views of mountain gorges and flowing waterfalls to be seen from the place that would be their home for the next six months.

This province was aptly called the Switzerland of China.

What a setting for an introduction to the language and culture of the people they believed God had called them to serve! The grandeur and beauty were balm to their souls after all the change and hectic activity of the past few months. A great new chapter was beginning.

Looking over the rooftops of Dali towards the mountains (Photo: FWF White)

Inside Dali (2014)
(Photo: S Joynt)

Inside Dali, looking towards the City Gate (2012) (Photo: R Joynt)

Chapter 14

THE 'SIMPKIN SCHOOL OF ORIENTAL STUDIES'

O live would have been very glad to get out of the bus. Travelling by bus was only minimally less unpleasant for her than being on board ship. Having the two small children to keep occupied and happy during the long hours of bumping along the newly 'made' Burma Road[1] would have helped to keep her mind off the effects of the bus's bumping and swaying on her 'internal equilibrium'. The times the bus had been bogged gave them all the opportunity to get out of the bus and enjoy some fresh air.

However, her thoughts would have kept running ahead to the task before them. In Wuding, it's true, she had run the mission home, but there had seldom been more than three or four visitors to accommodate at any one time, and now she had two small children. Her regular family in Dali would be twenty or more to house and feed, seven days a week, besides extra visitors.

She was not sure how well the mission home at Dali would suit this new purpose. She expected that, as with most Chinese homes, it would be built

---

1   The Yunnan-Burma Highway had been in operation for just over a year, the section to Kunming having been opened to traffic on 1 December, 1938. 'The sections from Kunming to the Burmese border were built by 200,000 Burmese and Chinese laborers during the Second Sino-Japanese War in 1937 and completed by 1938.' Wikipedia, The Free Encyclopedia, 2018, *Burma Road*, viewed 25 October 2016, en.wikipedia.org/wiki/Burma_Road.

on the four sides of a rectangular courtyard. She did not know how many rooms there would be, nor how conveniently they would be arranged. What would the kitchen facilities be like? How easy would it be to find and hire help in the kitchen, cleaning and laundry departments? Would there be people she could safely hire to help care for the children while she oversaw the household arrangements?

And while Olive was probably wondering about all this, Theo's mind would have been pondering where he would find Chinese teachers for his students, the party of eleven new workers. How many would he need? What classes should he himself take? Would any of the mission home rooms be suitable for use as classrooms? Which of the students would learn quickly, and which would find it a struggle? How would their spiritual lives progress as they encountered the daily grind of learning new vocabulary, and trying to understand the grammar and the culture it expressed? How would they handle the difficulties of being away from family and friends?

It is likely that his thoughts kept straying to the Lolo people for whom he had long prayed, and among whom he had hoped to work. Who would take them the good news of a Saviour who loved them and longed to bring them forgiveness and new life?

Upon reaching the Dali mission home, they found that the new workers

The courtyard of the mission home in Dali (Photo: FWF White)

had arrived several hours before them. There were rooms to be allocated, new partitions erected to sub-divide larger rooms, furniture to source or make, teachers and servants to be engaged, food and other stores to be purchased and meals prepared. The new chapter had begun.

Crucial beginnings and firm foundations

The first six months for new missionaries were crucial. This was the time when the foundations for their language were laid. Each was expected to complete successfully the first section of the Chinese language course. During this period, they were not permitted to take any active part in the ministry to the local community in order to focus fully on the language study[2].

There were still ways in which they could support the local church—such as befriending the children of the servants who shared the mission compound, and praying for them. Several of the men started English language Bible classes for local Chinese students who were eager to learn English.

Frank White, one of the new workers wrote about his delight when at last he was given an opportunity to go out on the streets to hand out tracts to the locals, and to invite them to the Sunday service:

We felt that we were getting somewhere. My first attempt to preach in Chinese was in front of a crowd of Chinese tribes-people, Tibetans and others at the annual market... I guess we were one of the popular sideshows. It was almost amusing to see how the people crowded around when one of our number struck up a tune on the piano accordion and we sang choruses in Chinese...[3]

None found the language easy to learn; some struggled, despite their best endeavours and those of their teachers. In recalling these struggles, Steve Knights, one of the boys from the UK, wrote:

I remember one day when I felt defeated in my lack of progress in the Chinese language. I went out on the city wall to talk to the Lord about it. Then the Lord seemed to talk to me. 'Who called you to your present task?' He then reminded me: 'Your questions and fears did not come from me but from your enemy. Trust me. I'll help you'. Then

---

2   This was stated in a prayer letter by Harry Gould. Theo sent a copy to his sister, Mary, dated April 1940.

3   Andrews, op. cit., p. 19.

alone on that city wall His peace flooded my soul.

He also reminded me, 'This may not be the last time the enemy will attempt to take away your sense of calling when difficulties arise'. Then I remembered Hebrew 13:5b ['...be content with what you have, because God has said, "Never will I leave you; never will I forsake you".' (Hebrews 13:5 NIV)] which He gave me when I first believed. I left the city wall that day rejoicing in our Lord's marvellous love and mercy to His children and from that day to this I have never doubted His call to China.[4]

A typical day in the life of Theo

The alarm rang and Theo rolled over, reaching out a hand to turn it off before it woke the children. Theo and Olive had both been late to bed the night before.

Neither had ever been so busy. Olive had been catching up on the accounts for the whole compound as well as each individual missionary's accounts. Theo had been trying to complete the preparation for all his classes the next day, as well as the weekly Bible class he ran for the local church.

He stretched and rubbed the sleep out of his eyes before hurrying to pour some cold water into the basin to wash his face. Tonight it would be his turn for a hot bath; Olive had hers yesterday. This morning they would both have to make do with a 'lick and a promise'.

Quickly dressing, Theo ran down the stairs and along the corridor to the kitchen to make sure the fire was lit. Already the new workers were moving about the house. Theo boiled a kettle and made a cup of tea to take back up to Olive. The children were now stirring, and soon she would have no time to herself.

While she drank her tea and got up, he sat down with his Bible. Gazing out the window at the snow-capped mountains, it was easy to reflect on the psalmist's words as recorded in Psalm 121:1–2 (NIV),

I lift up my eyes to the mountains—where does my help come from?
My help comes from the LORD, the Maker of heaven and earth.

He needed all the help God would give.

---

4 Unpublished memoirs sent to me by Steve's daughter.

Above: Inside the Dali church (Photo: FWF White)

Below: Dorothy and Helen inside the same church in 2012 with a friend.
It would have been over seventy years since Dorothy was last in the church
as a small child.

This morning it was his turn to lead the morning worship in Chinese for the Chinese servants. His Chinese was a bit rusty, and his brow wrinkled with concentration as he sought to remember the correct Chinese idioms. Tomorrow he would lead the English morning prayers for all in the mission home—that would be easier. There were the carpenters to check on—making and painting new tables, chairs and cupboards for the large community.

There were other responsibilities that fell on him as the senior missionary. Workers might be passing through and need to be met and transported to the mission home, or there might be other dignitaries in the region whom he and Olive should entertain.

On some days, things just didn't go according to routine or follow any sort of plan at all.

One day, Theo was to meet Miss Daisy Kemp at Xiaguan. She was coming to help in the mission home.

He borrowed a bicycle to ride the ten miles over to Xiaguan. She did not arrive, so he pedalled the ten miles back to Dali. The following day he repeated the ride—but again she did not arrive.

When he arrived back home in Dali late on that second day there was a telegram waiting for him to say she had *just* arrived in Xiaguan! Early the next morning, he returned to Xiaguan for the third time. Since the bicycle was not available, Theo had to walk the ten miles. When he finally met Miss Kemp, his blistered feet were a good enough reason for hiring a rickshaw to take them both back to Dali.

That night, his prayers on retiring might well have included a thanksgiving that Miss Kemp had finally arrived and he would not need to go back to Xiaguan again the following day!

A typical day in the life of Olive

Olive's days were filled with planning and preparation of meals for her large family in addition to caring for her own little family. She was very grateful for the help in the kitchen, first, of Miss Nellie DeWaard, an American missionary, and when she left, of Miss Daisy Kemp from England.

The international character of their kitchen staff was reflected in the variety of meals prepared. While Nellie DeWaard was with them, there was an introduction to the idea of a variety of salads such as carrot salads, and Waldorf salads, to be served with the meat. The Canadian boys enjoyed

Chinese women doubling as nursemaids for Dorothy as well as home help
(Photo: FWF White)

these, whereas the Britishers and the Australians didn't quite know what to make of them.

There were usually Chinese assistants in the kitchen, but when any of them left or got sick, Olive became 'chief cook and bottle-washer'. Washing, ironing, mending and darning had to be done for all on the compound. Olive tried to train up some of the local girls to take over these roles, and keep an eye on David and Dorothy in the garden while doing some mending. Life was so busy that she'd sometimes resort to leaving the children with one of the new missionaries.

On one particularly hectic day in April 1940, Olive wrote to her mother:

> We are so short of servants that I'm almost desperate and searching in every avenue possible for likely help, but still none are available. This is Friday night, and scarcely any of the week's ironing is started yet, and certainly no floors have been scrubbed.

The new missionaries rallied around for the various regular tasks they could undertake to lighten Olive's load. Geoff Malins, for example, was the 'Bath Steward'. It was his responsibility to ensure that sufficient water was heated for all the household to bath regularly, and to roster the baths. (He was the supposed author of a letter to the Editor of *The SSOOS Spotlight* regarding the inordinately large quantity of water some people seemed to require for their weekly bath![5])

The new workers had soon christened the Men's Training Home in Dali 'The Simpkin School Of Oriental Studies', and at the end of their six months together, published a light-hearted journal called *The SSOOS Spotlight*, each contributing something entertaining or serious. It is included as an Appendix to give an idea of the kind of young men who had sensed God's call to them to serve him in the mountains of Yunnan.

Olive soon came to discover how unsuited the house really was for their purposes. The family's living quarters were upstairs. To get to the dining room, kitchen and pantry areas, she had to go downstairs and then walk the length of three rooms along a veranda. The big store room (for bulk storage) was a long way from the pantry (with everyday usage stores), kitchen and dining room[6].

In the space of one day, while baking, jam-making, and caring for the children, Olive must have walked many miles and climbed the stairs dozens of times.

Special occasions

'All work and no play makes Jack a dull boy', so the saying goes, and the days in the Training Home were not solely given over to language study. There were many occasions, such as Christmas and birthdays, when there was something special to celebrate, and those celebrations became high points on their calendar.

These might be a picnic just within the CIM family. On other occasions, they joined with other foreign Christians who were in Dali to minister to the local community. Whether as hosts or guests, they delighted in the fun and fellowship they enjoyed as relaxation from the daily grind of language study.

Once when the CIM family were the hosts, the young men had planned an evening's program. There were charades by the northern hemisphere boys, and then by the southerners, who were not to be outdone.

One of the charades saw the boys acting out one of Theo's Chinese

---

5   *The SSOOS Spotlight*, pp. 17f. See Appendix, pp.386-398 below.

6   See Olive's letter to her mother dated 13 August, 1940.

New Year's Day picnic 1940 in Dali. Theo holding Dorothy and Olive with David on her lap are in the centre front. (Photo: FWF White)

lessons, mimicking his mannerisms beautifully. Another boy rushed in, pretending to be young David, bumping into the door and making a terrific row—as he did sometimes. Steve got up and said 'Go away David while the uncles are studying'.

There were various other acts. One told a fairy story about 'good King Theoss' (who got on well with everyone because he always did as he was told), and of his 'beautiful Queen Oh-lie' who sits so devoutly at the foot of the table with hands clasped (a favourite pose of Olive's). Everyone laughed so much their sides hurt.[7]

At Christmas, there were gifts to be distributed to everyone from the tree. The boys (i.e. the new missionaries or new workers) had already given the children gifts. Geoff Malins and Hec Hogarth had made David a little hobby horse. He was delighted with it, riding it around nearly all day, and bringing it dishes of sawdust and shavings to eat. Theo and Olive were given matching silver serviette rings each with their Chinese character names engraved on them. Then Theo was given a very heavy parcel which Father Christmas found almost too heavy to carry. Theo unwrapped it to discover a dirty old brick, at which Father Christmas hastily rushed up to replace it, full of apologies for the (intentional) 'mistake'. Then he handed Theo the right parcel. It contained two beautiful Dali marble bookends.

---

7   See Olive's letter to her mother dated 2 January, 1940 for all these details.

When four-year-old David was called up by Father Christmas to receive a gift from the tree, he was scared stiff and jumped over the back of the chair into his father's arms where he howled. After a while, however, he relaxed and eventually, at the 'old' man's request, was willing to stroke his beard and give him a kiss.

Once there was a huge market outside the West Gate of the city, and extending even partway up the mountain behind the town. It lasted about five days. Several times Theo and some of the boys went up to the market to hold open air services. Some of the boys were brave enough to try out their wee bit of Chinese for the first time. How exciting for them to be able to bear even halting witness to the love of God! This was what they had come to China for. They noticed how many Tibetans were present in the market and how much more friendly they seemed to be than the Chinese. And everywhere, there were beggars...

Birthdays were also special occasions that had to be acknowledged with a special meal. The menu for a birthday meal might include, as a special treat, a locally caught fish. There would, of course, be a birthday cake decorated with candles, 'hundreds and thousands' (i.e. nonpareils) and paper violets. There were scones, special desserts such as jellies set in egg cups and then turned out on a plate, and the meal might finish with oranges and walnuts.

A Dali North Gate market, 1940
(Photo: FWF White)

The CIM cook in Dali with a locally caught fish (Photo: FWF White)

A FOOT WIDE ON THE EDGE OF NOWHERE

Proper etiquette and braces

Olive was quite early christened the 'Mother Superior' at the Training Home, with her large family of young men to keep in order. With an international family like that, there were bound to be differences in what was accepted as proper.

One day the boys asked her if it was necessary to wear a coat to the meal-table during the summer. (Remember, this was back in 1940.)

'No', Olive replied seriously. 'So long as you don't come to the meal table with braces showing, a coat is not necessary. Make sure you are neatly attired in shirt and shorts with a belt, and you will be quite respectable.'

The next day when they came to dinner, there was something rather odd about the way each one was dressed. Frank Muir had a towel around his neck joined to an old strap and then to his trousers. Others had ordinary braces, but all on the *outside* of their pullovers. Some who did not have proper braces came with a piece of rope over their shoulders. David Johnson had his razor strop across one shoulder and string to make it long enough. All had manufactured some 'excuse' for braces to wear.

Frank explained that 'it was the order of the day'.

Olive soon dropped to the joke and wrote to her mother in a letter dated 30 April, 1940, 'Of course I pretended to be cross with such ridiculous children'.

David goes grave-digging

The new workers had very quickly become an integral part of the Simpkin family at Dali. Their birthdays were celebrated together in just the same way as the family birthdays. Together they commiserated and prayed over difficulties experienced each day—and rejoiced when a new Chinese language structure had been mastered. There were many laughs together, including family jokes which even repetition failed to blunt.

One lunch hour, Steve Knights and Dave Johnson took little David down to the nearby creek and caught thirty-nine little fish for him to put in a bottle. (Perhaps David overfed them, or there were too many for the bottle, since all except four died quite soon. However, the four lasted a bit longer once David realised he should not continually feed them and must change the water daily.)

Another day, Arthur Gunn took David for a long walk and brought him back with a big bunch of wildflowers and a daisy-chain around his neck.

Arthur became a firm favourite of David's, and one day, David was seen digging a hole in the yard.

When asked what he was doing, he replied that he was digging a grave. (Spending his first few years in Wuding where he often accompanied his parents out to the mountain villages, he probably would have seen people digging graves for loved ones who had died.)

'Who are you digging the grave for?' he was asked.

'For Uncle Arthur,' he replied seriously.

'Why are you digging a grave for Uncle Arthur?'

'Because I love him so much'.

Once when Steve fell ill, young David decided to be his doctor and visit him. He took his temperature with a spoon and then 'took out 1000 germs'. He followed this up with a service for Steve, singing and praying that 'the Lord Jesus would keep all the uncles from getting worms'. He finished one of his prayers with 'Hip hip hurray Lord Jesus!' (Theo thought this might be a modern equivalent to 'Hallelujah'.) Steve said young David's 'service' had been as good as a tonic.[8]

Theo, Olive and the children in the Moon Gate, CIM home in Dali
(Photo: WT Simpkin collection)

---

8   All these details are from Olive's letter to her mother dated 21 April 1940.

Safe amid the storm

The CIM directors had decided that Dali was the best place for the new workers' language school because it was not one of the areas where Japanese fighting was concentrated.

Theo wrote for *China's Millions*:

Although war rages in many other parts of the world, and even in this country too, everything is so peaceful here that we would know nothing of the death and destruction elsewhere were it not for wireless news which we receive from time to time. Yet Jesus is our confidence. In Him we have peace…We have been indeed thankful for the quietness and safety of this place; there has been only one air raid (a false alarm!) since we came.[9]

On the whole, the war's main effect in Dali was on the difficulty of obtaining supplies, and the constantly rising prices of goods. Early in 1940 the news told how the Japanese had warned the French that if their railway line[10] continued to be used to carry supplies into China, it would be bombed. In fact, the line *was* bombed several times and important bridges destroyed.

Yet, in a world at war, the beauty of Dali's physical environment would remind the missionaries, new and old, of the Creator of the ends of the earth. The Scriptures promised them that:

those who hope in the Lord will renew their strength.
They will soar on wings like eagles;
they will run and not grow weary,
they will walk and not be faint.

Isaiah 40:31 NIV

---

9   See WT Simpkin, 'Six Months with the Students', *China's Millions*, September 1, 1940, p. 134.

10   This was the railway line from Haiphong in French Indochina to Kunming in Yunnan, by which the CIM party had travelled in November 1939.

Chapter 15

HEIGHTS AND DEPTHS

One day in March, there was an unexpected and unusually cold snap which resulted in the mountains around Dali being not just snow-capped but clad in snow down to their knees. This was such a new experience for the Australian boys especially, that several of them had an early lunch on that Saturday and took off straight away to go up to the snow.

> *They revelled in pulling themselves up to the top by the rhododendrons on the ridge, and then sliding down on the seat of their pants, using sharp sticks to dig into the snow to act as a brake when they wanted to stop.*[1]

But reaching just the mountains 'knees' was not good enough for some of the young men. The summit was a continual invitation and challenge to them.

As summer approached and the end of their six months in Language School loomed before them, they kept watching the weather and looking up longingly at the mountain top. Would they be able to conquer it before it was time to leave Dali? The attempt had to be made.

A day or two before the end of the Language School, Frank White and Arthur Gunn set out early with a packed lunch to make the assault. As with

---

1   Andrews, op. cit., p. 13.

Snow on the mountains (Photo: FWF White)

Two of the Australians, Harry Gould (left) and Geoff Malins (right) enjoyed the rare treat of a snow fight in Dali. (Photo: FWF White)

all mountain peaks, what had looked, at first, like one mountain, became another and then another.

When one was in the valleys or under overhanging rocks or towering trees, the summit could no longer be seen. Were they taking the quickest and best route to the summit? Surely, if they kept going up they could be certain to come to a place where their height gave them better vision, but closely packed rhododendrons or clumps of bamboo impeded their way.

They struggled up and up for four hours, finally coming on a small icy mountain lake between themselves and the peak. Despite the snow around them, they were hot and sweaty from their exertions and accepted the invitation of the clear waters of the lake to strip off and dive in for a refreshingly icy dip, before continuing, re-invigorated, on the final climb.

At last they reached the top.

It was worth the thumping hearts and sore muscles. Frank White described the scene on the back of a photograph he sent home, and his daughter later put it into her own words like this:

> Dali sat to the east. Turning around they saw little snatches of cultivation and villages and the Burma Road winding away to the west. As far as the eye could see the ranges got dimmer and lost themselves in the hazy distance of Burma and Tibet.[2]

From the top of the highest peak

---

2   Andrews, op. cit., p. 20.

Triumphant, the mountaineers set off on the return journey. They discovered that going down, it was even harder to keep their bearings. Several times they were caught in a thicket of bamboo, and finally had to admit to themselves that they were lost.

Darkness fell. It was no use trying to find their way anymore. They had to wait until daybreak.

But where could they be safe for the night? There were many robber bands that hid in the mountains. They knew too, there were stories of wild animals in these ranges—animals such as snow leopards, red pandas, golden monkeys, black bears and the giant panda. Frank's story, told decades later by his daughter Marion Andrews, records that they took shelter in a cave, and the next morning, they saw what they believed to be panda pawprints outside their cave.[3]

Back at the Training Home, a worried CIM family gathered to pray for the missing pair and to decide what to do. They sent out a search party with lanterns, but they returned alone hours later after a fruitless search.

It was agreed that they could do nothing more before dawn when four of them set off again to look for the two climbers. While they were still searching, two rather sheepish and crestfallen wanderers arrived back home, to be welcomed by a very relieved CIM family.[4]

The next steps

When Theo and Olive initially accepted the invitation to take charge of the Dali Training Home, they had understood it would be for six months only. As April drew to a close, they were beginning to hope again that they might soon be free to take up the work among the Lolo tribespeople of central Yunnan.

They were quite disappointed to receive a letter saying that Theo and Olive would need to stay on at Dali until the new workers had all been relocated in August. Then Theo and Olive could have a brief period of respite before receiving the *next* lot of new workers. What a bombshell! The CIM leaders could see no other alternative but for the Simpkins to continue leading the Language Home in Dali for another year.

But was this the direction in which the Lord was leading Theo and Olive?

---

3 Andrews, loc. cit.

4 See 'The Magic Mountain', *SSOOS Spotlight,* Dali 1940, pp. 10, 11, Appendix 1 below and opposite, for an anonymous fairy-tale account of this event as written at the time.

THE MAGIC MOUNTAIN

Long, long ago, before ever people became so clever that they ceased to believe in fairies, and gnomes and hobgoblins, there was a magic mountain. At least people who ought to have known, said it was a magic one in spite of the fact that it looked just like any other mountain. Well, one day, two bold, dashing travellers came to the city of Ilad which was the city nearest to the magic mountain. They had come from as far away as possible and they told the citizens living in the joint that they were going to have a go at the mountain.

The first thing to do was to sneak some grub and then sneak off before the good fairy whose name was Sadie, could forbid them. And very early, while all the good people were still asleep they sneaked off and the grub. Up they went, and up and up, and I'm not so sure there wasn't another up. The snow grew deeper and the magic bushes plucked at them and tore pieces of their clothes off until it became a question whether they would be wearing anything at all when they arrived at the top. However the top did come. And they knew they were there because when they tried to go a bit higher there was nothing to go up.

Now near the top there was a lake, deep mysterious and very magic. "What about it?" they asked each other in their vulgar way. And believe me or believe me not, I don't care, before you could say 'Snakes alive' they found themselves in the lake and their clothes on the bank. The water looked just like the water they had once had in a bath when they were tiny. But it wasn't the same it was solid magic. And they were soon under a spell. They got out and dressed. And then the magic began to work.

In just about as long as it takes the Mother Superior to add 3 and 4 together correctly, they found they were lost. That sounds a bit funny but what is meant is they were in a horrible forest of bamboo that prodded them and mucked about with those who blokes so much they would have cried if they had been alone instead of together. Then

one of them had a brain wave. He remembered a magic word he had once heard when he was eating grubs in the bush. "Tutti-fruity' he said so softly to himself he could hardly hear what he said. And there they were out of the bamboo winding their way down the most beautiful valley you have ever seen, even if you have lived in Australia.

But that wasn't the end. Oh no, there's a bit more if your are not sick of listening. But anyway you needn't listen if you don't want to. I don't care. Well they went down that valley until suddenly the valley did a queer thing. It dropped, it just wasn't there: it was below them, miles below and the only way to go on was to fall over and they weren't sure how you pulled up when you dropped like that. So they thought they would go back to the path that they would have been on all the time if they had not been bewitched. You see the magic was beginning to wear off a little and they were as nearly sensible as they had ever been in their lives. It made them feel quite excited.

But would you credit it, Boys and Girls, no sooner did they try to climb up to the right path than the sky grew black and dark and they couldn't see and they didn't know what to do and they hadn't got the magic light that all the people of Ilad used to have whenever they went for a walk in the dark or anything like that. All the birds and the beasts laughed like mad at them and came along to have a free smell as these two adventurers fell asleep in the bamboo. What you say? Oh, yes, they had got back to the bamboo again.

That night long after Mummy has tucked you up in bed, four good fairies set out with a glow worm to try to find the missing links but the dark magic of the night drove them back. The next morning the citizens of Ilad had a meeting and from their number they chose the four bravest and nicest and most handsome and best liked citizens and sent them off on the search. But that is another story.

P.S. The two travellers got back all right. But during the night they turned into little baa-lambs and that is why their smiles were sheepish.

'The Magic Mountain', SSOOS Spotlight, Dali 1940, pp. 10-11.

Olive wrote in detail about their dilemma to her mother in a letter dated 5 April, 1940.[5].

> In my last letter I said I hoped to be able to tell you when we would be moving on as we were expecting Mister Sinton [the CIM Assistant China Director]. Well, he has not come out, and will not be coming, as he was recalled to Shanghai owing to Mr Gibb's [CIM General Director] illness and great pressure of work there...
>
> Mister Sinton dropped one or two bombshells in his letter though, saying that we would all be staying here until after the summer, and that designations will be round about August, when all the men would get off to their respective stations shortly afterwards, leaving us with a breathing space before the next lot of new workers arrived!! He said that he can see no alternative but to ask us to carry on for another year here in this training home.
>
> Just about the same time as we got his letter we had letters from Tom and Isa who are already in [Chuxiong] and are waiting for us to come too, and also from Mrs Morgan of the mid-Yunnan Bethel Mission in [Chuxiong], who longs for us to come and work the tribes-people [i.e. the Lolo] in her district. She only works the Chinese people. She has been asking the CIM for long enough to send workers for the tribes in her district and was overjoyed when Mulhollands and we were appointed. Now she is very upset at our delay. I don't know what she will say when we write and tell her we may not be able to come for some time. There is a saying in the CIM something like this, 'take on a temporary job and it almost invariably turns to a permanent one'... The boys are all teasing us here and telling us we will be here for years too.
>
> Today we were talking about having a proper group photo taken and someone said 'Oh yes, we must have a photo of the pioneers of the SSOOS'. They picture a row of such photos on the dining room wall with the ones in years to come of Theo with a beard. They tell me I'm an ideal matron, and that we both are just absolutely fitted for this work!!
>
> Yet we ourselves, cannot feel as yet that it is our work even for

5   Olive told her mother this in a letter dated 5 April, 1940.

another year when the work among the tribes is so urgent. Surely there are some older missionaries who could take on this work who could not go to tribes land. However we have not decided as to how to write to Mister Sinton about the matter—we feel we must pray a bit more about it first. You might ask the folk at home to remember this matter in prayer too, that we may know definitely what the Lord would have us to do.

I must write to Mister Sinton to tell him what I consider must be done to this place if it is to be a more or less permanent training home. We have managed with many inconveniences thinking it was only to be for six months. The Mission certainly is up against things just now in these abnormal times, and I suppose they just don't know where else to have the training home nor who else to be in charge of it. Daisy will be leaving here in June and says definitely she will not be coming back. Maybe I could manage if I had better staff, but where to find a better cook and helpers is the question. So that is how things stand at the present.

A month or so later, there was another letter from Mr Sinton. Designations for the new missionaries had been finalised, and the CIM was trying to make alternative arrangements for the future of the Training Home. Theo and Olive were asked to stay in Dali until all the new workers had completed their first section of language and were able to move on to their newly designated fields of service.

Once the new workers had been able to move on to their designated places, Theo and Olive would be free to return to the work among the Lolo to which they had been designated before they went home on furlough in 1938. Other arrangements had apparently been made for the men's language school, but this was not explained in the letters which got through to Theo's sister and Olive's mother.

The SSOOS

As the end of their time in the Training Home approached, the group of new missionaries decided to mark it by the publication of a journal called *The SSOOS Spotlight*. They wanted to have official photographs taken to commemorate their first six months in China. They were a lively lot, and mealtimes and all social occasions had always been entertaining.

In one article entitled 'Valete', they wrote the following:

If we did but remember each day separately, we should recall the grace given us that day...There has been peace that is rare in this troubled world, there has been the daily bread and the daily strength; often times prayer made on our behalf has been answered, all un-known, perhaps, to the maker of it; and there has been given us the Father's best gift which is love, making us a family indeed.

We came to study Chinese intensively and that task has been accom-plished in its first stage by the grace of God. What we know now, we know because His help was given in a common task. We know that the Lord Himself will reward Mr and Mrs Simpkin for every help they gave to us, and compared with that, our thanks have but little value. But each of us is grateful and although 'thank you' are trite and conventional words, they best express what each sincerely wants to express.[6]

The Dali Training Home Community 1940
Back row: WH Pape, DC Johnson, H Hogarth, SD Knights, AG Gunn, FWF White
Centre: DA Muir, DA Cunningham, GH Malins, FH Muir, HG Gould
Front row: Miss N De Waard, EO Holmes, Olive, David, Dorothy and Theo
Simpkin, Miss DEF Kemp, Mrs VJ Christianson (a CIM missionary who
happened to be in Dali when the photo was taken)
(Photo: *China's Millions*, 1 August 1940, p. 115)

---

6 See 'Valete', *The SSOOS Spotlight*, op. cit., p. 21 in Appendix, p. 397 below.

'To the ends of the earth'

For a moment, let us look at the work of these new missionaries over the following decades. Eight decades later, is it possible to measure the value of the service given by this dozen or so new missionaries? Where did they go? What was the nature of their contribution to the growth of the Kingdom of God?

In their time at Dali they emerged as a diverse and exceptional group of young men. Some were quiet and retiring, others were usually the centre of whatever mischief was being hatched. Some were lively and physically robust while others were more studious. All were compassionate and caring, deeply committed to their calling to make Christ known where people had not yet heard of him. To that end they threw themselves into the daunting task of learning a language and culture vastly different from their own. They were prepared to endure struggles, privation, ridicule and poverty for the amazing privilege of introducing people to the One who gave his life for them.

In the main they were designated to work in the south western provinces. Arthur Gunn, Doug and Frank Muir and David Johnson were designated to Yunnan, with Harry Gould appointed initially to local secretary work in Kunming. Bill Pape, Steve Knights and Don Cunningham were designated to Sichuan. Hec Hogarth was designated to Guizhou. Geoff Malins and Frank White went further north and east to Shanxi.

It was a dangerous time to be in China. The Japanese were making determined efforts to extend their control. The fighting did not discriminate between missionaries, innocent civilians and soldiers. In 1943, Bill Pape was asked by the Mission to lead a group of women missionaries into the mountainous Lisu tribal area where it was thought they might be safer.

News from the rest of the world about the progress of World War II was sporadic and unsettling. After a couple of years of service in China, two of the new missionaries, Frank White and Arthur Gunn, decided they should resign from the Mission in order to join their own country's armed forces to defend their homeland in time of war.

The rest of the group remained in China as long as possible, until the rise of Communist China forced them all to return to their home countries (mostly in 1951) or to be redeployed elsewhere.

It is not certain what direction their lives all took subsequently. However, several of the Dali group later embarked on the formidable task of learning another language to serve in yet another country such as Japan, the Philippines, Indonesia, Singapore or Malaysia. Some served on the homeside in Canada, New Zealand and Australia, representing the Mission there, caring for missionaries' children in the Mission's hostels, teaching in theological or Bible colleges, or pastoring churches. Steve Knights was instrumental in setting up Ambassadors for Christ, an organisation ministering to the spiritual needs of the many Chinese students flocking to Canada to study.

In many ways, the words of the writer of the letter to the Hebrews come to mind when thinking of these young men:

> *Should I go on...Through faith they fought whole countries and won. They did what was right and received what God had promised. They shut the mouths of lions, put out fierce fires, escaped being killed by the sword. They were weak, but became strong...*
>
> *The world was not good enough for them!*
>
> *What a record all of these have won by their faith!*
>
> From Hebrews 11:32–39 GNT

Chapter 16

BACK INTO THE MOUNTAINS

Theo was eager to be off, champing at the bit, now that he and Tom had been given the green light by the CIM leaders to proceed with work among the Lolo. Yes, he had enjoyed the past months with the new workers as they tackled their language study. What a delight it had been to see the light slowly dawn as they engaged with the language's new structures and this new culture. They had gone through days of dark depression when they had wondered if they would ever understand the way the Chinese people thought, or remember the vocabulary and characters[1].

And then there had been the moments of delight when they were understood by a Chinese person, or when they could grasp the gist of a conversation. Yes, it had been satisfying.

Now, as 1940 was drawing to a close, Theo was itching to get back into the mountains, to seek out the Lolo tribespeople he and Tom Mulholland had first visited over two years ago, just before his furlough. As soon as he could make arrangements with Tom, they would be off for a second visit.

---

1   See for example comments in Olive and Theo's letters dated 3 December 1939, 6 March 1940, as well as a report by Steve Knights, sent to me by his daughter. This is also referred to in Theo's article 'Six months with the students' in *China's Millions*, 1 September, 1940, p. 134.

Theo and Tom visit mountain villages

First, Theo packed for a couple of months on the road with Tom[2]. There would have been a light on his face, a spring in his step and he probably whistled as he set off. This was where his first love was—bringing the light of the Gospel to these mountain people. The weather was fine, and the sunshine was matched by the joy in their hearts as Theo and Tom told the 'old old story of Jesus and His love' to men, women and children in the villages and market towns of Yao'an County in the province of Yunnan.

Many responded positively, but how firm would their faith be when persecution came? Theo and Tom realised they needed to stay in the area to teach these new believers and help consolidate their commitment to Jesus. They began making enquiries about suitable houses to rent so the Mulholland and Simpkin families could move into the area[3].

Olive stayed on in the mission home in Dali, making apple jelly[4], until Theo returned from this trip. She was determined to leave the pantry full for the next mission home hostess before moving onto their next assignment. Her task in Dali had been mammoth with so many to feed and provide for with so little help. The boys had been an entertaining expansion to her family. Olive was glad she and Theo had been able to help them through their first year in China. But now she looked forward[5] to a much smaller ménage, where she could give more time to her family and to ministry among her Chinese neighbours. She had been experiencing severe indigestion[6] and was sure all she needed was rest, and a lot of it.

Soon Theo was back from his trip into the Lolo territory, however, and it was time to pack up all their belongings again.

On the Burma Road

The day dawned bright and clear on 18 October 1940. The Simpkins were about to leave Dali permanently. Pack animals were used to carry all their

---

2   See Theo's letter to his sister, Mary, dated 9 August, and Olive's letter of 13 August 1940 to her mother. This is also referred to in Theo's article 'A prosperous journey' in *China's Millions* 1 April, 1940, p.52.

3   The information for this section and the following one comes from Theo's article 'Moving to a new sphere' in *China's Millions*, 1 May, 1941, p. 72.

4   See Olive's letter to her mother dated 13 August 1940.

5   See Olive's letter to her mother dated 13 August 1940.

6   See Olive's letters to her mother dated 29 July and 13 August 1940.

luggage for the eight-day journey to Yao-An County where they would stay while looking for more permanent accommodation. They followed the Burma Road most of the first day.

Theo and Olive rode ponies, and the children were carried in baskets on men's backs.

David, who was nearly five years old, had travelled like this before and quite enjoyed the novelty. He had a few books and toys with him in the basket to while away the hours, as well as some biscuits and a drink to which he could help himself whenever he chose.

For Dorothy, aged just a year-and-a-half, this was quite a new experience. To begin with, Olive would have made sure she was

David asleep in his basket
(Photo: WT Simpkin collection)

close by to reassure her daughter. Perhaps this is what she said:

'Hello girly-girl[7]. Are you comfy in there? Are you enjoying your ride? Can you see the houses we are passing, and all the people going to market? What do you think of my pony? Isn't he good-looking?'

It wasn't long before Dorothy lay back among the cushions in the basket with her favourite soft toy and, like David, had nodded off to sleep.

Theo was not having such a restful ride. The saddle for his pony was a rough Chinese one with only rough rope stirrups for his feet. His pony was not good-tempered and suddenly reared up and bolted, bucking as it went. Theo tried to hold on, but as the animal careered down the road Theo was thrown off, one foot catching in the rope stirrup. The animal was even

---

7   David was often nicknamed 'Sonny Jim' and Dorothy was 'Girly-girl'.

more alarmed at the unusual weight bumping and bouncing along against its side, and took off at a gallop, dragging Theo along with it.

It was fifty metres or so before a Chinese policeman, seeing Theo's predicament, managed to bring the beast under control and release Theo from the ropes. He managed to gather up all that he had lost—except some precious bits of skin—and was able to continue, bruised, bleeding and shaken, but not too much worse for wear.

Although Theo had no further trouble from his pony, the animals carrying their luggage were not so well-behaved. One nervous mule bucked its load off about forty or fifty times during the day, every time a motor lorry passed them. Motor traffic was still relatively new in this area, since the Burma Road had only been opened for some months, and pack animals had not yet become used to the sudden influx of lorries taking advantage of this new means of transportation into the mountains of Yunnan.

The next day they cut across country, sometimes finding main horse roads, but often following narrow rough tracks over the steep mountains. Even here the animals often kicked up and threw off their loads; horses and loads sometimes rolling down steep banks together, on one occasion nearly killing a muleteer. The party was constantly stopping to settle the fractious animals and retrieve what possessions they could.

They had to ford two swiftly flowing rivers whose beds were scattered with huge boulders. The scenery was rugged and beautiful, but Olive's heart would have been in her mouth as she watched the men carrying her precious children, negotiating the steep and rocky tracks and the river crossings.

'Dear Lord, please give your angels charge over them lest they dash their feet against a stone.'

The carriers seemed much more sure-footed than the animals, however, and the family arrived safely.

Settling in Guanglu Zhen

Eventually, in a big Chinese market village called Guanglu Zhen, Theo found a man willing to rent to them a new three-storey house, built in a semi-foreign style. The house was quite imposing-looking, but it was dirty, draughty and not built for the convenience of the inhabitants. It needed a lot of alterations and additions, as well as much cleaning up, to make it suitable as a base for their operations. The house had very thick mud brick walls—at least 60 cm thick so the window ledges were very wide and inviting for a small child to perch on.

Surrounding the house was a high mud brick wall. Inside the wall there was a garden with a pond filled with waterweed, and a bridge over the pond.

The brick wall gave an illusion of safety inside, but David remembered an occasion when a servant was severely reprimanded by Theo. She had left the washing hanging on the clothesline in the yard overnight instead of bringing it in at nightfall. In the morning, the clothes were gone. A thief had dug a hole under the back gate, slithered through into the courtyard, stolen the clothes and taken them back under the gate. They never saw the clothes again.

Seeing the hole under the gate, David, who was not yet five years old, felt quite vulnerable[8]. He was glad his dad seemed able to handle the danger.

A new commission

The tribal minority groups in Yunnan are many and varied. Theo and Olive were familiar with some of them, such as the Nosu whom they had met in Salaowu and the Miao at Sapushan. They were also getting to know the Lisu, who are the descendants of Yi or Lolo ethnic groups.

In those days, the believers in these minority groups had established

Theo with three tribal evangelists, three porters and a local guide.
(Photo from *China's Millions*, 1 September 1941, p. 135.)

8   See David Simpkin's reminiscences of his life in an unpublished document he shared with the author, 'DMS Life story'.

annual conferences in various tribal centres, usually attended by hundreds of people. Theo attended one of these conferences and his heart was warmed as he heard how new believers had been baptised as the Holy Spirit had brought new life to them.

Many of these centres held Short Term Bible Schools, and Theo had already been involved in some of these at both Salaowu and Sapushan. The missionaries had long believed there needed to be a permanent Bible School for the tribes-people, to train up leaders for the tribal churches. Now the tribal churches were coming to the same conclusion. The decision was finally taken, at a United Tribes Conference, that setting up such a permanent Bible School was of paramount importance.[9]

It was suggested that Theo could be set aside for leading such a Bible School, at Taogu, for instance. What would that mean for Theo and Olive? Theo would not be as free to go out on evangelistic trips into the mountain villages if he were running the Bible School. Perhaps evangelists from among the tribal groups would be more effective than a foreigner. Would Theo be better serving as a teacher of the future evangelists and pastors rather than as an evangelist? Theo's training and experience as a teacher were clear. His teaching had met with great acceptance in the places he had been. Was this need of the tribal churches God's call to Theo to teach rather than directly to evangelise?

In addition, were they to take up this role, Olive would be able to share the ministry to the female students. Since returning to China this time, her role had been that of housekeeper, nurse, chief cook, accountant, encourager and comforter to the new missionaries in Dali. Apart from her contacts with the Chinese women whom she employed to help with the housework and cooking etc., she had had no opportunities for ministry to the people she had come to serve.

Olive never referred to this in her letters. She was just too busy. But she did care that the ministry to the Lolo, which she and Theo believed God had laid on their hearts, had had to wait. In Guanglu Zhen, she and Theo had commenced a Sunday School for the children of the town, some of whom may have been tribes-people. It is probable that she would have shared in running the Sunday School, seeing an added role for herself in the contacts this afforded with the mothers of the children.

---

9 The information in this section comes from Theo's article, 'What God hath wrought among the tribes' in *China's Millions*, 1 July, 1941, p. 104.

While Theo was in the midst of this soul-searching, a request came from the CIM for him to go to the neighbouring province of Guizhou for six months, to run the Bible School among the tribes-people there. There are tribes-people in many of China's provinces, but Yunnan and Guizhou have the highest populations of them. So far, all of Theo's service had been in the province of Yunnan. This request would probably have been made in order to allow the movement of missionaries who might be overdue for furlough, or who needed to travel to receive medical treatment. Trying to find enough missionaries to keep successful programs going without overtaxing them or taking them out of programs that were just being started, was always a challenge for the Mission leaders. At the end of that six months Theo would be released so he could take over the running of the new Bible School in Taogu, Yunnan, from Tom Binks who was currently running it until he took furlough. What should Theo's answer be?

The CIM always took very seriously each missionary's personal sense of conviction regarding God's call and leading.

Transferring to Guizhou[10]

About this time, Olive realised that she was pregnant again. It would certainly be easier for her to manage the early months of morning sickness and then a larger family if they were settled in one place, not doing itinerant ministry in the mountain villages. Although Theo sometimes embarked on more extended trips through the mountains without Olive (such as his trip late in 1940 with Tom Mulholland), there was always value in having Olive and the children with him, and they joined him where this could be managed.

For Theo and Olive, the call to run the Bible School seemed to be answered by an inner sense that this was God's leading for them at this time.

But Theo did not want to leave Olive with the children on her own for so long while he went to Guizhou. Would the Mission be willing for the whole family to travel to the neighbouring province for these six months? Permission was granted; the business of sorting and packing was commenced again, and the family set off for what they expected would be a

---

10 Information for this section comes from Theo's article, 'An uncomfortable journey', in *China's Millions,* 1 September, 1941, p. 135. Unfortunately, no letters from Theo or Olive survived from this year.

new experience in a different province. (They left the bulk of their possessions in the rented house until their return.)

There was no 'public transport' (as we know it) at that time in the village of Guanglu Zhen. Neither did trains run in the direction they would need from Yunnan into the neighbouring province of Guizhou. People 'hitched' rides on passing vehicles. Anyone requiring transport had to sit on the roadside and hope that a truck would come along with room to take them on board. There would be the usual haggling about the price for carrying the people and their luggage, and then they would climb onto the back of the truck with their baggage, finding some place to sit or stand among the other passengers and produce already there. Theo and Olive and the

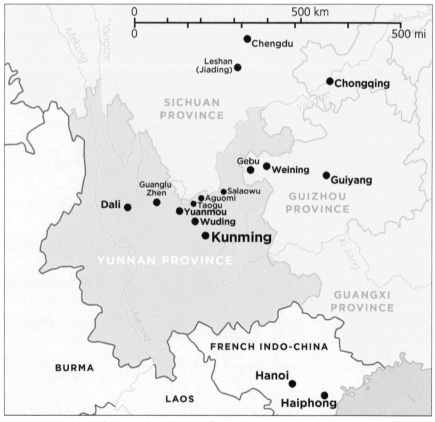

Map showing locations of selected cities and villages

children reached Yao-An like this with no great difficulty, but the next stage of the nearly 700 km journey was different.

No driver could be found willing to take the family any further.

After sitting by the side of the road for six long hours, both David and Dorothy were becoming tired and fractious. How much longer would they have to sit there? Did the family need to change their plans?

A local man who saw their predicament told Theo there was no way they would get a truck to stop for a whole family with a whole family's luggage. What should they do?

Theo and Olive prayed, and thought, and thought and prayed...The hours dragged on. Olive would have been dreading the hours, indeed days of travelling with the children in the back of a heavily loaded truck over such rough and bumpy roads. As the hours of waiting lengthened, bouts of nausea would make her stomach bunch up. If it was this bad just sitting on the side of the road thinking about it, what would it be like on the truck?

Very reluctantly, Olive and Theo concluded that she and the children would have to return to their rented house in Guanglu Zhen for the six months, while Theo went on to Guizhou alone.

No-one was happy about that decision, but it couldn't be helped.

Theo remained at Yao-An for the night with his share of the baggage, while a disconsolate Olive, David and Dorothy finally found a truck returning to Guanglu Zhen, willing to take them back home with their luggage.

Theo's journey continued. It took until 3.00 pm the next day for him to find a truck driver willing to take him up for the next stage. He climbed up to join more than forty other people crammed into the back of the lorry. With such a heavy load, the truck was extremely slow, and the passengers were expected to alight and walk up the hills. It took four hours to cover what should have been just a one-hour trip, and they arrived after dark.

Travelling like this was neither quick nor comfortable, but it would cut the travel time by a month or more in comparison with walking. It was out of the question to try to hire carriers willing to walk for many weeks over the mountains, carrying the luggage. That would have been prohibitively expensive if possible at all.

The following day was bitterly cold with intermittent misty showers.

Theo sat by the side of the road from 7 am until 3 pm, not daring to leave the road, as he hailed forty or fifty trucks, asking for a lift. None was willing to take him on without charging an exorbitant fee.

'Lord, how am I to get to Guizhou? If you want me there, you will have to provide the transport.'

Just then a Christian truck driver stopped and offered to give him a free ride to Kunming, despite the truck having three broken springs from being overloaded. He did it for the Lord's sake, he told Theo, and refused to take any money for it. Theo breathed a heartfelt thanks to him and to the Lord, and climbed up.

After Kunming, there were four more days of this bone-shaking, lung-choking, smelly, dusty, smoky ride north-west, before reaching Weining just over the border in the province of Guizhou. The next lap of the ride was on the back of a heavily loaded crude-oil truck. Fortunately, Theo was hardly ever afflicted by travel sickness as Olive would have been, and he occasionally dozed off.

Suddenly the truck stopped. Theo described what happened next.

> The driver and others began to climb out, shouting 'Fei, Fei' (robbers). Sure enough, a quarter of a mile down the road we could see a group of eleven robbers just in the act of robbing a foot traveller.[11]

The noise of the truck and the shouting scared the thieves who quickly made off up a steep mountain side with their loot and their guns. The travellers climbed back up into the truck and proceeded on their way. Theo breathed a quick 'Thank you' prayer.

Bible School in Guizhou

Finally, without further incident, Theo reached Weining, the county in Guizhou province with the largest populations of Yi, Hui and Miao tribes-people. From there, Theo probably had to walk the last lap up the mountains to Gebu. The Bible School was held in the town of Gebu, where for the next five months or so, Theo would be teaching. There were about thirty young men from these tribal groups staying in Gebu, eager to study the Word of God in order to take it back to teach their own local communities.

The running of these Bible schools was very dependent on the availability of missionaries to teach there. (As yet, there were no tribal believers with sufficient training to staff these Bible Schools, though it was hoped there soon would be.) So they were more 'permanent' than the Short Term

---

11 Simpkin, WT, loc. cit.

Bible Schools, but still did not run continuously from year to year in the one place. Besides, the various tribal believers were all eager for the Bible School to sometimes be located in their own area so they would not have to travel so far to reach it. So the location was apt to move every few years.

Theo was given the task of taking the students through studies in Ezekiel, the Gospel of John and the book of Revelation. What a pleasure it was to open the Scriptures to these young men, so keen to become well-equipped to serve the Lord among the rugged and lonely hills around Weining!

One Sunday early in his time at Gebu, Theo went out to an outlying village where 67 new believers were to be baptised. It was wet and bitterly cold yet the baptism, outdoors by full immersion, took place amid great rejoicing. Theo described the service:

> *Six hundred or more crammed into the church, where I was privileged to minister the Word, while two hundred were unable to get in and stood in the misty rain, listening at the doors and windows. Yes, God's Word is precious to them. It is the joy and rejoicing of their hearts.*[12]

How many folk at home would be willing to stand for hours in the cold and rain to hear the Word of God, Theo wondered. But he knew that his presence in Guizhou was only a stop-gap measure, and he saw it as preparation for his next step. He was due to return to Yunnan at the end of the Bible School, to run the Taogu Bible School.

As the Bible School term in Gebu approached its end, Theo began to prepare for his return journey to Yunnan. He packed some of his clothes and sent them on ahead, to lighten his luggage for the trip back.

In Guanglu Zhen

Back in Guanglu Zhen, Olive and the two children had settled into a quieter life. It fell to Olive to keep young David occupied without his father there to give him simple lessons. And Dorothy was growing apace, increasing her vocabulary in both Chinese and English every day. Olive's pregnancy continued smoothly—or as smoothly as the familiar daily nausea permitted.

On the day when the box of his father's clothes arrived, as Olive unpacked

---

12 Simpkin, WT, loc. cit.

them, David buried his face in the clothes. A wave of homesickness and longing swept over him.[13]

'They're Daddy's clothes! When will we see him again?' he pleaded longingly. 'It won't be long now, son', Olive replied. 'Perhaps he is already on the way back to us.'

A note on 1941

No letters from Theo or Olive have survived from this year 1941. Elements of the story have been pieced together from articles that Theo wrote at that time for *China's Millions*, as well as from stories of other missionaries living in the mountains of Yunnan (such as Grace Reed Liddell Cox[14]) and from David's childhood memories.

Despite the ongoing war in China, it seems likely that villages such as Guanglu Zhen and Taogu were thought to be relatively safe centres for CIM outreach, in part because they were off the main supply routes, such as the Burma Road, and less likely to be targeted by the Japanese. Further south and west in the area of Baoshan and Longling, war was a terrible daily reality. The Japanese had bombed the railroad, and the Burma Road was impassable. Very little mail was getting through. Even the capital of the province of Yunnan, Kunming, was bombed several times by the Japanese.

The scenes of devastation[15] after these bombing raids were gut-wrenching. The smell of gunpowder and dust filled the air, and demolished houses, dismembered corpses, and grieving families following the bombing raids were common sights. Travel was extremely risky, especially if it required joining up with main roads, but the relative safety of the more northern tribal villages was slightly offset by increased inconvenience—food and other supplies became expensive, often unavailable and hard to transport.

However, Theo negotiated the trip back from Guizhou safely, and arrived in Guanglu Zhen, to be welcomed with delight by his wife and children. It was good to have the family together—and soon it would be expanding.

---

13 Simpkin, DM, loc. cit.

14 Grace's story is told by her daughter in Moran, MG 2015, *Someone to be with Roxie*, Lulu Publishing Services.

15 See, for example, Moran, op. cit., p. 197.

Chapter 17

TRIUMPHS AND TRIALS
IN TAOGU

Another member of the family

Olive and Theo had arranged for the CIM nurse, Dorothy Burrows, to attend Olive during the birth of her third child. So, in due course, after Theo's return to Guanglu Zhen, Nurse Burrows took up residence there with the Simpkin family.

As with all village homes, there was no running water or electricity, and with no telephone or doctor to call on, the resources were limited. But Olive and Theo trusted in the boundless resources of the Almighty, and they were content to leave it in His hands.

Marjorie Helen was born safely in the house on Bai Ta Road[1] on 16 September 1941— named 'Marjorie' after Olive's younger sister Marjorie, but always known in the family as 'Helen', or, to Olive and Theo, as

---

1　This road is currently called BaitaLu. The family had always said Helen was born in Pehtakai, pronounced 'Beh-ta-gai', but no such town could be found. Her birth certificate gave the name of the town as Kwangluchen (now written, in Pinyin, as Guanglu Zhen). When Helen and Robert visited China in 2012, a friend helped them discover a town in the right area called Guanglu Zhen. In that town, as they made enquiries, they found a road called 'BaitaLu', meaning 'Bai-ta Road', 'Bai' meaning 'white' and 'lu' meaning 'road'. Seventy years ago, 'beh' was the word used for 'white' and 'gai' for 'road'. When the residents were asked where Beh-ta-gai was, they pointed to the road they were standing on. So Helen's birth town and road (though not the house) had been located.

Dorothy with David holding baby
sister Helen
(Photo: WT Simpkin collection)

'Little 'un'. David, who turned six a couple of months after Helen's birth, was very proud of his little sister, and was very careful to hold her tightly when given the chance.

As Theo and Olive gave thanks for this new life entrusted to them, their hearts echoed the words of Proverbs 10:22 (CEV) 'When the Lord blesses you with riches, you have nothing to regret'.

The CIM came to be known affectionately among its members as 'Constantly In Motion'. The volatile political situation in China combined with the unpredictable needs of the church meant that the missionaries' plans or locations changed frequently. It was so for Theo and Olive. A few months after Helen's birth, the family was busy packing up again, this time, for the projected move to Taogu.

Taogu was a small, very remote Lisu village perched on a sloping 'shelf'

The village of Taogu as seen from the other side of the gorge
(Photo: WT Simpkin collection)

A FOOT WIDE ON THE EDGE OF NOWHERE

on the hill side. It was situated about 7000 feet up in the mountains of north-west Yunnan. In Taogu, Mr and Mrs Metcalf were in charge of the local mission station work, and Theo was to take over the Bible School from Mr Binks when he and his family went on furlough.

Travelling to Taogu

Travelling for the whole family with all their possessions was a gargantuan task. Although Guanglu Zhen was off the beaten track, there was a road through the town that led out to the motor road.

This motor road, however, did not go all the way to Taogu. In fact the nearest motor road to Taogu was a day's journey away, up and down rugged mountains, and across several rivers. Carriers with mules had to be hired to shoulder all the luggage and household goods, as well as the baskets holding the precious cargo of their three children. Theo and Olive rode ponies, often slipping off and preferring to proceed on foot when the track became steep and the footing precarious.

When writing about western Yunnan, Miriam Moran quotes her mother's description:

The only way to many villages in Yunnan is on foot along narrow tracks.
(Photo from a private collection)

For miles and miles all around us we could see mountain peaks all gaily bedecked with cumulus clouds, tiny and great, like tufts of cotton scattered at random… All along the way were white lilies, orchids, eidelweiss, ferns and many other like flora…[2]

Feeding a family of five

The journey came to an end—they had arrived! The building that would be their new home in Taogu was a two-storey mud brick house.

The village was surrounded by small terraced rice-fields, wherever a level patch of ground could be found or made. So rice and some other grains were locally grown, but there were no supermarkets or greengrocers near Taogu. If you wanted fresh fruit or vegetables, either you went on a two- or three-days' journey to an area where there was a harvest of that product, or else you dug a vegetable garden and grew your own fresh food.

So, when they heard that oranges were available, Theo would set off on the long journey to the town where they were being sold, and would buy a sackful. This had to be carried home and then each orange carefully checked, wrapped in clean paper and stored away. Periodically he or Olive

The village of Taogu as seen from above (Photo: WT Simpkin)

2   Moran, op. cit., p. 105.

would go and check the oranges in case one had started to go bad, in which case it had to be separated from the others. This way, the oranges could be stored for over a month. Having fresh fruit such as oranges was essential if they were to remain healthy and strong. And all the family enjoyed marmalade!

Theo had always enjoyed growing fruit and vegetables as he had done in Wuding—and his father had been a keen gardener—so he looked forward to the challenge again here in Taogu. He wrote asking his sister to post him packets of various seeds. There were established apricot and pomegranate trees in the garden too. They also planned to buy another cow or some goats so they could have fresh milk and butter.

The Simpkins' home and garden in Taogu (Photo: WT Simpkin collection)

To get fresh bread here in Taogu, they had to buy the grain, mill it (sometimes even having their own millstones constructed for them first by a man in the village), make their own yeast, and then make and bake the bread. Olive was used to having to bake her own bread, but this would take the process back several steps further. Now they would have to keep their ears open for when grain was available somewhere, and send a servant off to buy a bag and then carry it back, up and down the steep mountains and across the rivers, to Taogu where they would grind it into flour.

The Taogu Bible School

The number of Bible School students in Taogu fluctuated according to which family members could be spared from demands for war service, the farming or other family affairs. Over 50 students were accepted for study, although the most they had at any one time was 37.

The Bible School accepted students from a very wide area in Yunnan.

Some of these lived several days' journey away from Taogu. In fact, some, such as the Gebu and Nosu churches who lived at the other side of the East Yunnan field, were pressing for the transfer of the Bible School to Sapushan for a two-year period. After that, they suggested it could move to another centre such as Salaowu. These were questions that the tribal churches had to address at their United Tribes Conference each year.

Most of Theo's time in Taogu was spent in teaching. He had two or three classes to prepare and teach every day, and four classes on some days. The teaching was in Chinese, which the students from different tribal groups could all understand.

Classes were held in Biblical texts including Leviticus, Exodus and Acts, besides sessions on Singing, Personal Work, Sunday School and Church Organization. All required Theo to put in hours of preparation. He also arranged practical work for the students to lead outdoor services in Taogu on market day, as well as in neighbouring villages.

Being very musical, the students were trained at the Bible School to sing in quartets. The singing would start in the church. Heads would appear out of village doorways. Soon many came running to listen. Imagine a world with no radio, no CDs, no iTunes! Music spoke to the hearts, and often people responded with deep emotion to the song. Outlying villages requested that a team of students might be sent out to them to conduct worship and evangelistic services each week that would include Gospel music, so that was incorporated into the students' practical program.

At the end of each year there was a special graduation meeting. They were inspiring occasions as the young people testified to how the Lord had supplied their needs so they could come to the Bible School. Most came from extremely poor families, but they were eager to support their young people who had heard the call of God to service. Their local village fellowships also helped to support them.

When the Lisu church held its annual meeting following the graduation, they decided to offer four of the Lisu graduates a permanent position as evangelists, if they were willing to take it on. It was so good for Theo and Olive to see their work in Taogu bearing fruit. It was their prayer that these young people would become effective teachers and servants of the church, for the glory of God.

While much of Olive's time was taken up with running her household and caring for the children, she would probably have held classes with the women students also. These might have incorporated simple lessons on hygiene and child care, but it is probable that she also taught the students how to run a Sunday School, and how to minister to women in the villages.

Family life in Taogu

For the children, this was a special time in their lives. It was a simple family lifestyle—no McDonalds, no television, no Mars bars—but they were a loving and happy family. There were frequent walks out across the surrounding hills, punctuated by picnics. There were books to read and stories to tell. Now and then the whole family went with Theo on one of his evangelistic trips to nearby towns and villages...a real adventure.

For special treats their mother would make lollies— 'snowballs', peanut toffee, marshmallow or even honeycomb. Toys came by post unless Olive or Theo made them. For decades afterwards, Dorothy and Helen treasured soft knitted toys each had been given: for Dorothy a white-tusked grey elephant which she named Kentucky (Tucky for short), and for Helen a white lamb (Lamby).

David alone had memories of life in Australia where there was running water, power, sewerage, and clean streets, but his memories were distant and hazy. Here, learning about the 'technology' in use in Taogu made a distinct impression on him. He saw how the local people constructed their own millstones to grind grain to flour for bread and noodles.

He also learnt how water was supplied to the village, there being no reservoirs or dams anywhere near Taogu. The village people relied on water from nearby snow-fed streams. Flowing down from the higher mountains, these streams brought usually clear, fresh water to the village. Split lengths of bamboo, with the 'section' divisions removed, diverted the water down the mountain from these streams to the village.

Because Theo and Olive's house was on the higher side of the village, theirs was the first house in the 'supply line'. There was a 'switch' on the main line (composed of another piece of bamboo) which re-directed the water from the main pipeline to their house or else to other houses below. When they had filled their large water pots, they re-adjusted the bamboos so the water continued to flow on to the rest of the village.

There was no local school that David could attend, or a kindergarten, but his mother and father provided a rich educational environment for him. While Olive bathed baby Helen or dressed little Dorothy, she would ask

David to read, or to spell or write words, or add up simple numbers. He delighted in the challenge. His development was going ahead in leaps and bounds. Now, at six years of age, he was not only able to tell his mother which hand of the clock was on which number, but to 'tell the time properly' (and this was on an analogue, not a digital clock).

It was in Taogu that David found out about the relative speeds of light and sound. Although there was no internet, few books, no *Encyclopædia Britannica*—David learnt from personal experience and his parents' general knowledge. He later recalled[3] it like this:

> Sometimes when we were out we could see a man digging in the fields a good distance away. In the quietness of the hill side we could hear the noise of the hoe as he swung it over his shoulder and then down to dig into the ground. I can remember that I noticed that the sound of the hoe hitting the ground arrived quite a bit after we had seen the hoe hit the ground and my father explained that this was because sound travels much more slowly than light..

One day David was out in the garden playing. Having no permanent water supply, Theo had dug some 'irrigation ponds' around the house which could store water for the garden. They were not deep—perhaps 15–20 cm—but had a lot of fine silt at the bottom.

Somehow or other, David managed to fall into one and was covered in mud from head to toe. He was a sorry mess, and Olive couldn't help laughing at the woebegone little figure. She took him out to the yard and threw water over him to rinse off the worst mud, peeled his muddy clothes off and then popped him into a bath. By now he was able to enjoy the adventure too.

Although it was not quite teatime, Olive suggested putting him in his pyjamas straight away, and putting him to bed early, since he was nice and clean. He thought that was 'jolly fine splendid' so long as he could have his paper and pencils for drawing and colouring. He came down for tea, but then went back to bed, making it an early night for everyone.

When David lost another of his baby teeth, Olive put it in a glass of water by his bed, and he was most intrigued at the silver coin he found in the glass the next morning.

'Is that how you make money, Mummy?' he asked. 'It must be, because I

---

3 Simpkin, DM, op. cit.

remember in Australia there was Australian money when one of my teeth came out, but here in China it makes Chinese money!'

Still he hadn't worked it out. He rushed down to the Bible School grounds to show the students. He couldn't understand why some would not believe him. Olive promised to tell him how it happened the next time he lost a tooth.

The three children enjoyed playing together in their home. The inside walls were all white-washed, and it became quite a temptation to draw on the walls with their pencils. Then they discovered that some flower petals could be crushed and used to colour their pictures. Olive decided the simplest way to manage this was to allocate the laundry room walls as the permitted easel for their 'artworks'—nowhere else in the house. Problem solved!

Another favourite family pastime was playing hide-and-seek. There were so many places to hide—under and behind beds and other furniture, behind doors, under blankets, in cupboards, 'upstairs and downstairs and in my lady's chamber'. Once when it was Olive's turn to hide, she took up her position in plain view on top of the dressing table, standing perfectly still. The children hunted everywhere they could think of and could not find her. In the end, to their great embarrassment, Theo had to point her out to them. How could they have missed her?!

Dorothy's third birthday passed and was marked by a late birthday party since she was suffering from measles on her actual birthday. The birthday menu started with macaroni and cheese, for which Olive opened a tin of cheese—the first they had tasted for about a year. A tin of apricot and pineapple jam was another treat on the birthday menu, as well as snow-balls and nut Florentines. Olive described this occasion in a letter to her mother dated 15 April, 1942.

> The dessert was preserved peaches, jelly and angels' food (the latter a milk jelly). The cake was a chocolate one with a mock cream filling and iced with brown sugar icing. Theo had the brain wave that I could use his medical syringe to write Dorothy's name on the cake, so I scoured it out well, and put a white icing in it, and before it was dry, scattered 100's and 1000's on it, so that her name and the date showed up in these. It was not very clear in spots, but still not too bad at all. Three candles and three little Australian flags finished it off.
>
> We had the tea rather late so as we could use candlelight. Mrs Binks

had given us before they left two big pink candles. Theo fixed these up on a piece of board, and this was our lighting arrangement. Flower decorations were big bowls of sweet peas and nasturtiums [out of the garden].

Of course we all had to dress up for the occasion, much to the children's pleasure! I have four paper caps which I keep for such occasions so we all donned one again for this party. Helen sat in the high chair and seemed to enjoy watching it all too.

Sundays under the stars

Sunday evenings stood out from the rest of the week. The whole family walked down to the local church together for the evening service. There was no street lighting in the village, of course, and very little lighting of any kind in the houses. That quiet walk through the darkened village under the starry sky seemed part of the whole worship experience for the family.

The church was also in pitch darkness. The only light came from a small pine-chip fire[4] on the side of the pulpit where the Scripture was read and preached. It was a vivid reminder of the Light of the Gospel which Theo and Olive had come there to share.

---

4   Simpkin, DM, op. cit.

Chapter 18

LIFE AND LOVE IN AN ERA OF CHOLERA

Although the CIM policy was for its missionaries to live among the people to whom they ministered[1], their children were not usually free to play unsupervised. At that time there was no sanitation in these remote villages, and outdoor latrines consisted usually of a deep open pit with a couple of planks across on which to squat. Bacterial diseases were common. Often home gardens were fertilised with human waste, and fruit and vegetables might be offered unwashed to the children, along with unboiled water to drink. There were too many examples of local children contracting diseases and dying very quickly.

Having no access to antibiotics, Olive and Theo kept close supervision of their children.

The cholera epidemic in Yunnan

Adults and children alike were susceptible to disease. With limited

---

1   'The China Inland Mission was more insistent that [sic] most missionary organizations that its representatives blend into Chinese society. The CIM was the first missionary organization to require that missionaries dress in traditional Chinese clothing.'
    Thompson, LC 2014, *Missionary Children in China: The Chefoo School and a Japanese Prison*, Academia.edu, viewed 2 November, 2018, www.academia.edu/8994079/ Missionary_Children_in_China_The_Chefoo_School_and_a_Japanese_Prison.

understanding of hygiene, and only rudimentary sanitation, infections were spread rapidly in the villages.

Late in 1942 a devastating cholera epidemic[2] swept through Yunnan, killing thousands. The germs of cholera (like typhoid) enter the body through the mouth in contaminated food or water. They set up infection in the small intestine followed by purging diarrhoea and copious vomiting, resulting in massive dehydration. Death often ended the suffering speedily.

The incubation period of the germ was very short—sometimes only one day—so the hope of help for these tribes-people was very small once they were showing signs of infection. Only inoculation would help—and then only for those not yet infected. (Theo was glad his own family had been protected in this way, since all CIM workers and their families were required to be inoculated, usually by the CIM nurse.)

There were no doctors anywhere near, and none who would travel to such remote and inaccessible places. Who would help? The church leaders begged Theo and Olive to do something.

Theo had found a place where there was very good quality clay. He made tablets out of it for them to take to stem the diarrhoea and minimise the dehydration. But that was only mildly effective. The best course was prevention by inoculation. Having learnt how to inoculate, he ordered supplies of anti-cholera vaccine, and when they finally arrived, he set out on a 17-day trip to inoculate 1300 people in eleven villages. It was an eventful journey.

One night, he was lost in the mountains and almost had to camp out. At last he found the track to Aguomi, arriving there tired and hungry at 9.30 pm.

Another day, when climbing a precipitous track, Theo dismounted to tackle the hill on foot. The pony missed its footing and tumbled, turning several somersaults before finally coming to rest 50 feet down. Theo thought it would have broken its back and been killed, but amazingly it survived[3].

Twice, huge floods of dark angry waters released by thunder storms in

---

2   See Theo's letter to his younger sister, Myrtle, dated 26 August, 1942.
    See also World Health Organisation, Cholera, February 2018, viewed 20 October, 2018, www.who.int/news-room/fact-sheets/detail/cholera.

3   See Theo's letter to his younger sister, Myrtle, dated 26 August, 1942.

mountain valleys further up came rushing down rivers just after he had crossed.

Tragically, many had already died before Theo arrived to bring them hope. Along the road, people had set up numerous devices aimed at keeping the 'cholera demon' away. Doorways were arched with thorns and prickly pear leaves. Others were covered with white handprints made by dipping hands in lime and then pressing them to the doors. Across some roads rough grass ropes had been strung supporting grass figures of men holding a tiny bow and arrow with which to shoot the demon. Elsewhere a dog had been killed and left on the road, either to frighten or placate the demon.

In many villages, courtyards were filled with manure in preparation for fertilising the fields. These dung piles became a fertile breeding place for the cholera germs. The folk had some understanding of quarantine, so people from 'unclean' villages were forbidden to enter 'clean' villages. This meant that on some occasions Theo did the inoculating in a shady spot outside the village, while people sheltered in makeshift huts until they dared return home.

It was heart-wrenching when people brought already infected family members to Theo for help. In most cases, this was just too late.

Everywhere there were good opportunities for practical talks on hygiene, how to avoid infection, and how to treat patients. He had numerous opportunities, also, for preaching and teaching.

Without the missionaries, most people in that area would have gone to locals with a reputation for treating sick people. But without medical training, results were very mixed and often their suggested treatments were useless or worse than useless, especially for those who had a chronic problem. There was one patient Theo and Olive treated in Taogu who had a chronic ulcer on his leg. The local witch doctor thought there must be an evil spirit causing the problem, so he got some dog's faeces to rub into the ulcer to expel the evil spirit. Not surprisingly, the ulcer only got worse not better[4].

On their first furlough Theo had obtained a set of dental instruments. Extracting teeth with dental forceps (though without any anaesthetic) hurt

---

4   A personal reminiscence sent to the author in an email dated 20 April, 2017, from Dr David Simpkin.

less than going to the local blacksmith who would knock the tooth out with a hammer and chisel, perhaps with the help of some pliers[5].

While Theo was out in the villages inoculating folk, the Metcalfs and Miss Kemp (who moved between various mission stations according to medical need) inoculated more than 3000 people at the home centre in Taogu. And so, the epidemic abated in that region.

Difficult conversations

During the evenings, however, after the children were asleep, a recurring conversation along these lines was taking place.

'Olive, it's time we thought about school for David.'

'But you are the best teacher he could have. You can teach him any-thing he needs to know.'

'But I can't give him enough time and still be able to do my job in the Bible School.'

'That's when I can supervise him. If you leave some work for him to get on with.'

'But he needs the company of other children his own age. He needs to learn how to get on with others. Anyway, you know the Mission policy. The children have to go away to boarding school so their parents are free to do their work. You know that's what we agreed to when we joined the Mission.'

'But he's so little. He's only six years old. He has never been away from home without us before. How can we let him go? And how would he cope if the school were interned as the former school at Chefoo was?[6]'

---

5   Referred to in David Simpkin's email of 20 April, 2017.

6   The China Inland Mission School (the 'Chefoo' school), was a Christian boarding school established in 1880 by the China Inland Mission—under James Hudson Taylor—at Chefoo (Yantai), in Shandong, a province in northern China. It had been set up primarily to provide an education for the children of missionaries in China. With children away at school (but usually able to visit their parents once a year) the mothers as well as the fathers would be able to take on a full missionary program. Staff of the school were required to be full members of the CIM. When Japan invaded China in 1937, the Chefoo school was not initially disrupted very much, although it became increasingly difficult for the children to travel home to their

And so the discussion continued. It was a challenge they had seen other missionary parents struggle with. Hadn't God given them their precious children? Didn't they have the responsibility, the right, to care for their little ones themselves?

Yet they acknowledged the Lord's prior claim on their lives. In applying to join the CIM, they had accepted its policies as the framework within which they would serve the Lord.

They thought back to the first exciting days after David's birth. They had known then that one day he would have to go away to school. But that day had seemed so far away. There had been an air of unreality about their conversations on this subject. Now it couldn't be avoided.

Previously, God had provided for them in seemingly impossible situations. They were experiencing his abundant blessings now because of their willingness to put God first in their lives, instead of grasping for the blessings in a time of their own choosing. Wouldn't he also provide grace for them to make this decision, and protection and provision for little David as he went away to school?

At last the unwelcome decision was made. Plans were made for David to go to the CIM boarding school at Jiading, a small walled city in the Sichuan province of south west China, a little north east of Yunnan. He was to leave soon after his seventh birthday in 1942.

Olive was immediately immersed in all the necessary preparations. She was supplied with a huge 'outfit' list of items David would need: suits, shirts, trousers, coats, underwear, socks, shoes that fitted him now, and more for when he outgrew them. None of these could be bought ready made, and even the cheapest material was prohibitively expensive. Olive had to become bargainer, designer, cutter and seamstress, and every stitch was sewn in love and watered with tears.

While Olive stitched, Theo made the travel arrangements. He would accompany David until they could meet up with others travelling from

---

parents for the holidays. After the Japanese attack on Pearl Harbour, however, in December 1941, the Japanese army took control of the school property at Yantai, and a year later the staff and students were interned at the school, meaning they could not leave, nor could family members visit them. This situation lasted until the war ended in 1945 when they were finally liberated by American paratroopers. By that stage, some children had not seen their parents for seven years. After the war, the Communist forces occupied north China and the school never returned to Yantai. Parts of the school were opened temporarily at Jiading in Sichuan province from 1941-1944, and this is where it was planned to send David.

Yunnan to the school. From there on Theo would return to Taogu, and the children and accompanying adults would travel on as a party.

Perhaps the greatest parting gift Theo and Olive gave David at this time was the example of a trusting confidence in the goodness and power of their Lord. Since going away to school was part of the life to which God had called them, there was nothing to be feared. It was a great adventure! God would be with them all: with David at school, and with the rest of the family back at Taogu. He would undertake for them in every circumstance.

Olive taught David some verses from Psalm 121, particularly verses one and two[7]:

> *I will lift up mine eyes unto the hills, from whence cometh my help?*
> *My help cometh from the Lord which made heaven and earth. [KJV]*

It was not easy for either the parents or the children. In her letter to her mother, dated 27 July, 1943, Olive wrote:

> *We miss him terribly, and wish it were possible to have him home occasionally, but travelling will continue to be very difficult until the war is over, and he is best where he is in school for the time being. He is wonderfully happy, and getting on well with his schoolwork. His first report said he works hard and steady and has made progress. No exams were held on account of a measles epidemic in the school... This will give you an idea of travel difficulties. It took Harry and David almost a month to get to [Jiading] too. You see, there are no passenger buses these days, just a few transport trucks and you have to almost fight your way on to get a seat, and sometimes have to wait for days or weeks for such a means of travel.*

When David set off on his long journey to Jiading, it was with a sense of anticipation and excitement that he started this next step in his life's adventure. For Olive and Theo, it was just the next big opportunity to renew their commitment to put God first in all they did, and prove his faithfulness to them and the precious children he had given them.

---

7   Simpkin, DM, op. cit.

Chapter 19

TAOGU TO JIADING

After the upheaval of getting David off to school in Jiading, life set-tled into a more predictable routine in Taogu. Theo was fully occupied teaching the Bible School students, arranging evangelistic trips for them, or accompanying them on such events.

Several villages had asked for a week of Bible teaching, so one week of term (which often lengthened out to two as additional openings arose) was spent by students going out to these villages and teaching the Bible there.

Other villages asked for students to be sent to them each week to con-duct worship services, so that also had to be incorporated into the Bible School program. How good it was to see the young people ministering to their own people, witnessing their joy and delight in sharing the good news of the love of God!

Olive was kept busy with household duties: baking bread every second day, preparing meals, making cakes and biscuits, and washing and sewing for Dorothy and Helen. On top of that, she taught classes for the female students on how to prepare Sunday School lessons, or took meetings for women, incorporating simple hygiene and child care as well as Bible teach-ing. Occasionally she and the girls would join Theo in visits out to even more remote villages.

Invisible dangers

Illness was always a risk in village life, and cholera and typhoid were not the only diseases to be wary of in Yunnan. Typhus is contracted differently—from the bite of an infected louse, tick or flea. It occurs particularly where people live in crowded or unsanitary surroundings. When Theo and the students travelled to remote villages to preach, they were exposed to such dangers.

Perhaps it was following one such trip that first Olive, and then Theo contracted typhus which laid them low for weeks. Typhus typically is accompanied by high temperature, chills, severe headache, and muscular pain. In some cases there may be a severe cough, haemorrhagic rash and delirium. The latter was Theo's experience. He was so ill that another missionary, Mr Hatton, came to Taogu to take over Theo's classes in the Bible School.

As the days passed, Theo's temperature kept rising stubbornly. His thirst seemed insatiable, but he couldn't face food. His weight fell drastically. Mrs Metcalf helped by cooking tempting treats for the invalid. Miss Daisy Kemp (the CIM nurse who attended Olive at the birth of David in Wuding) was sent for as well. She relieved Olive of some of the overnight nursing, since Olive herself was still weak from her earlier bout of typhus.

Theo's headaches were fearful. The fever left him weak and thin. He often woke at night, burning up with the fever, and calling for a sip of water. At the height of the fever, in his delirium, he imagined people were offering him juicy bunches of grapes, but they were always just out of his reach[1].

Fearful thoughts distressed Olive.

'How will we survive if anything happens to Theo. How would it affect David, away at school without his Mummy or Daddy?'

'Almighty God, you are the Divine Healer. Please bring Theo through this so that he may continue to serve you and your church here in Yunnan. But not my will but Yours be done.'

And in the Lord's goodness, Theo began to improve. The fever subsided. Gradually he was able to endure the sunlight and began to read again. It

---

1   Some details are given in Olive's letter to her mother dated 27 July, 1943. The same letter refers to a previous letter that contained more details. Sadly that letter has not survived. Theo also referred to his illness in a letter dated 13 September, 1943 to his older sister, Mary. Some of these details had become part of family lore.

was a new experience for him to be served and waited on by others instead of serving them. For this period, Mr Hatton was teaching his students at the Bible School. It was a lesson for Theo that no-one is indispensable in the Lord's work.

In a letter to his sister dated 13 September, 1943, Theo wrote as follows:

> God has others he can and will use, and can get along without us if needs be! So I have been amusing myself reading magazines, playing Chinese checkers, helping Olive bottle peaches and pears and so on.

When he first commented on all the weeds he could see in the overgrown garden which had not been tended for weeks, Olive knew he was back! Praise the Lord.

David at school in Jiading

Theo and Olive heard that war clouds were gathering over Yunnan, but they scarcely made any impact on the people around Taogu. Theo wrote:

> In this secluded mountain village, overlooking huge valleys and deep gorges, which run steeply into the Yangtze River, we have been kept in peace and quietness as though there were no war going on not so very far away.[2]

But through it all there was an ache in their hearts. Something was missing. Someone was missing! The girls missed their big brother—someone close enough to their age to have time to play with them but old enough to be the resident authority.

Every letter from David, and each report that arrived from the school was pored over and read and re-read by Theo and Olive. They longed to have him home to visit them occasionally, but travel to and from their remote location was so difficult.

He did manage to get back to Taogu during one school vacation, but it had taken him nearly a month to return to the school, and all travel was risky. Theo and Olive had to make do with his letters, and reports of his progress and how happy he was at school.

They heard about his journey to the school, starting in an army convoy of trucks, with an ex-missionary who had joined the army as their escort.

---

2   See WT Simpkin 'A Tribal Bible Institute' in *According to plan, Part of the story of the China Inland Mission in 1943*, compiled by Bishop Frank Houghton, St John Bacon, Melbourne.

Part of the trip was in an unpressurised bomber which went so high the passengers had to be given oxygen periodically. The last part of their travel was by boat, since Jiading was at the junction of two rivers, the Min and the Dadu. One carried clear water, and the other, muddy water. The waters mingled as they reached Jiading and a combined larger Min river proceeded to flow down into the Yangtze.

Boarding school days—and nights[3]

The teachers at David's school were two Australian women: Ruth Porteous, whose father had been Theo's Field Superintendent for some years before his death, and Elizabeth Swanton who would later marry Harry Gould—one of the new workers Theo and Olive had mentored in Dali. The housekeeper was Isa Mulholland, the wife of Theo's great friend Tom, whose first child Douglas was born in Wuding not long after David had been born there. So Douglas was at the school as well.

The boys slept in one dormitory, and the girls in another in a different building, after having dinner together in the dining room. At night, the staff dined together in the main house after 'lights out' in the dormitories.

When the teacher on duty disappeared down the stairs from the dormitory for dinner, the boys would post a look-out at the top to give warning of her return. In the meantime, one of the older boys was deputed to tell stories, making up yarns of adventure and daring for an enthralled audience of little boys.

On other occasions, the teacher on duty might play a record such as Handel's *Messiah,* or some negro spirituals, on a portable gramophone. David often went to sleep to this stirring accompaniment.

The children at the school went through the normal stages of childhood development, but without the immediate personal comfort and support of their own understanding and sympathetic parents. Some children found this extremely difficult. Teachers tried to be kind, but discipline was important in their overloaded lives as well as compassion. Bedwetting became a source of anxiety for several children who were reprimanded by the teachers for such 'carelessness'.

---

3 The details regarding David's time in Jiading are derived from David's personal memories, as well as those of a slightly older friend, Keith Butler, who was at school in Jiading with David. A copy of both of these reminiscences is in the author's possession. They are referred to as Simpkin, DM, op. cit., and Butler, KJD, op. cit.

The discipline of finishing the food on one's plate, no matter how distasteful it might be, was considered an important habit to form. So various children, David among them, found themselves still sitting at the meal table an hour after others had left while they tried to force down the hated boiled eggplant, or some foul-tasting meat.

A more enjoyable experience for David was when the children gathered round the open fire in the staff sitting room on a Sunday evening, singing hymns from the school *Golden Bells* hymnbook. David enjoyed music which had always been an integral part of his home, and it was at Jiading that he began to learn to play the little pedal organ, following in the footsteps of his father, Theo, his Grandfather Simpkin, and Grandma Kettle.

Along with many other children, David succumbed to many childhood complaints while at school, some being conditions which—if he had been home in Australia—he would never have encountered. He had mumps, intestinal worms, hepatitis, and tonsillitis, and he became familiar with the school's sick bay. Antibiotics were either unknown or unavailable, so bed rest and good nutrition were the usual treatment, apart from the hated enemas as worm treatment. Theo and Olive's evening prayers always included a heartfelt petition that David would be kept well.

School excursions

School life at Jiading was not all difficult. Strong friendships began to develop among the children, some of which endured for decades. And they had a lot of fun together.

There were plenty of mud banks beside roads and walking tracks around Jiading, and one enterprising child started to carve a 'highway' for his toy cars in the mudbanks. The idea quickly took root and soon many other children were constructing their roads and highways. These were guarded jealously, and seldom was another child allowed to drive his or her cars on another child's roads. A lot of energy and inventiveness was invested in this road-making enterprise and much pride was taken in the end results.

One day the teachers took David and the other children for a walk to see a huge seated Buddha[4] carved into the stone mountain, above the confluence of the Min and Dadu rivers. The statue is over 70 metres high,

---

4   United Nations Educational, Scientific and Cultural Organization (UNESCO), *Mount Emei Scenic Area, including Leshan Giant Buddha Scenic Area,* viewed 2 November, 2018, whc.unesco.org/en/list/779.

having over 1000 spiral curls carved on its head. A small child can stand up inside its ear. It was immense. David could not help thinking of the words of Psalm 115 which his parents had often read to him after seeing some of the idols feared and worshipped by people in the villages.

Describing man-made idols, the Psalmist said the following:

They have a mouth and eyes,
*   but they can't speak or see.*
Their ears can't hear,
*   and their noses can't smell.*
Their hands have no feeling,
their legs don't move,
*   and they can't make a sound.*
Everyone who made the idols
*   and all who trust them*
*   are just as helpless*
*   as those useless gods.*

People of Israel,
you must trust the Lord
*   to help and protect you.*

Psalm 115:5-9 CEV

In the school holidays, when it was not possible for some children, like David, to return to where their parents were serving, other arrangements had to be made.

On one occasion, David and the others left at the school were taken for a holiday to Omei, a well-known summer destination in Sichuan not far from Jiading.

Mount Omei is a very important cultural site in China, since it is the place where Buddhism first became established in China. In fact, the first Buddhist temple in China was built on the top of Mt Omei, in the first century AD. It is a strikingly beautiful area and the children delighted in going for walks up the steep mountains, past splashing waterfalls and clear streams.

David's letters home from this holiday were full of the places and things he had seen. There were the beautiful rainbow beetles he saw while walking through fields of maize. Once he discovered quartz crystals in the fields.

Sichuan crystals, a variety of quartz (silicon dioxide) are usually clear, double-ended crystals, having triangular faces at the pointed ends and rectangular faces around the middle. Often they had other material trapped within the crystal. These aroused in David a simple wonder and delight in the natural world. This and awe at their Creator stayed with him throughout his life.

Letters to and from home

Every week the children would be given pens and paper and instructed to write their weekly letter to their parents. The fortunate children, like David, who regularly had letters from their parents to answer had a good starting point: answer any questions, comment on events their parents had written about, and then tell about their own week.

David's letters from his father often included a little sketch of something funny that had happened in Taogu. The family's dog, Caesar, sometimes featured in these drawings. As was his wont, he had been out in the village on one occasion, taking on all and sundry of the village dogs in a free-for-all fight. His heart was bigger than his fighting skill however, and he had limped back home looking decidedly worse for wear.

Or there was a picture illustrating a story about the man in the village who had a watch. He was almost the only one in Taogu to have one, and

Dorothy and Helen on a pony, travelling to an outlying village
(Photo: WT Simpkin collection)

he was very proud of his possession. But he was never able to learn not to overwind the watch. When the spring was wound too tight, it broke, and the owner took it down to Theo to have it mended. This had happened so often, Theo was afraid the time would come when there would barely be enough spring left for the watch to work.

Olive's letters to David mentioned any special occasion in the home, such as a birthday meal, visitors who had come, or a trip out to another village. She told him what flowers were out in the garden at present, and most letters included a dried pressed flower, such as a pansy from her pansy patch.

Sometimes the family had been out to a village to preach, or teach, or give medical help. Every letter reminded David to trust in the Lord, the ruler of the nations, even those nations that did not acknowledge him. And always, he was told that his mother and father loved him dearly.

Too close for comfort

Although Jiading was well away from the centre of fighting between the Japanese and the Chinese, air-raid sirens were frequently heard. The school staff were taking no risks, and constructed an air-raid shelter, tunnelled into the rock wall behind the school.

The children were drilled in their expected response to the siren. They practised tossing their mattresses and soft toys out of the dormitory windows, and, in case the stairway was on fire, escaping down a rope ladder through an emergency hatch in the staff member's bedroom. Once on the ground they lugged their stuff into the pitch-black air-raid shelter, lit only by the teachers' storm lanterns. For most of the children, this was just a game with the grown-ups joining in.

Fortunately, the city was never actually bombed during the period the school was there, though the fighting between the Chinese and Japanese continued.

The CIM had long since realised that the war would affect its operations, so it had transferred most of its administration from Shanghai to Chongqing, China's wartime capital. The war had divided China and the CIM's field of operations into two regions: 'Occupied China' and 'Free China'. The Japanese occupied the eastern part of the country, but the Chinese government had moved inland and was resisting the Japanese advance in the western mountainous provinces.

As the Japanese made a concerted push towards Chongqing, it was felt that the war was getting too close for comfort.

The Mission leaders decided that the school in Jiading must be closed and the children and staff would join the general exodus from China. The route now used routinely for evacuating to the west was over 'the Hump' (i.e. the Himalayas) to India and from there to all points of the compass.

Just before Christmas 1944, the children, staff and luggage were stowed into American army trucks which roared out from Jiading bound for Chengdu. The Americans at the US airforce base in Chengdu treated the Jiading party to the most lavish Christmas dinner they had ever eaten.

From Chengdu, the school was split between two planes bound for Kunming, where they would be transferred to planes heading towards India. One plane arrived in Kunming from Chengdu within a couple of hours as expected.

David was on the other plane. His experience was very different.

Chapter 20

ON A WING AND A PRAYER

David, now nine years old, was taken aboard a small, two-engined transport plane. This was no passenger plane. The corrugated iron floor was piled high with their luggage, and benches along the sides served as seating for the passengers.[1]

The flight to Kunming should have taken only two hours. But it took much longer, and it was not Kunming where they eventually landed, but a small minor airfield, Yunnanyi. What had happened?

Before taking off, the pilot had to wait for a faulty pressure gauge to be repaired on the plane. To fill in time while waiting for the repair to be done, and for the children and adults to board with their luggage, the pilot decided to fill the plane's fuel tanks. (Normally, for such a small flight he would not have bothered refuelling until he reached Kunming.) He reasoned that refuelling now would make his return trip from Kunming quicker.

Once all were safely stowed aboard, the plane took off.

As he approached Kunming, the pilot discovered that there was a

---

1 The details in this chapter come largely from Simpkin, DM op. cit., Butler, KJD op. cit., and from the description given by Steve Knights. These memoirs were sent to the author in a personal email by Steve's daughter on 30 October, 2016, referred to as Knights, op. cit. The author also remembers travelling in planes like this. It was not an enjoyable experience!

Japanese air-raid taking place. He climbed to a higher altitude to avoid enemy aircraft, and circled around, waiting for the Japanese planes to leave. Since the airforce had no children's parachutes, the crew had refused to take any for themselves.

The plane was not pressurised and the oxygen level was low. Many of the passengers were unable to control their airsickness, but there were no 'sick bags' to distribute. Soon the floor of the plane was running with vomit.

Night fell, and the city lights were switched off to hinder the Japanese planes in any planned bombing raid. Without radio beacons or lights, and in dense low cloud, the pilot of the small plane found it hard to get his bearings. He flew around, searching for a gap in the clouds. He became increasingly desperate as the flight time lengthened and the fuel became dangerously low.

How much did the adults in the plane or the parents of the children understand all of this? It is unlikely that either the children or their parents knew anything of this until very much later. But without doubt, the parents were praying for the Lord's protection of their children in all their journeys, as were the missionaries accompanying the children on the flight.

None of Theo and Olive's letters from this period have survived, so we do not know how much they knew of this story, nor when they heard it. At least, they would probably have received a telegram, informing them that the school was being evacuated, and would then have to wait for letters to fill in the gaps.

At last, with only a very few minutes of fuel left, the pilot saw an opening in the clouds, and descending through it, saw a small less frequently used airfield (Yunnanyi), and managed to bring down his plane safely there.

Was it just by chance that he had decided to refuel the plane before leaving Chengdu? The CIM family saw this as another indication of God's over-ruling power and care for his children. In his life story, David put it this way: 'But for that faulty pressure gauge, I would not be here today'[2]. When the plane came to a standstill, the pilot jumped out and kissed the ground.[3]

---

2 Simpkin, DM, op. cit.

3 See Knights, op. cit. Steve was a missionary who joined the party in its onward flight from Kunming to India. He was one of the 1939 new workers with whom Theo and Olive had worked in Dali, and was now married. His wife (Edith) was expecting their first child and had been advised by the CIM doctor that she should go to India for a Caesarean birth. Steve and Edith were in Kunming, waiting anxiously for that plane to arrive. In fact, their daughter was

Up, up and away

The plane refuelled and flew on to Kunming, Yunnan, where they joined the other children and staff. The combined party from Jiading then had to try to find a plane to Calcutta. They were joined by another missionary couple, Steve and Edith Knights (Steve had been one of the new workers Theo and Olive mentored in Dali).

All the British aircraft had been confiscated by the Chinese, to utilise in their war with the Japanese. Furthermore, the Chinese government did not want to admit that they were unable to keep the foreigners safe in China. They did not want people fleeing China for India.

Nevertheless, the British Consul in Kunming went to extraordinary lengths to locate a plane for the CIM party of adults and children, about forty in number. They were loaded onto army trucks, hiding among boxes of goods, and were secretly transported to an airfield where they found a plane waiting for them. All of this was done surreptitiously, before the Chinese authorities could prevent them, and the British Consul later got into great trouble over the affair.

Thus the Jiading CIM School was evacuated to Calcutta, India, stopping to refuel in Burma. The flight path was over the Himalayas. (The Himalaya Range is the highest mountain system in the world, separating the plains of the Indian subcontinent from the Tibetan Plateau.)

In between bouts of air-sickness, David looked out in awe at the grandeur and beauty of the mountains below. Range upon range of soaring, snow-covered peaks were separated by valleys and huge alpine glaciers. The cabin of the plane had small round windows that could be opened, and David remembers putting his hand out and feeling the rush of the air past the plane as it travelled at, perhaps, 200 km per hour. However, his reaction to the scenery was overpowered by his extreme airsickness.

Flying in Calcutta, India

The party from Jiading was heartily glad to land in Calcutta, where very crowded but temporary accommodation was provided for them in and around the Calcutta Yacht Club. While enquiries for more permanent accommodation were made, the children and teachers had some time to explore the fascinating city of Calcutta.

---

born in Calcutta, in 1945. They returned to China, serving there until 1951.

David blinked. What a vibrant, colourful place this huge city was, so different from the Chinese wartime cities he'd seen. Were those giant butterflies fluttering around the tall buildings? Or brilliant birds, swooping and diving in the sky above? Yet each seemed to be tethered, anchored to the earth. He blinked again, as the soaring, dancing shapes came into focus.

Then it dawned on him. They were kites. All shapes, sizes and hues. Wherever he looked he saw them, flying from the streets, out windows, from the rooftops.

As the days in Calcutta went by, David discovered that kite-flying was serious business. To those with a few annas in their pockets, string coated with powdered glass could be purchased for the kite string. Then, with a bit of practice, the owner was able to wage war on other kites. With a swift pull on the string, just as it crossed the path of another kite's string, the owner could sever the other string, and the competitor's kite would be lost. With any luck, the victor could retrieve yards of the opponent's string to add to his own store.

Kites were not the only lively thing to be seen around the tall buildings. There were monkeys everywhere too. And the monkeys were expert thieves, especially where food was concerned. It didn't take the children long to realise it was safest to finish eating something before going out on the streets.

In the botanical gardens they were amazed by a giant banyan tree. At that time, it was over 200 years old, and had thousands of aerial roots giving it the appearance of a forest rather than a single tree. The tree survives (as a clonal colony) without its main trunk, which decayed following damage by cyclones and was removed in 1925. The whole tree covers three or four acres.

On another occasion, the school visited various temples, including a burial site where the Hindu practice of burning the bodies of the dead was in progress. It was a gruesome sight, seeing the human flesh burning, and some of the children had recurring nightmares about it.

'The Lord will provide'

Where could more permanent housing be found for the school party of 35 children plus several adults in wartime India? The CIM family had often proved that God is the one called *Jehovah Jireh*, 'The Lord will provide' (Genesis 22:14 CEV), and so he provided again.

Mr Bernard Studd was president of the St Andrew's Colonial Homes in Kalimpong[4] at this time. The homes had been set up to provide for destitute Anglo-Indian children but some of the houses were now made available to the CIM party.

Their accommodation was to be in 'The Hills', Kalimpong, just across the valley from Darjeeling. It was 300 miles north of Calcutta and within sight of Mount Kanchenjunga, the third highest mountain in the world. At last the party proceeded by train from Calcutta to Siliguri, and then by taxi to Kalimpong. School was in again!

This is how another child in the CIM school party, Keith Butler[5], described this last part of the journey from Jiading:

> So by crowded train across the Indian plains, past working elephants and held up by sacred cows on the line, then by taxi up the winding monkey-draped jungle road, we arrived at paradise—a landscape of the world's highest mountains, glistening white in the cool clean crisp air, deep valleys, and the church and Swiss-like cottages dotting the slopes. There was a half-hearted attempt at lessons, but most of the time seemed to be spent exploring, always carrying a small packet of salt to melt off the huge black leaches which often fastened themselves onto our bare feet or legs.

Scholastic shenanigans

The children in the St Andrews Homes all went barefoot, and it didn't take the CIM children long to follow suit. After a few weeks they were able to take a flying leap from a veranda onto a gravel path without turning a hair.

Just as David's letters home from Jiading had referred to occasional childhood complaints, so too did his letters from Kalimpong.

Tonsillitis was still a frequent part of his life, keeping him out of action several weeks every term. Eventually, when a visiting surgeon came to the St Andrew's Colonial Homes, it was decided that the CIM children who were susceptible to tonsillitis should be added to his operating list. David's

---

4   Dr. Graham's Homes, *over a century of caring for children,* 2010, viewed 2 November, 2018, www.drgrahamshomes.net/milestone.php.

5   Butler, KJD, op. cit.

was one of well over a hundred tonsillectomies the surgeon did at Kalimpong. At least, there were no sore throats after that.[6]

Many of the CIM children also developed trachoma. There was a very nice swimming pool at the St Andrew's Colonial Homes, and the CIM children loved using it. All of them vied to be able to swim the length of the pool under water without coming up for a breath. David later wondered if this was what caused the trachoma.

The treatment at that time involved rubbing a copper sulphate crystal along the inside of the eyelids. The children hated this remedy which caused their eyes to sting badly for several hours. So they were given a lolly and spent the next couple of hours in bed resting, with their eyes closed.

Often the children would play on a bank under a big tree. Some of its branches hung over the bank, and it was great fun leaping off the bank, catching hold of a branch and swinging back and forth before letting go and dropping to the ground.

Once when David was doing this, the branch he grabbed was too flimsy. It broke, and he fell awkwardly, breaking his left wrist. There were no X-rays available, and no plaster of Paris to immobilise the fracture. So, his arm was set without the benefit of anaesthetic, and bandaged onto a padded board for several weeks. He was a bit of a hero for a few weeks, and fortunately his arm healed without any apparent problems.

A French (or spool) knitting craze went through the school in Kalimpong, and teachers were kept busy finding empty cotton reels, hammering four or five tacks into the top, sourcing some wool, and then teaching the children—boys and girls—how to do the French knitting.

It became a competition to see who could make the longest 'tail'. These multi-coloured 'tails' could then be used to decorate all kinds of objects.

World War 2 ends

One highlight of the school's stay in Kalimpong was hearing of the end of the Second World War. Keith Butler, one of David's friends at the CIM school, recalled it like this:

> Highlight of our two months stay in Kalimpong was the news of the victory of the Allies in Europe. The whole community celebrated VE-Day with a huge bonfire on the top of the ridge, with the backdrop,

6 Simpkin, DM, op. cit.

across a 40 mile wide valley, of the sunset glow on Kanchenjunga.
An incredible thunderstorm followed, flashing and reverberating
between those same icy walls.[7]

But even on such a night of celebration and peace, there were more imme-diate concerns and dangers. Walking back to the mission home on that starless black night by the light of torches, the children and staff hoped that the panther recently seen close to the village was not prowling unseen in the shadows.

The aftermath of the war

Back in Taogu, Theo and Olive realised that in a couple of years, they would be due to take furlough again. It was now late 1944, five years since they had returned to China—five years they had spent in Dali, Guanglu Zhen, Gebu and Taogu.

The school continued in Kalimpong through 1945, during which time David never saw the rest of his family. Mail had been sporadic throughout the war years, and even after the end of the Second World War, it was slow and uncertain. None of Theo and Olive's letters have survived between 1943 and 1947.

As 1946 commenced, the CIM leaders disbanded the Kalimpong school. Since the war had ended, it should be possible for a school to again be opened somewhere in China. In the meantime, parents were asked to take charge of their own children.

Theo and Olive were due to return to Australia late that year, since it would then be seven years since they left Australia. With the school in Kalimpong closing, they would need to travel to India, pick David up, and all travel on to Australia together. The trouble was that transport from India to Australia was totally inadequate for the demand. How would they all get home? Where would the funds come from to pay for the whole fam-ily's travel from China to India to Australia?

As God had shown them in the past, where God led, he would provide. So they believed he would supply all these needs now.

The family travels from Taogu to Kalimpong

In Taogu, Olive and Theo commenced the familiar routine of sorting and

---

7 Butler, KJD, op. cit.

packing in preparation for travelling. They expected to be away for a year, though their past experience had shown them that this was by no means certain. When they returnèd to China, would they be going back to Taogu? Or would the local church and the CIM feel they would best serve somewhere else? And who would take their place in the Bible School in Taogu while they returned to Australia?

Weeks of travel ensued: long hours walking or riding the ponies over the mountains; days of bumping and jolting in smelly noisy trucks; nights trying to fit the whole family into a room in noisy Chinese inns; frustrating days at the Kunming Mission Home trying to arrange travel for the four of them to India via Burma, and at the same time keep the children from getting under the feet of other missionaries.

And finally, they were up in the air, flying out of Yunnan—the only way to get from China to India. But for how long? Only God knew.

The plane landed in Calcutta, and the family's senses were assailed by all the different sights, sounds and smells there.

Dorothy found the resident monkey population quite alarming, being especially concerned for her little sister from whose hand a bold monkey stole a biscuit quite early in their stay there. They loved watching the Indian children flying their kites from the rooftops of the high-rise buildings, though they never acquired the same expertise.

On another day when the family was out walking in the market, four-year-old Helen let go of her mother's hand, and for a heart-stopping few minutes, her family was out of sight. They quickly found her in the crowds, and ever after she remembered this as one of her first experiences of the protecting care of her heavenly Father.

Theo and Olive immediately started trying to make arrangements for the family's travel to Australia. But so many people had been displaced worldwide through the war—and so many ships destroyed or sunk—that it became apparent that it would be months rather than days before they could find space on a ship. It would be better to join David in Kalimpong. From there they could maintain telephone contact with shipping agents and even the British Consul in Calcutta, trying to book the family on a ship to Australia.

They were allocated one of the St Andrew's Colonial Homes cottages, Mount House, for their use in Kalimpong, and they were all soon together again. What a wonderful reunion it was!

David had grown so much in the two years since they last saw him. His sisters' awe of their big brother disappeared quickly, though, and was soon replaced by admiration and devotion. David's shyness and reserve with his parents probably took a bit longer to overcome.

Theo and Olive arranged with the St Andrew's School for David and Dorothy—who was now about seven years old and ready for school—to attend classes there. When it became apparent that the passage home would take considerable time to arrange, Theo accepted a request from the principal at the St. Andrew's School to join the staff.

The three Simpkin children in Kalimpong, India, 1946: David (10), Dorothy (7), Helen (4)
(Photo: WT Simpkin collection)

The days of waiting continued. Helen celebrated her fifth birthday while in India. She was a fairly precocious child and had learnt to read despite not having attended school yet—a result perhaps of being the third child in the family with two older siblings to try to keep up with. Still, she was free to run around and play while the others were at school. One warm day when she swung on the down-pipe beside their house on her way out the door, she disturbed a hive of wasps which had nested in the downpipe. The angry creatures swarmed all around her, attacking her. Whatever remedy her parents applied must have been successful, though, since she did not have a severe reaction to the many stings.

Theo was always ready to accept any invitation he was given to share the story of the people of China whom he had served, as well as to tell the 'old old story of Jesus and his love'. When invited to go and preach to the American soldiers in their barracks in Kalimpong one Sunday he accepted with alacrity. He took the family along with him and Helen happily sang 'Jesus loves me' to the men, many of whom had been separated by war from their own children, and whose hearts were touched by this little child.

Back to Australia

At long last the family's eight-month interlude in Kalimpong came to an end. Bookings were finally able to be made, and they travelled down to Calcutta and boarded a ship bound for Australia. They celebrated Christmas on board before arriving in Australia in the summer of January 1947.

Theo and Olive had not seen their families for over seven years.

Chapter 21

A WORLD ACROSS THE SEA

The Australia to which Theo and Olive returned in 1947 was very differ-ent from the Australia they had left behind late in 1939. The Second World War had intervened. Conscription had been introduced and almost a million Australians—more than a tenth of the entire population, men and women—had taken part in the War.[1]

Hardly a family had been untouched. Many sons and daughters, fathers, mothers, brothers and sisters had fought in campaigns against Germany and Italy in Europe, in the Mediterranean and North Africa. Olive's younger brother, Murray was one. He had enlisted and trained as a pilot and died in the Middle East, less than a year after Helen's birth. Theo's younger brother, Ray, had also fought in the war and survived. Others had been involved in the ugly conflicts closer to home in south-east Asia and the Pacific.

The Australian mainland itself had come under attack.[2] Japanese air-craft had bombed Darwin and other places in northern Australia. Japan-ese submarines shelled Sydney and Newcastle, and torpedoed and sank

---

1   The Australian War Memorial, London, *Second World War, 1939-45*, n.d., viewed 2 November, 2018, www.awm.gov.au/articles/second-world-war.

2   The Australian War Memorial, London, 2017, *Air raids on Australian mainland – Second World War*, viewed 3 November, 2018, www.awm.gov.au/articles/encyclopedia/air_raids.

a hospital ship off North Stradbroke Island, Queensland. The Australian Government had turned increasingly towards the United States for support in the Pacific area, although not cutting its ties with Britain.

Every home had been impacted by the rationing of food, clothing and petrol[3]. The 'Land of Plenty' was now suffering privations of its own, although the shortages of food were never as severe as those in the United Kingdom. Air-raid drills took place in schools, and some families dug air-raid shelters in their back yards in case of attack.

But by 1947, the war memories were slowly receding, and Australia was looking to a new future. Women had for the first time been elected to federal parliament. The Australian Government embarked on an intensive promotional campaign encouraging migration from Britain, and then from Eastern Europe to Australia.

The first major post-war wave of migration was of Displaced Persons—people who had fled from their own countries because of the war and were hoping for a new start. There was still a strongly 'White Australia' mentality, with Asians often belittled. Even so, Australia's population was developing a more diverse ethnic character.

Theo's and Olive's experiences had been different. The land they had been living in had been invaded by the Japanese years before the Nazis invaded Poland. The resultant sufferings of China, whose war was longer and more violent than many in the West realised, were largely unknown in Australia.

Whereas the World War had concluded and Australia was looking towards a hopeful future, China's part in the global war was followed by civil war which was even then being waged across the land. China had suffered millions of casualties and was continuing to suffer. Its economy had collapsed—fuelled by soaring inflation and corruption—and millions of Chinese people had become refugees. This had impacted Theo and Olive, away out in the high mountains of Yunnan, in the scarcity and high cost of food and other necessities, and in the paucity of news from outside. Newspapers probably didn't reach the mountain villages, though they would be pasted up on big walls in the larger towns, where the public could read them. So news might be brought into the villages and shared by travellers.

---

3   The Australian War Memorial, London, 2017, *Rationing of food and clothing during the Second World War*, viewed 22 October, 2018,
    www.awm.gov.au/articles/encyclopedia/homefront/rationing.

A FOOT WIDE ON THE EDGE OF NOWHERE

Mail had arrived only sporadically. Transport—unreliable at the best of times—had become even more unpredictable. This had meant anything they needed to have brought in would take many days to reach them. And their son David had seldom been able to travel home from school to spend the holidays with them. In the end, war had meant that his school had been evacuated to India where Theo and Olive and the girls finally caught up with him enroute to Australia for furlough.

Nevertheless, it was so good to be home in Australia. There was clean drinking water at the turn of a tap, and electric light and power at the flick of a switch. The gutters ran with water on rainy days, but never with raw sewage. There were doctors and hospitals that could be reached, in the cities at least, within minutes. Papers were delivered each week day, and it was possible to read what was going on within Australia and further afield.

This was how they described what it was like for them to return to Australia.[4]

> *After living in troubled China all through the war years, experiencing some Japanese air-raids over Kunming, living under the threat of Japanese invasion, and enduring the insecurity of a rapidly soaring cost of living due to the crashing values of the Chinese dollar, followed by the anxiety of eight months in India, you can imagine the relief to be under the Australian flag again. Though, really our hearts have been kept in 'perfect peace'—'kept by the power of God through faith'.*

Best of all, they could catch up with family members and friends they had not seen for seven years. David had been only three or four when they were last at home, and Dorothy was just a baby. Helen was not then even a 'twinkle in her father's eye'. Now they were children of eleven, seven and five years of age.

What a delight it was to introduce them to their Grandma Kettle, as well as to aunts, uncles and cousins! Their home base in Melbourne was again with Olive's mother, Grandma Kettle, who lived in Carnegie. When it was time to visit Theo's relatives, they would stay with one or other of his sisters in Maryborough or Lexton.

---

4   Excerpt from their prayer letter on returning to China the following year, 1948.

School a world away

There were medical check-ups for the whole family on arrival, and arrangements had to be made regarding schooling for the three children for this year in Australia.

Theo and Olive investigated the local government schools. Education in Australia was free, compulsory and secular, and in the Melbourne suburbs, there were numerous schools. The Simpkins could not consider private schools for the children. They did not have the money for the fees. Both Theo and Olive had been educated in State Schools, and had no reason to be discontented with their education.

David was enrolled with other lads of his age at Gardenvale Central School in East Brighton, in Grade 7. Theo bought him a second-hand bicycle and he mastered bike-riding very quickly. He rode to and from the school (about 4 km each way) every day. Dorothy and Helen were both enrolled at Ormond East State School, and every day—like the majority of the children—they walked to and from school. Grandma Kettle's home was over a kilometre from the school.

David soon discovered that school in secular Australia was very different from the CIM school he had attended in Jiading and Kalimpong. There were no prayers at the start or end of the day, and no understanding or appreciation of what their parents had been doing in China. Punishment by the strap or ruler was not uncommon for even minor infringements such as turning round in class.

David started having piano lessons. He wanted to learn about the theory of harmony so that he could try his hand at composing his own music. His teacher, however, was not impressed by this suggestion, saying she felt David needed to concentrate more on his actual piano practice at this stage. (Perhaps it may have been stretching her own musical knowledge further than was comfortable for her!)

For Dorothy and Helen at the Primary school, there was (Christian) Religious Instruction (RI) once a week, given usually by an elderly and rather uninspiring clergyman.

Helen had early learnt to read so found no difficulty with her school work. She delighted in being called on to read a Bible reading in church. She was no shy retiring violet when it came to displaying her abilities. A couple of older ladies in the church were so taken with her that they offered to adopt her, to relieve Theo and Olive of at least one of their children while in China. Fortunately for Helen, her parents didn't give the generous offer a moment's thought.

On Sundays, the family accompanied Grandma Kettle to the Glen Huntly Methodist church where she was a member. There was Sunday School for the children—a somewhat more enjoyable experience than RI at school.

At home after the evening meal, the family gathered around the piano for *libai*, or family prayers. After singing a hymn, accompanied on the piano by Grandma Kettle or Theo, they would read a Bible passage and then anyone who wanted to (including the children) could pray. Any matters that had arisen during the day could be made the subject of prayer. It was never doubted that the God who had created them loved and cared for them deeply.

Still, this was a new experience for Olive and Theo—living like a normal family, with the children going to school every day and returning at the end of the school day. There was schoolwork to be looked at, homework for the children to do, reading to listen to, reports to read. They valued education and expected each child to work as hard as they could and do their best.

Partners in mission

Neither Theo nor Olive had a guaranteed income. The CIM's policy regarding finance was that they would never enter into debt, nor would they solicit funds from the public. Rather, they would make their needs known to God in faithful, believing prayer, and trust that God would move people to give. Whatever came in to the Mission was divided equally between the members, from the newest recruit to the General Director. So, the money allocated to each of its members fluctuated according to the giving of the Mission's supporters. Theo's and Olive's testimony was that, in all the time they had served in the CIM, their needs had been met.

Seeing the hardship some had experienced through the war, they valued all the more the sacrificial gifts of their partners in mission. Even the very small amounts, which were all some could afford, were precious in the sight of the Lord.

Whenever an opportunity arose, Theo and Olive went on deputation, telling stories of their past seven years in China—speaking of the students in the Taogu Bible School, and the service those students would now be giving to the local tribal churches in the mountain villages of Yunnan—sharing the countless moments they had seen the Lord provide and protect.

Where to next, Lord?

While in Australia, Theo and Olive received a letter from Bishop Frank Houghton, CIM General Director, asking if they felt able to accept a call to return, not to Yunnan but to the Bible School in Guizhou province where Theo had been for six months or so before Helen was born.

As they were thinking and praying about this request, some letters arrived from China, from Yunnan tribal Christians.

A Miao pastor wrote to Theo, full of appreciation of his Bible teaching. He said the students Theo had trained were just the sort of men the tribal churches needed. He gave a very earnest appeal to Theo

The Simpkin family out on deputation
(Photo: WT Simpkin collection)

and Olive to return to resume Bible teaching in their midst.

Another letter—this one to Olive—was from a Lisu girl who had been their home helper while she attended the Bible School in Taogu. She told Olive of her grief when her bonny baby son had fallen ill and died at the age of ten months. There had been no-one to whom she could go for help. She wrote to Olive saying:

If you had been here, my baby would not have died.
If I had been a bird I would long ago have flown to you![5]

How this touched Olive's heart! She and Theo saw these letters as a further confirmation that the Lord still wanted them in Yunnan.

Eventually they were asked to go back, not to Taogu, but to Sapushan to resume their Bible teaching there. Whether this would be a permanent Bible School, or simply various Short Term Bible Schools would depend on the decision of the United Tribes Conference.

---

5   Quoted in Theo's letter to his younger sister, Myrtle, dated 27 July, 1947.

Chapter 22

ACROSS CHINA BY AMBULANCE

Olive was aware that when they returned, she would have three children to provide for at the CIM school. Following the Japanese surrender, the CIM had taken steps to re-establish a school in China for the missionaries' children.

A disused school that had belonged to the American Church Mission became available to the CIM. The Americans handed over the property for the nominal sum of US$1 with the stipulation that children from their Mission also be admitted to the school along with the CIM children.

The school was in a scenic tourist resort, Guling village, on a strikingly beautiful mountain, Lushan, in Jiangxi province. The climate in Guling was generally cooler than the hot steamy plains at the bottom of the mountain, and would be more suitable for children to grow and develop. The area was one of great geological significance, and being off the beaten track, should be safer. A wonderful place for a school!

Necessary preparations

Preparing for the children to go to the boarding school meant three lists of clothes and other supplies for several years had to be sourced, named and packed. So while the children were at school each day in Melbourne, Olive frequented material stores to buy cloth for the children's clothes, and wool shops to buy knitting patterns and wool for their jumpers. Evenings were taken up with knitting and sewing, stitching and packing.

In order to help keep track of clothing and other items belonging to so many children, it was the CIM school policy to give each child a number. Every article of clothing and every item they brought to the school had to be labelled with the child's name and number. When the Simpkin children returned to China in 1948, David's number was red 25, Dorothy's was blue 48, and Helen's blue 140.

Olive's fingers must have felt like a pincushion after the hours and hours she spent, just sewing names and numbers onto countless pieces of underwear, socks and outerwear, as well as towels, sheets and blankets. Theo's single sisters, Mary and Myrtle, as well as other friends, periodically came to stay and helped in these sewing evenings.

They did not know the latest about the political situation in China, nor how long it would be possible for Christian work to continue there, yet they were strongly convinced of God's call to them to follow the example of Jesus by 'teaching, preaching the good news of the kingdom, and healing', wherever they could in China.

In a prayer letter sent out as they returned to China, Theo acknowledged the dangers and difficulties they might encounter[1].

> And now our faces are turned China-wards once more. The boat on which we have been offered passage is the "Yunnan," and it is due to sail from Sydney to Hong-Kong before Christmas. So we hope that early in the New Year, if the Lord will, we shall be once again among the Tribes-people of Yunnan.
>
> Those of you who have seen our lantern slides will be able to visualize these primitive people with their picturesque dress and very poor dwellings, and also the wonderful beauty of the grand old mountains.
>
> Our three children will be at the C.I.M. school in Kuling, 1500 miles away. So we are under no illusion as regards the dangers and difficulties we shall have to meet, the partings and separations, the loneliness and privations. If it were not for the fact that our Lord has said, "My Grace is sufficient for thee," I suppose we would not be

---

1   Taken from their prayer letter on returning to China in 1948.

able to face it. But that grace given to us freely in every time of need, through your prayers, will enable us to be more than conquerors.

The boat's departure was delayed and it was early 1948 when the family packed up and said their goodbyes again to family, friends, and Australia. So, they enjoyed their first Christmas in Australia as a family—and their first Australian Christmas since Theo had left in 1929, and Olive in 1933.

They disembarked at Shanghai where arrangements were still being finalised for the opening of the school in Guling. For about a month the family joined other returning CIM families at the Shanghai CIM headquarters while travel plans were made, and they were updated on conditions in China.

Before a word was spoken...

On board ship on their way out to China, Olive raised her concerns about sending their three young children to boarding school, especially since the youngest was only six years old, and neither of the girls had ever been away from their parents before. Perhaps this is how the conversation ran.

'If only I could go to the school with them, Theo. I'm sure I could help at the school with all the children there, at least until the girls settle in.'

'Let's talk to the Directors about it when we reach Shanghai, Olive', replied Theo. 'But first, let's pray about it.'

Olive and Theo spent much time in prayer that the Lord would reveal his will to them, and, if possible, open a way for Olive to accompany the children to Guling at the beginning of term. On arriving in Shanghai, they had meetings with the Directors to decide how best they should be deployed in Yunnan during this term of service.

Now it so happened that the American Mission to Lepers had heard of the need for an ambulance in Yunnan and had raised the money to purchase one. It had been shipped to Hong Kong and from there to Shanghai, and there it was still, awaiting a driver to take it across the more than two and a half thousand kilometres of winding roads from Shanghai to Yunnan.

Mr Stead, a CIM missionary, had agreed to drive it, but he needed another driver to accompany him and share the task. Would Theo be willing to do this? It would take him weeks, or even months to negotiate the journey, as well as to arrange for the transport of the Simpkin family's goods to Yunnan.

Perhaps Olive could accompany the children to Guling and help them settle in there while Theo and Mr Stead drove the ambulance to Yunnan. In fact, the ambulance would be an ideal way for them to transport the family's luggage. It could all be stacked inside the ambulance!

Once again, Olive and Theo discovered that the concerns of their hearts for the children, made known to God in prayer, had been matched by provision made months ago in the loving providence of a sovereign God.[2]

Across China to tribesland in Yunnan

Theo and Mr Stead set off from Shanghai, having obtained all the necessary travel permits for the long journey across China. Near the cities, there were surfaced roads, though most of these were in a poor condition after so many years of war. Once in rural areas, roads were mostly dirt and stones, full of potholes. As they approached the mountains, the roads began the long winding course up, around, over and down, on and on.

There were countless rivers to cross. Sometimes there were bridges. Sometimes they had to find a shallow part of the riverbed and drive through. At least once they had to drive the ambulance up some wooden planks onto a ferry which took them to the other side of the river, where the reverse process had to take place.

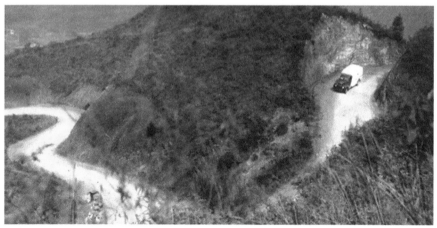

The ambulance on its trip across China (Photo: WT Simpkin collection)

2 Sadly, no letters have survived from this period, and I have had to rely on existing photos and family memories for this section.

Theo and Mr Stead drove along this road beside rice paddy fields when bringing the ambulance from Shanghai to Kunming (Photo: WT Simpkin collection)

Ambulance crossing a river on a ferry (Photo: WT Simpkin collection)

Theo and Mr Stead with the ambulance they drove across China in 1948 (Photo: WT Simpkin collection)

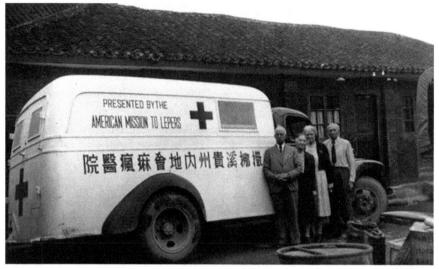

The ambulance was handed over in Kunming after their arrival there.
(Photo: WT Simpkin collection)

Once the ambulance arrived in Kunming, it had to be handed over, so Theo then needed to find a truck that would take the luggage on up from Kunming to Wuding. From Wuding, he hired porters to carry all the luggage up the hill to Sapushan. He described this last leg of the journey like this[3]:

> *As you climb the long, steep track, the air becomes clearer and cooler, the sky becomes a deeper entrancing shade of blue, green grass and wildflowers appear at the roadside, while azaleas and rhododendrons grow wild on the mountain slopes. At the precipice you cannot ride the pony up the steep stone steps, but he will not object if you hang on to his tail and get a little help that way. Otherwise at such altitudes, you will soon be exhausted.*
>
> *From here on you will see several herds of cattle and goats feeding, with a few skinny runts of pigs, and some shaggy dogs...Sometimes a wolf, or leopard, or a deer is sighted and chased, for these [i.e. the Miao] are intrepid hunters from childhood. Then a little further on you are sure to see several Miao hoeing up their maize or potatoes, or perhaps ploughing the mountain-side to plant buck-wheat or oats.*

---

3   From their prayer letter on returning to China, 1948.

These are the crops on which they depend for food. The soil is poor, the yield very small, rent for the land takes maybe half or more of the harvest, and taxes are heavy, so there isn't much left for the family larder.

What strikes you most everywhere is the warmth of the welcome. Nearly everyone you see calls out to you (in Miao) a cheery greeting, and there are plenty of smiles and chuckles of delight if you happen to know the appropriate answer in their language. But then the barrage of questions in Miao which follows leaves you stunned, so you smile your pleasure at being there and hurry on.

...If it happens to be the Harvest Thanksgiving the chapel will be packed with nearly 1000 people. You will be amazed to see the huge baskets set to receive the offerings, for these people, though poor, give liberally for the Lord's work. Indeed, they give so liberally that right from the beginning of the work 40 odd years ago, the Miao church has been self-supporting.

Sapushan village women, 2014 (Photo: S Joynt)

Maize harvest in Sapushan, 2014 (Photo: S Joynt)

On one occasion Mrs Nicholls [a fellow-CIM missionary] pointed out to me an old Miao woman tipping her offering of corn or buckwheat into the basket. 'In less than three months that family will have eaten all their grain, and will have to dig fern roots for food till the next harvest is reaped!' And yet she would not 'appear before the Lord empty'—she must give sacrificially to Him who loved them and gave Himself for them.

Theo had arrived in Sapushan.

Chapter 23

SCHOOL ON THE MOUNTAIN TOP

While Theo and Mr Stead were negotiating the roads from Shanghai to Kunming, Olive joined a party of children and teachers on their journey from Shanghai up to Guling. They boarded a river steamer travelling about 500 miles up the Yangtze to Jiujiang in the plain below Lushan mountain. Here, the river was still about a mile wide, and was navigable for a further 1000 miles upstream.

A new name at a new school

For many of the children in the group, going to boarding school was a totally new experience. Others, like David, were returning to something familiar, even though the school was now in a new location.

Another child in the party enroute to Guling was also called 'Helen'. Someone in the group suggested that it was going to be confusing having two 'Helens' at the school. Since the youngest Simpkin was actually Marjorie Helen, they thought she ought to be called Marjorie to avoid confusion. Somehow the idea stuck. Helen had no objection. It was quite a novel idea—going to a new school and having a new name! By the time they arrived in Guling, Helen had become 'Marjorie' to everyone at the school except her immediate family, who still called her 'Helen'. (To this day, anyone who was acquainted with her solely from the period she was at the school knows her only as 'Marjorie'.)

From Jiujiang the children and adults all clambered up into trucks which drove them to the foot of the mountain. There was no motor road any further, so the last long climb was on foot for those able to manage it. Most of the women and children were carried up in *huagans* (sedan chairs), with the smaller children allocated two to a chair.

One of the children, writing years later, remembered it like this:

> *The [carriers] hoisted the poles of our chair to their sweaty shoulders. After a brief moment of imbalance they secured their positions and set off in short quick steps. The poles holding the chair acted like giant springs, and we bounced rhythmically with their stride. Up the red clay path, up the Thousand Steps where the straw sandals of the front coolie were level with the hat of the last. Round angled corners swinging over the cliff below. Past the coolies, straining with a pole across their shoulders with our luggage dangling at both ends. For nearly three hours M and I silently sat while the coolies strained upwards.*
>
> *The path levelled out near a small t'ing-tze (decorated pavilion). Our speed quickened as we came to the Gap—the small and only cluster of shops on the mountain. We sped down the last gentle descent to the school in the darkening afternoon. Past the rushing stream, round the last bend; through the school gateway, down the concrete steps. We were lowered onto the stony path in front of the school.[1]*

Olive had never enjoyed riding in a *huagan*. It was too much like being in a ship riding the waves, and she always ended up being sick. But there was no alternative, unless she felt able to get out and go on foot, climbing up and up and up the 14 kilometres to their destination on the mountain top. That would have held up the entire party, so she had to endure the bouncing swaying ride and the resultant nausea. She was very glad, at last, to climb out of the *huagan* on her own two shaky legs.

---

1 FRK, in Martin, G 1990, *Chefoo School 1881-1951*, Merlin Books Ltd., Braunton Devon, pp. 140-141. Reprinted with permission through the auspices of the Chefoo Schools Association in 2009, Kwik Kopy Design & Print Centre, Barrie, Ontario, Canada.

Sedan chairs (*huagans*) carrying people up to Guling
(Photo: Chefoo Schools Association, used by permission)

The party on the path up to Guling
(Photo: Chefoo Schools Association, used by permission)

The Guling school

The school consisted of two large stone and brick buildings with numerous other cottages and workshops on the hillside. Further downhill, screened by some very tall plane trees, and below a big retaining wall, was the school oval. The party was taken up the big stone steps into the school where they were soon shown their accommodation.

The dormitories for the small boys and girls were on the top floor of the main building, McCarthy House; the boys down one end and the girls up the other. Dorothy and Helen were both in this area, though in different dormitories since Dorothy was with the older girls. They were shown their beds, each nicely made up and covered with a plain bedspread. It was quite an adventure for the girls. They had never slept in a dormitory with other girls like this before. David was with the older boys at a lower level in McCarthy House.

The second large building, behind McCarthy House, was Bruce House. The senior girls' dormitories were there, as well as the Sick Bay. Lower down in McCarthy House were the classrooms, art room and library. The dining-room, kitchen and laundry were in the semi-basement.

Up in the attic of McCarthy House, above the junior dormitories was the

In 2012, the school was being used as a hotel (Photo: H Joynt)

A FOOT WIDE ON THE EDGE OF NOWHERE

luggage area where all the trunks and suitcases were stored. Now that this group of children had arrived, their clothes needed to be sorted through, and garments appropriate to the current season brought down to the dormitories. Each year, at the change of season, the winter clothes were packed away and the summer clothes checked for size and condition and then brought down to the dormitories. This was done in reverse at the end of summer. Helping in tasks like this kept Olive occupied during her three months at Guling along with providing supervision of younger children at playtime and on walks and outings. Olive enjoyed seeing how the school ran, and how her 'three chickens' behaved.

At first, Olive made sure she was there to tuck her daughters in at night, until they felt more sure of themselves. She also went to other children as well, giving a cuddle where it was needed, since some of them were missing their mothers terribly. She wondered how Dorothy and Helen would cope when she left. It was good to see David catching up with children he had known in Jiading and Kalimpong, and the friendships growing.

Nature study in a wonderful environment

The climate and beautiful environment of Guling meant there was a strong emphasis on outdoor activities and nature study. Any excuse for a picnic was good enough. One day it might be all the Australian and New Zealand children who would climb up the hill behind the school to the tiger-lily-covered hilltop, Monkey Ridge, where the teachers would spread out the meal. Another day, the children whose parents worked in Yunnan might go dancing down the hill beside the stream to picnic under the giant, thousand-year-old Three Trees, while those from other provinces picnicked elsewhere.

On balmy summer evenings, the children were sometimes free to take their plate of food outside and eat it, perched on a rock or even up on a tree-branch. The

The ancient Three Trees in 2012
(Photo: H Joynt)

variety of native plants, flowers and insects enriched every nature study lesson, arousing in many of the children a life-long love of the natural world.

Olive was aware that through the whole of the school program there ran a thread of love and compassion that was rooted in the teachers' devotion to God. Hardly a child was unhappy but someone noticed and tried to comfort that child.

And yet, there were some unhappy children at the school[2].

The three Simpkin children were not among them, not even aware of those children's unhappiness which, it has since emerged, arose from their enforced separation from their parents. Some felt resentment that persisted into their adult lives. They felt 'rejected' by their parents.

David, Dorothy and Helen never felt that way. They enjoyed studying in an international school, rubbing shoulders with teachers and children from many different countries. The physical environment was superb. They received quality education from committed Christian teachers, who believed they were called to their job.

There were still meals which every child, at one time or another, struggled to get down. There might be one teacher who rubbed them up the wrong way. There were occasional tears, longings to be enfolded again in their mother's arms or sat on their father's knee. For the Simpkin children, those moments did not last, and they had no doubt that their parents loved them deeply.[3]

Olive returns to Yunnan

As the first term at Guling drew to a close, Olive realised it was now time for her to leave Guling and re-join Theo. On the first night of Olive's journey back to Yunnan, at bedtime, her thoughts were irresistibly drawn to her children. How were they feeling without their mother to kiss them

---

2   In fact, a whole new movement, called 'Chefoo reconsidered', has been established under the OMF umbrella, to provide help and resources for people who felt their lives were adversely affected by their experiences at the Chefoo schools. OMF International, *Chefoo Reconsidered—The Story Continues*, October 2016, viewed 2 November 2018, omf.org/blog/2016/10/11/chefoo-reconsidered-story-continues/.

3   I have often wondered why this was the case. Could it be because a week never went by without each of the three of us receiving a personal note from each of our parents? Our parents were very faithful letter-writers, often including a drawing, or a dried flower from their garden in the letter.

goodnight? Would they cry themselves to sleep? Would they be afraid? Her heart was heavy. How she had enjoyed spending these months at the school!

Not long after she commenced her journey back across China to get back to Theo in Yunnan, she received letters both from the principal (Mr Stanley Houghton, the brother of Bishop Frank Houghton who was, at that time, General Director of the CIM) and from Miss Ailsa Carr, the teacher in charge of the junior school, setting her heart at rest about how the children were coping now that their mother had left. Ailsa's letter, dated 4 May 1948, said:

> *Dear Mrs Simpkin,*
>
> *Mr Houghton shared with us your kind letter, and I feel that it is we all on the staff, and especially on the 'top floor', who want to say thank you to you for all you did for us while you were here. You certainly saw the works from the inside, and got underneath a lot of it, and if it will help you to pray with the understanding, we will be more than ever grateful. We miss you and all your help...*
>
> *Your children have been marvellous since you left, so brave and sensible and cheerful. Dorothy put out her arms for a hug the first night, but Marjorie [i.e. Helen] though very friendly, has seemed more independent. They came to Church with me on Sunday, David occupying an exalted position in the choir.*
>
> *It must have been frightfully hard to leave them, and as we realise again the sacrifice entailed, we realise too how great is our responsibility and our privilege. We shall value your prayers and also your confidence, and you will have ours, being labourers together in a very real sense.*
>
> *With every good wish, and again thanking you for all you did for us,*
>
> *Yours sincerely,*
>
> *Ailsa Carr.*

How much Olive appreciated these thoughtful personal notes from busy staff members!

Months later, when Olive's birthday came round, the Deputy Head Master, Mr Gordon Martin drew a picture of Olive riding a pony over the mountains of Yunnan. He gave it to Dorothy and Helen to colour for their mother. David added an inscription on the back, and Mr Martin posted it on to Olive, together with a letter giving her encouraging news of her three children, their place in the school and the development of their character. He wrote:

> We have had our most successful close to the term, with a fine program in spite of very inadequate practices in the big Tu Shu Guan [Library] Hall just across the stream from the school, lent to us for the day: it holds 1000, but we must have had more than 500, so that the hall looked reasonably filled. Dorothy and Marjorie[4], I noticed, were leaders of various parts of the school in the rather complicated ascending and descending of the platform, which needed self-possessed and sensible children to take the lead.
>
> At one point in the preliminary practising Mr Houghton said, 'We seem to be entirely depending on the Simpkin family to keep us straight', and they did their part admirably. We had to cut out a lot of stuff which had been projected for the occasion (even so our program lasted 1¾ hours): So David's form found themselves cut out of reciting Milton's Nativity Ode. But David had his share of the singing, and did well...
>
> Today we went out with the boys and girls of the form, (including David) for a picnic to the Temple in the Clouds...Heather and Dick [Mr Martin's younger children] were with us, and walk slower than the long legged fourth formers, and I was very pleased to see that David was the one who chose to go at their pace and pick flowers and make conversation with Heather, instead of doing what the crowd did and go at his own pace. I know that you will be glad to hear of this; it is the sort of thing that shows what family upbringing a boy has had as well as what sort of a boy he is becoming. Well done David.[5]

---

4   i.e. Helen

5   Excerpt from a personal communication from Mr Martin to Olive dated 29 July, 1948.

Sapushan countryside, 2014 (Photo: S Joynt)

Theo and Olive re-united

The travelling from Jiangxi to Yunnan took weeks, probably by *huagan*, river boat, bus and plane. Olive was glad finally to be back in Sapushan with Theo. They had so much to talk about.

Theo would have told her all about his long drive across China, and the hair-raising experiences he had driving the ambulance. 'You would not have liked it, Olive', he would have told her. She probably responded by telling him about the mischief one or other of the children had got up to at the school.

Now it was time for them to get on with the job of teaching. As they embarked on their new assignment in Sapushan, it was under stormy skies, with the distant grumble of thunder an ever-present reminder of the new political environment.

Chapter 24

INTO THE UNKNOWN

The sounds of Japanese aeroplanes, bombings and guns had ceased in China. At first there was hope that now peace might return to the Middle Kingdom[1]. But the peace was short-lived. Very soon the National-ist Government and the Chinese Communist Party resumed fighting each other for the control of China. Who would prevail?

A tremor ran through the CIM ranks when they heard how, in a Com-munist-controlled region, a woman missionary from another mission had been arrested, taken before a People's Tribunal, and summarily executed. There followed news of the violent deaths of four members of other mis-sions[2] in Communist-controlled regions.

Was this the direction the future might take? Theo and Olive knew that their lives were not their own. They had counted the cost of serving the Lord in China. Would they be called on to make the ultimate sacrifice?

---

1   The Chinese word for China is 'Zhongguo', literally 'Middle Kingdom', since China saw itself as the centre of the world.

2   Thompson, P 2000, *China: The Reluctant Exodus, The story of the China Inland Mission's withdrawal from Communist China,* ed. Tewksbury, ME, OMF International, Littleton, Colorado, USA, pp. 9–10.

Sapushan

At first, it seemed that the Communist soldiers in the Sapushan area were behaving with restraint and courtesy. Perhaps it would be possible to still function in areas under Communist control. After much earnest prayer and soul-searching discussions, the CIM determined that their missionaries would remain in China as long as it was still possible to serve the Chinese church. Any decision to pull people out would be taken by the Mission's directors, or the superintendent of specific regions, who would convey the message to the missionaries.

In Yunnan, there was still work to be done, and a warm welcome from the tribal churches greeted them. So, Theo and Olive settled down. Their letters from this time were, of necessity, very guarded. Who knew when mail might be opened and read by the authorities? Nothing must be included that could bring harm to the local believers.[3]

For Olive, not a day went by that she did not think—with a pang—of her children, so far away from them in Guling.

How had David gone in the pole-vault[4] at the school athletics last week?

The mission home in Sapushan (now disused) (Photo: H Joynt)

---

3   This was Theo and Olive's message to the family when they returned to Australia in 1951. See also Thompson, P, op. cit., pp. 66-67.

4   While at Jiading, David had won a prize for pole-vaulting. (See Simpkin, DM, op. cit.) It is likely that his enjoyment of this sport continued in Guling.

He had so hoped he would excel. On his birthday in November 1948 he entered his teens. What direction would his life take? Would he, like his parents, choose to seek God's guidance about what his life's work should be?[5]

Dorothy was preparing for the test for one of her badges in Brownies. Had she been able to complete the task?

Helen—Little'un—was she learning to knuckle under to school routines and obey the school bell promptly instead of considering her own activities of greater importance?

Working as a team

Olive was able to be more 'hands-on' at Sapushan than she had been able to be in Taogu. Now she could take on a full load of teaching and helping, alongside Theo. She would have been much more confident, now, in her language, and accepted the challenge of preparing for classes. There was a great need for lesson plans, visual aids, flannelgraph and other materials to be used in the Sunday Schools, Christian Endeavour groups, Young People's groups and Choirs of the local churches.[6]

The Miao Pastor in Sapushan was eager that Theo and Olive should hold regular Short Term Bible Schools (STBS) to train the local leaders who conducted worship, as well as taking nightly meetings in one of a hundred or so places in the region around Sapushan.

Theo and Olive made frequent trips out to surrounding villages, organising classes for local leaders, and gathering together any believers who were eager to help their own people understand more of the Gospel, in addition to providing simple medical care. They travelled mostly on horseback, which was one means of transport that never made Olive sick. The fresh mountain air on their faces brought a glow to their cheeks. Olive felt like a girl again, encouraging her horse to speed up to a canter when there was a straight bit of track ahead.

She smiled as she remembered how she and her brother Howard, as teenagers, had raced each other across the hills near Gisborne in Victoria—a world away from Sapushan.

As the sun sank lower in the sky, Theo and Olive would look for any village that might welcome them for the night. They were becoming

---

5   See Olive's letter to David dated 8 November, 1948.

6   See note about this in Theo and Olive's prayer letter on returning to China in 1948.

well-known in the mountains around Sapushan, and frequently they were met, long before they came to the village, by children and young people begging them to stay.

Whenever he had free time, Theo loved working in the garden. On the 11 September 1949, Theo wrote the following to his younger sister, Myrtle:

> Yesterday afternoon I had 'time off' from teaching or study and put in an hour or two working in the flower garden at the side of the house. We have quite a lot of pansies planted out (50 odd plants) and sweet peas and stocks etc. But I put seed in a new bed: pansies, sweet peas, stocks, larkspurs. So Christmas time or later we should have plenty of flowers. We could gather cart-loads of dahlias which grow wild around here. In a fortnight there will be cart-loads of wild cosmos too!! Praise the Lord for flowers. We could do with lettuce, carrot or cabbage seed though.

Olive helped in the garden too, and the children thought of the pansy bed as her domain.

Home for the Christmas holidays

The letters regularly exchanged with the children now included plans for them to visit Sapushan for the Christmas holidays. It was the general practice in the CIM that children would go to their parents for school holidays once a year, if traveling conditions were safe enough, and the distance not too great. They might even arrive close to David's birthday. It was a special birthday, for he was entering his teens in November. In her birthday letter to David dated 8 November, 1948, Olive wrote:

> Happy Birthday to you. You are growing up, son, aren't you? You have entered your 'teens' and before you're out of them, you will no doubt have begun your life's work, so we, and you too, will need to pray much that the Lord will very definitely guide you in the way that He wants you to go, and that you may have no doubt at all as to what He wishes you to do, as well as being willing to do whatever He would have you do.

But as his birthday approached, David, like so many at Guling, contracted chickenpox. Disaster! Would he be well enough to travel? Would he be allowed?[7] Eventually the school decreed that he could manage the journey if he rested as much as possible on the trip.

First the children were carried down the mountain by carriers. Then they boarded a boat and proceeded up the Yangtze to Hankou where the party had to spend a day or two waiting for a plane to take them on to Kunming in Yunnan. After a day or two their plane arrived and the Yunnan party boarded for the flight to Kunming.

From Kunming, they were driven to Wuding and finally carried up the hill to Sapushan, where they were greeted by a very happy Theo and Olive. The family was together again.

A late birthday party for the new teenager was how they started their Christmas holidays. Olive had been planning for this occasion for months. She ended her birthday letter to David, saying:

> ...we will pray much that the Lord will open the way for you all for the 26th, so that you could be home with us here on the 27th. Shall we have your birthday party that night, or wait until you are all a bit rested up after your journey?

The life of the village continued normally while the children were home and they were included in all that was going on. As winter approached, the schools broke up for the winter recess. There were no schools in many of the villages[8]. If children in those places wanted an education, their families had to arrange for the child to be boarded in a village that had a school. Sapushan, being a bigger centre, had a school. When school broke up at the end of term, those children who had been boarding returned to their own homes and Sapushan became a quieter place.

One day, it had been decided to fell some of the huge gum trees, planted in the area decades earlier by an Australian missionary. Theo showed the local men how to take the thick bark off the trees in sheets and smoke it to preserve it. (He had probably seen his own father do this decades earlier in Australia.) The big sheet of bark then made an excellent roofing material. And the children had a ready-made playground, climbing in and out of all the fallen branches.

On other days, the children might accompany the local Miao girl whom

---

7   Simpkin, DM, op. cit.

8   See Theo's prayer letter dated September 1930, where it was noted that the CIM established some schools for tribal children.

Theo and Olive had employed to care for the goats they had purchased when they first settled in Sapushan. She would take the goats out onto the hillside to find pasture during the day after having first milked them. The children could not communicate with her except by gestures, since they had so little Chinese, but they enjoyed running up and down the hills together with the goats, Fidget, Black Billy, Midget, Black Major, Black Minor and Madam Black.

The Miao folk loved having feasts, and when there was a wedding in the village, the whole Simpkin family was invited. The dirt floor of the house where the wedding feast was to be served was carpeted with fresh pine needles from the many pine trees on the hillside. The fresh fragrance of the pine needles combined with the delicious festive food made these unforgettable occasions.[9]

There were traditional special Christmas services in the church as well. Hundreds of people streamed in from villages all around, despite the cold winter weather. The mountains echoed to their singing, and sermons were not just quarter hour homilies. They were much more likely to go on for an hour or two.

For the girls, whose Chinese language had largely disappeared during the time in India and then on furlough in Australia, it meant sitting for a long

Believers gathered outside the church in Sapushan after a service
(Photo: WT Simpkin collection)

9   Simpkin, DM, op. cit.

Guests at a Miao wedding feast in Sapushan, 2014 (Photo: S Joynt)

time, listening to an incomprehensible language. Occasionally, a familiar phrase might pop back into their minds, if the preacher was using Mandarin. David remembered more, but not a lot. If, however, the preacher was speaking in the Miao language, they would understand almost nothing. But it gave them a glimpse of what their parents were engaged in while they were at school, and there was no mistaking the joy in the faces of the worshippers.

At one stage during their holiday, Theo suggested taking the older two children with him to visit a neighbouring village, Daqing. Seven-year-old Helen stayed in Sapushan with Olive, enjoying this

The Simpkin family together in Sapushan
(Photo: WT Simpkin collection)

rare one-to-one time with her mother, and learning some cooking skills at the same time.

One very cold day, Olive thought she would try making ice cream. Of course there was no refrigerator, no freezer, but water left outside overnight was frozen by the morning. So Olive made up the ice cream mixture and set it outside overnight to freeze. The following day she took it inside, beat it up, and then placed it outside again the following night. The next day it was ready. It may not have been like ice cream from a big city shop, but the children thought it was wonderful.

All too soon, however, the end of the holidays loomed. After all the last picnics, parties and outings, it was time for the children to pack up and return to the school. Theo escorted them to Kunming where they joined the other Yunnan children returning to Guling for the new school term.

Making the most of each opportunity

Following Mao's proclamation of the People's Republic on 1 October, 1949, all of China including Yunnan came under Communist control. The new government was installed, and at first things seemed to proceed smoothly and peacefully. The new officials in Wuding were very friendly. Theo and Arthur Glasser (who with his wife, Alice—new CIM missionaries—were stationed in Wuding) had several interviews with the officials.

'We are here to protect the foreigners and the church', they told Theo. [10]

There was no way of knowing how long this situation would last, but while it did, Theo and Olive wanted to take advantage of every opportunity to serve the church. The Short Term Bible Schools, and classes for local believers who might become leaders in their churches, continued.

This is what Olive wrote to her mother in a letter dated 18 January 1950:

> *We have been through Wuting recently several times, and all things are as usual, so you will see there is nothing, at present, to worry about. Just whether their attitude will remain as at present remains to be seen, but anyway for the present we are permitted to remain in this land, and so it behoves us to be up and doing while the door is open. There may come a time when it will not be possible to remain here but that time is not yet.*

---

10 See Olive's letter to her mother dated 18 January, 1950. A similar sentiment is noted in Thompson, P, op. cit., pp. 34 f.

Olive and her Miao Bible School students[11]

In September 1949, a Miao Girls' Bible School commenced in Sapushan, attended by girls from surrounding villages. Theo wrote (11 September, 1949) to his sister Myrtle about one group of young girls attending the Bible School:

> These girls at the Bible School aren't much like students—yet! They have never been to school, and are rather untamed, or rather undisciplined. They pray earnestly and intelligently; they sing well and seem to enjoy it immensely; and above all show that they love the Lord. One of them said, 'If it was an ordinary school we wouldn't have time to come. There's too much farm work to be done at home. But because it is a Bible School, we just HAVE to come and let the farm work go.'

The subjects taught in the Bible School by Theo and Olive were Scripture, Chinese and Miao language, Arithmetic and Knitting.[12] For practical work, the girls conducted a small Sunday School, taking it in turns to teach the children while watched by their fellow students. The classes were followed up by a time to critique one another's teaching under Olive's guidance, and

---

11   A friend has recently met a lady in Yunnan who knew the girls in this photo. Although several have left the faith, there are some who remain believing.

12   See Theo and Olive's prayer letter dated 8 June, 1950.

thus learn new teaching approaches. They also participated in the weekly women's meeting, and alternated in leading their daily morning worship.

Some days, Theo and Olive had six or eight classes to teach between them, as well as participating in worship. Theo often played the pedal organ or taught the choir new hymns. What a delight it was to see eager young believers giving up their time to study God's Word!

The daily knock

Almost every day brought someone to their door who needed medical help. One day it was a woman with her jaw[13] out of joint and unable to close her mouth; another day, a young mother with her baby with a fever, a cough and a rattly chest. In a letter dated 3 June 1950, Olive wrote the following:

> *We are kept busy some days in our own medicine room with sore eyes, dog bites, sores, etc. Of course there are the usual ones who just come in for a dose of malaria medicine (a course of it I mean), or headache medicine. There has been a peculiar kind of flu going round that gives folk rheumatic pains. Our woman had it, and could not move her neck for a week or more. Others had it in the joints of legs or arms. We are treating one baby with a burnt head that was burnt 4 or 5 months ago, and never had any treatment until we started on it a week or so ago. You can perhaps imagine the mess it was in (or can you?). Anyway, it was just a whole head of black messy scabs, with pus oozing out from underneath. First we just put a softening ointment on to get the old black scabs off, and then began a course of sulphur treatment. He comes in every week now from about 10 English miles distant; he was in yesterday, and it is healing up nicely, but slowly, and we take care to impress upon the parent who brings him in that they must be patient to the end and bring him every week until he is absolutely healed. I hope they do, as there will be no hope for him if they don't.*

Theo and Olive did the best they could for their sick visitors, and were so thankful when the Mission decided to place a doctor in Sapushan.

Dr Max Gray brought a very welcome service to the Chinese and tribes-people of the area[14]. There was some local traditional medical help available in Wuding, about eight kilometres down the hill, but no hospital

---

13 Theo's letter to his younger sister, Myrtle, dated 11 September, 1949.
14 See Theo's letter to his younger sister Myrtle, dated 11 September, 1949.

or Western trained doctors any closer than Kunming, three days' journey away. Dr Gray ran a small dispensary from the side of the house in Sapushan, where he also performed simple procedures. He did not discriminate among his patients, so besides the hundred or more Chinese who came to the dispensary for treatment each week, there were also numerous tribes-people.

For each one, there was, in addition to the medical treatment, a simple reminder of the care of the Good Shepherd who loved even the poorest of the tribes-people of Yunnan.

Olive regularly dressed the burns on this small child who had fallen into the fire
(Photo: WT Simpkin collection)

Changing winds

Although some other missions in China were pulling their missionaries out, this was not yet the case for the China Inland Mission. In fact, 1949 saw forty-nine new missionaries arriving in China, believing God had called them to serve him there. Despite being criticised by some for this decision, the CIM leaders were convinced God was calling them to remain for the present. [15]

When the People's Republic was proclaimed, however, and the Nationalists fled, the revolution entered a new phase in the civilian arena. Travel permits[16] were required for people to travel outside their own district. This became especially difficult for foreigners in China. The processes of applying for permits and granting them provided ample opportunity for local authorities to ruffle or humiliate the foreigners—by delaying, or insisting on complex bureaucratic procedures.

Away in the mountains of Yunnan, Olive's and Theo's hearts were heavy

---

15 Thompson, P, op. cit., pp. 40-46.

16 Mentioned in Theo and Olive's letters dated 12 December, 1950 and 8 January, 1951.

as they read letters and telegrams from the school and the CIM leaders, saying the children would not be able to return to Sapushan for Christmas this year. Travel permits were just too difficult to obtain.

This would be the first time the girls had ever spent Christmas apart from them. Just two months before Christmas (25 October, 1949), Olive had written this hopeful note to David:

> *Just now, too, we are trusting the Lord to make a way for you all to come home at Christmas time. He can. We know that, don't we, and I believe He will. Last year you 'broke up' on your birthday, didn't you, but we have not heard this year when you are to 'break up'. Anyway we'll be looking forward to your homecoming in about six weeks time and then what a lovely time we'll have, won't we, so goodbye for now and may your new year be the best yet!*
>
> *Much love, Mother.*

Now the tone of her letters had changed. They couldn't understand how they had misunderstood what they had believed God was telling them. Just a few weeks after Christmas 1949 Olive wrote this to her mother:

> *Of course they were not able to come home. It was a big disappointment, but we are trying to take it as 'His appointment', though it still is a mystery why conditions had to be as they are seeing the Lord seemed to give the assurance that He was working for us and that he would bring the children home to us. So now, it is a case of still trusting where we cannot trace, and to patiently await the Lord's time for the answer to our prayers. It would have been impossible for them to get to Kunming, as it has been bombed a number of times and the CIM folks there have had a rather nerve wracking few days. It is a fortnight now since they have had air raids[17] so we trust it is all over and things will soon settle down to normal again.*

Why was God allowing this to happen? Yet not one word of complaint ever found its way into their letters to the children. Instead, they reminded them how much they loved them, and that in his good time, God would surely bring them together again.

---

17 The air raids were probably Communist air raids, aimed to wipe out any remaining pockets of resistance in Yunnan.

A vivid parable

In Guling, the children were aware that the situation was changing. David, being older, understood more about what was happening. There were armed Communist soldiers stationed at the gates of a big local property which had been the summer residence of the Nationalist leader. Their property was quite near the school, and each Sunday, when the children walked to church in the village (the Church of the Ascension), they had to pass the soldiers. Helen never felt safe until they were out of sight of the guards.

The staff of the school made sure that Christmas was celebrated in style with the children who had been unable to travel to be with their parents for the holidays. There were Christmas trees and parties hosted by staff members, special treats and presents as well as Christmas carols.

The unforgettable climax for Helen was an end-of-year concert. After all the items had ended, a door quietly opened at one side of the hall. A decrepit, grey-bearded Old Year, leaning on a walking stick, was ushered out through that door. On the other side of the hall, in the hush, another door opened. Standing in the doorway was a young child—representing the New Year.

The fresh New Year was welcomed in by a staff member, reading the words spoken by King George VI in his Christmas 1939 broadcast to the British Empire as the Second World War was beginning.

And I said to the man who stood at the gate of the year:
'Give me a light that I may tread safely into the unknown'.
And he replied:
'Go out into the darkness and put your hand into the Hand of God.
That shall be to you better than light and safer than a known way'.
So I went forth, and finding the Hand of God,
trod gladly into the night.
And He led me towards the hills
and the breaking of day in the lone East.[18]

It was a vivid parable that, in the current very unsettled political climate, God—not political leaders—was in control of the future. The new year

---

18 From the poem by Minnie Louise Haskins, see Kate Shrewsday, *The Gate of the Year: A Present for my Mother,* March 7 2012, viewed 2 November, 2018, kateshrewsday.com/2012/03/07/the-gate-of-the-year-a-present-for-my-mother/.

promised new opportunities to prove God's faithfulness in all its unknown moments.

A Christmas apart

The Christmas school holidays were in the depths of the Guling winter, and the children were entranced. The silently drifting snowflakes, and the delicate tracery of snow and icicles on bare winter branches aroused in the children delight in the beauty of the world. Woolly scarves, mittens and beanies were unpacked from the trunks in the attic and donned, and the hillside rang with the shouts and laughter of children throwing snowballs at each other, building snowmen, and tobogganing.

There was a long straight driveway running down the hill past several staff houses and the main school buildings, ending at steps down to the playing field below. During winter, a wooden ramp was placed over the steps from the drive down to the playing field. The ramp was covered with snow, and the driveway (christened Pennsylvania Avenue by the school) became the winter toboggan run.

A wall of snow was banked up from one side of the bottom of the ramp, curving around onto the playing field to deflect tobogganers from crashing into the wall on the far side. Small children like Helen were held within the encircling arms of older children on the toboggans. Down the drive they sped, over the ramp onto the field below, their hair and scarves flying, and their faces glowing. The speed was both terrifying and intoxicating.

Meantime, in Sapushan, Theo and Olive scarcely had the heart for celebrations. Without any of the children for the first time at Christmas, it was hard to be enthusiastic.

The local believers, however, had not forgotten them.

Early on Christmas morning, at about 4 am, Theo and Olive were woken by some of the Bible School girls standing outside their window in the bitterly cold night, singing Christmas Carols. The Simpkins struggled out of bed into thick overcoats and scarves, and hurried downstairs to greet the singers. Their voices may have been thin in the freezing night air, but their joy was infectious.

Olive offered them all some peanut brittle she had made in preparation for the children coming home. The crunching, as they went on their way to the next house to sing, told how much they relished the toffee.

Even without the children present, however, Theo managed to inject some laughter into their Christmas Day. At the breakfast table, Olive discovered at her place a pretty little hair clip with a card and a long string attached. 'Pull the string!' instructed the card.

Obediently, Olive pulled, and pulled, and pulled. Yards of string kept coming. At last, she got up and went to see what was at the other end of the string.

Out in the kitchen she was greeted by a loud 'Quack!' from a live duck, attached to the end of the string. She looked at it quizzically. Was it a Christmas present or Christmas dinner?

Olive took it out to join the hens in the chook yard while she pondered the problem. When she discovered a duck egg in the henhouse the following day, Olive decided that Mrs Duck had won a reprieve from gracing this year's Christmas dinner table.[19]

After a special Christmas service in the chapel with the local believers, they were invited to have Christmas dinner with their fellow-missionaries, Dr and Mrs Gray and their family, who lived in the other end of their house in Sapushan. Theo, who had to go down to Wuding, to attend to some business matters with the Glassers, was invited to stay and have Christmas dinner with them also. By the time he went to bed that night, he was more than replete.

Reading together the age-old story of the birth of the Babe at Bethlehem that night, Theo and Olive marvelled at the love that was willing to relinquish power and privilege, to bring life and hope to humankind. Since disaster and loss had been the lot of their Master, was it surprising that it also became their experience? Seasoned missionaries though they were, they needed daily to bring their disappointments to the Lord, and to learn the lesson of the writer of the letter to the Philippians (Phil. 4:11 NIV) who said, '... I have learned to be content whatever the circumstances'.

---

19 See Olive's letter to her mother dated 18 January, 1950.

Chapter 25

STORM CLOUDS GATHER

Missionary work in the new Republic

A week after Christmas 1949 Olive and Theo rode their ponies to a village seventeen miles past Wuding. The church was celebrating its Harvest Festival. About four hundred people attended. A group from Daqing church sang Handel's Hallelujah Chorus, unaccompanied, in the service[1]. On their way home, the young folk from Daqing went on ahead to line the road.

Theo and Olive dismounted as they reached the group, and passed between the rows of saluting young people who were blowing bugles as a greeting and farewell. Did the young people sense that change was coming, that soon the time would come when they would never see Olive and Theo again?

The new year dawned and the Simpkins' work in the surrounding villages continued. But—for how long would that be possible?

---

1   This has become almost a signature anthem for this church group who sang it for a recent visitor to the church in the early years of the 21st century.

Growing unease

On the surface, everything seemed normal. People were going about their daily lives and business as usual. Olive and Theo were greeted politely wherever they went. Yet there was an uneasiness in the air; there were the occasional side glances, or averted eyes. What were people thinking? What did it all mean? [2]

The revolution taking place in China seemed far away from village life in the mountains of Yunnan. The authorities had assured the missionaries that nothing would change. Life could continue as before. Nevertheless, disturbing news filtered through of political meetings at which the people of a village were expected to be present. They would be addressed by someone aggressively criticising landowners or foreign imperialists as exploiters of the people, and encouraging the poor to take matters into their own hands. They urged people to complain against officials who had deceived them, in particular, any who had been supporters of the Guomindang.

Accusation meetings were held, and people who did not show enough enthusiasm for the revolutionary message found themselves being accused. It was safer to voice an accusation stridently for a very minor fault, than to keep silent. The assembled crowds were challenged to take on the role of judge and jury. Let the people decide the sentence.

Sometimes these meetings were followed by public executions. In some places, schools were instructed to take their students to vilify those being punished, and to watch these executions.

Theo and Olive heard disquieting news of some 'visitors' arriving in a local village where the Christians were celebrating Harvest Festival. The visitors stopped the meeting and strung up the preacher and some others from the village. They beat them savagely and burned their books, cautioning the villagers not to worship in this way again. [3]

How were they to be true to their Lord now, if they had no Scriptures and were not able to worship? And how would the presence of the foreign missionaries play into the prevailing political situation?

Few, if any, of the local believers understood the ordeal awaiting them which was so at odds with the promises made by the Communists.

---

2   This was confirmed in private and confidential reports to family and to the CIM when Theo and Olive were once again in Australia late in 1951. It is also described in *The Reluctant Exodus* by Phyllis Thompson.

3   Olive mentions this in her letter to her mother dated 12 December, 1950.

Life goes on

Still, life did continue. People were born, grew, married and died. And so it was that Theo and Olive were invited to four or five weddings in nearby villages in the early months of 1950.

One was the marriage of a Kunming Bible School student to a girl who had attended the Sapushan Bible School for several weeks. It was to be held only ten miles away.

Theo and Olive decided they could make do with one pony between the two of them, taking turns to ride and to walk. A couple of the hills were extremely rugged, bordering on the precipitous. The paths were rutted and rocky.

As they commenced the last climb, Olive chose to dismount and continue on hands and feet, scrambling up the steep track, puffing and panting unceasingly, rather than trust the pony.

The wedding ceremony was held out under the stars on a cold, frosty night. There were two big bonfires around which they huddled, but still the locals shivered in their thin cotton clothes. There were hymns, Bible readings and prayers, and Theo was asked to preach.

Finally, a bowl of tea was handed to the bridegroom who gave it to the bride. After bowing in prayer, she sipped the tea and gave it to her new husband who also bowed in prayer and sipped the tea. The worship leader read out the marriage certificate and gave it to the bridegroom. At the end of the service, Theo congratulated them.[4]

Another wedding ceremony and feast held in a local village was a bit of a novelty, using the style of service that was current in Methodist churches in Australia. It was the first one Olive had attended where the bride and groom were asked to say a Miao 'I will' as part of the ceremony.[5]

United Tribes Conference in Aguomi[6]

About a month later, Theo and Olive set out from Sapushan to attend the United Tribes Conference in Aguomi. Olive rode their pony (named 'Black Beauty' by Dorothy when the children had been in Sapushan for Christmas 1948) and Theo had borrowed a mule for the trip.

---

4   See Olive's letter to her mother dated 18 January, 1950.

5   See Olive's letter to her mother dated 14 February, 1950.

6   This is described in a long prayer letter from Olive dated 13 March, 1950.

Both animals were male and quite mettlesome. They became very lively whenever they met a mare or a donkey on the road. (None of these animals would be the tame, well-trained animals one might see when out riding in Australia.). Theo's strategy when this happened was to assert his authority by whipping up his mount and making it gallop past the offending animal.

Although she was quite an experienced horsewoman, Olive didn't have the confidence to follow suit. She preferred to dismount, tossing the reins to one of the boys to lead the pony. She picked up a stick or branch and used it to chase off the other animal, while she continued on 'Shanks's Pony', walking until the danger was past. At that point she remounted. Describing this to her mother in March 1950, Olive wrote:

> I don't mind how steep the hill is, though I prefer to walk if the track is only about a foot wide on the edge of nowhere, but actually, the only thing I am really fearful of are these wretched animals that we might meet straying along some mountainside, or as we pass through some village.

They spent that night in a Miao village where the folk had prepared a delicious meal of maize, bean curd, fat pork and soup to share with them before a short meeting. A space had been cleared for them to sleep in the village's tiny chapel, and they were glad to turn in after the day's travelling. They woke before five the next morning, having breakfast and packing up to leave before the sun had risen.

It was a long, long day's riding and scrambling up one mountainside and down the other for hour upon hour. They stopped for lunch at a big Nosu village, selling worm medicine, ointments for sore eyes and itch, and pulling teeth for a couple of women (all without anaesthetic of course).

For the last few hours of the way, no-one in the group knew the road, so time after time they had to ask the way from passers-by, often needing to re-trace their steps since they had inadvertently taken a wrong turn. It took them nearly twelve hours to cover the thirty-six miles to Aguomi that day.

The village was crowded with delegates for the conference from every direction. There were Lisu, Nosu, Laka, Miao and Chinese delegates, many of whom Theo and Olive knew well. They were the only foreigners present. They attended most of the conference sessions, and Theo himself spoke three or four times. The morning meetings were generally focused on Bible teaching and devotional, while the afternoon meetings dealt with church

United Tribes Conference, Aguomi, 1950. Olive is on the far right
(Photo taken by Theo Simpkin)

matters. It was good to hear how the churches were doing and what were the hopes and fears of their leaders.

In between times, there was a steady stream of visitors to Theo and Olive's room as people came asking for medicine, or just wanting to talk.

One group from Taogu wanted Theo to return and re-open the Bible School there, but Theo felt he should not do so since it might seem to be in opposition to the Bible School already running in Salaowu. The future location of the Tribes Bible School as well as who would staff it was a major topic of conversation at the conference.

A Short Term Bible School

At the conference's conclusion, Theo and Olive set off for a Laka village called Fu Yin Cun, 'Gospel Village'. They were to run a two weeks' Short Term Bible School there. This is how Olive remembered that day's travelling:

> Our horses had gone on to await us at the river at the foot of that awful hill. One boy with a load waited to show us the way and he told us Mrs Binks[7] had cried over these terrible tracks. I didn't manage to squeeze any tears out, but drops of perspiration were continually dropping from me. All good for reducing, as Theo remind-

---

7   Another CIM missionary who with her husband and family was stationed at Aguomi for years.

ed me. But I don't think I've ever been down such a steep hill or over such an awful road. The mountains all around there are mostly rock and on these tracks, there are loose stones (for you to slip on) as well as huge boulders everywhere to make natural horse-shoe bends as you go down. We could see the boys with the horses as specks down below us, and eventually we got to them and were able to ride along the rocky river bed for a short way before ascending the other side up another terrifically steep hill.[8]

They were stopped now and then by people asking for medicine. Just before sunset they arrived at Gospel Village. They were to stay with an old Laka pastor and his family of four boys and two girls. The two older boys were married, one with a three-year-old child, and their wives also lived there, together with the bride-to-be of the third son.

Theo and Olive were given the bedroom over the stable. There was a thick earthen floor between the stable and bedroom. To get to this room they had to climb a ladder from the ground floor. Olive's tree-climbing days were long gone, and the Laka family often enjoyed a good laugh at her awkward attempts to go up or down. Indeed, one of the sons hung a rope from a rafter to give her something to hold onto as she came down the ladder.

Each day Theo and Olive were kept busy with the Short Term Bible School in Gospel Village. Theo taught the church leaders and potential leaders while Olive held classes with the children.

The oldest son of the pastor, who with his younger brother conducted Sunday School classes several times a week, helped Olive. He had little understanding of how to arouse and maintain the children's interest, so Olive was able to show him how to use flannelgraphs and pictures in telling Bible stories and give him some practice as well. She took the children out on the hillside with her to find samples of both wheat and tares to illustrate Jesus' parable. [9]

Since most of these children did not attend school, Olive began teaching them some Chinese characters as well, starting with the numbers, so they could find their place in the hymnbook. They spent a lot of time memorising Scripture. Olive left lots of lesson topics and plans with the pastor's sons. She hoped they would use them, and learn how to develop their own.

---

8   Olive's long prayer letter dated 13 March, 1950.
9   Details from Olive's prayer letter dated 13 March, 1950.

Trouble in the Church and a return to Salaowu[10]

In the tribal churches, however, not all was rosy.

When Theo and Olive moved out of Taogu (a Lisu area) for furlough in 1946, the Tribes Bible School relocated to Salaowu, in a largely Nosu area. The Bible School was there for some years. Dan and Cathie Smith had been the CIM missionaries on the staff at Salaowu for some time.

However, Cathie's health had meant they had to leave and return home to Australia. Who would take their place?

Perhaps Theo and Olive should leave Sapushan and resume teaching in the Bible School in Salaowu. Yet they were not happy at the thought of leaving the Miao in the Sapushan area.

New missionaries—Arthur and Alice Glasser—were willing to leave Wuding and go to Salaowu, but their language was still quite elementary. There was a Chinese Principal of the Bible School, so he could give a strong lead until the Glassers' language improved. Would that be satisfactory?

While the Simpkins were at Gospel Village, urgent news was brought to them that this Chinese principal might be retiring. Various Mission leaders recommended that Theo and Olive should go to Salaowu to carry on the work in the Bible School instead of the Glassers.

The matter seemed pressing, so they packed up to go to Salaowu immediately.

Wolves lurking

It was a hard two days trip through wild and rugged mountains. They saw a wolf on the way, and there was great excitement when someone spotted a big weasel, shouting 'Catch it! Catch it!' to folk nearby.

The first day seemed never-ending. They clambered over and around huge boulders up a long narrow gully, and then up another steep mountain side. But still they were a long way from any village where they could stay the night. The sun set, and still they rode on. By now it was quite dark, and the track was along a narrow gully sloping down beside a big river. Olive could not see the path ahead. Theo and the men assured her that the pony could see, but her courage failed her. She dismounted, preferring to trust to her own limited eyesight and feet. So they trudged on and on.

'Aren't we near a village yet?' Olive asked, time and again.

---

10 See Olive's long prayer letter dated 13 March, 1950, for this whole section.

The reply was always 'It's a long way to go yet'.

Suddenly, in the dark, they heard dogs barking. Straining their eyes, they could see a hut or two beside the track. The men said it would be no fit place to stay for the night, but Olive had come to the end of her strength. 'Please ask them if we can stay here', she pleaded.

It was no village, just some huts and stables housing the cows which three little boys were minding. They had never seen 'foreigners' before and were hugely interested in everything they did. The boys offered Theo and Olive one room to sleep in, but it was full of soot and smoke from the fire. The Simpkins did not relish the idea of trying to sleep in that atmosphere.

They hurriedly cooked some porridge, bacon and eggs, over the fire, and took it outside to eat under the stars.

As they ate, their eyes became accustomed to the dark. They saw that between two stables, opposite the room where the fire was, stood an old tumble-down cowshed, with not much in the way of a roof. 'That would be perfect for us to sleep in', said Olive. The men and the little boys thought this was very odd.

Olive and Theo enjoyed seeing the moon and stars shining down on them as they went to sleep. The next morning, they were up and out on the road early. More mountains, hills, plains and rivers had to be crossed, but at last, well into the afternoon, they arrived at Salaowu.

Olive in their 'hotel' for the night with one of the cowherds
(Photo: WT Simpkin collection)

Olive crossing a stream near Salaowu (Photo: WT Simpkin collection)

A crowd of Nosu were there for revival meetings.

Theo immediately called a meeting of the pastors and elders and told them that the Mission leaders had asked them rather than the Glassers to go to Salaowu.

His words were greeted with a pregnant silence. Something was wrong.

Apparently the Chinese principal had said he would remain in Salaowu if the inexperienced Glassers were appointed to the staff. If the Simpkins came, he would go.

What was this all about? Did this Chinese Principal feel that the Bible School was his particular fiefdom, where he could have the final say more easily with an inexperienced missionary with only basic language on staff? Or did he want to return to his home town?

Perhaps it was because at the recent United Tribes Conference, Theo had urged the church leaders to think about where the Bible School should be, giving some consideration to the different tribes' regions? It had been in Taogu (a Lisu region) and was now in Salaowu (a Nosu area). Was it time for the Miao to have the Bible School in their region? Or another tribe?

In fact, the Conference had recorded their decision that the next year, the Bible School would be moved from Salaowu to another tribe's region.

Unfortunately a previous missionary was said to have promised the Nosu that the Bible School would remain in their area forever. Perhaps the Nosu leaders felt that Theo favoured tribes other than the Nosu. As the days went on, there were heated and hurtful words, despite the revival meetings each morning. It was with very heavy hearts that Theo and Olive listened to all this.

The ringleader seemed to be a particular Nosu man who had been a problem in the Nosu church for years. He was an Assistant Pastor who professed to be so humble and earnest in the Lord's work, yet had caused dissension in the church for a long time. Eventually, it became clear that this man was the only one who objected to Theo being appointed to the Salaowu Bible School. The elders, deacons and pastor came to Theo, individually and as a group, and told him they had deposed this man, and the man would have just the same rank as the travelling preachers. They begged Theo to come to Salaowu. They all wanted him there.

What should Theo do? Where was the Lord in all this? As he and Olive talked and prayed together about this, they had no peace that this was the Lord's leading for them at this time.

They packed up to leave Salaowu sadly. The Bible School had done so much good work in the past, training evangelists, pastors and other Christian workers. What would happen to it now? Could this discord, the work of the enemy of Christ's Church, be turned to good by the sovereign Lord?

Returning to Sapushan

They called at the new government headquarters in Salaowu, to inform the officials of their travel back to Sapushan, and to ask for an escort since the road from Salaowu to Wuding was notorious for robber bands. It was on this road that fellow missionaries Dan and Stella Kirkman had been held up by bandits who stole all their possessions, even requiring Dan to give up his good trousers. They relented enough to allow him to keep his pyjama pants to ride home in.

The Communist officials told Theo and Olive they would have to wait another day if they wanted an escort. So, feeling that they had done all that might be required of them, they chose to proceed unescorted, trusting the Lord to care for them.

All was quiet and peaceful as they rode on. They met the postman on his lonely trek, and he told them how the previous night he had been robbed right on that spot. Two days of constant travel brought them safely to Wuding for afternoon tea with the Glassers, before the final push up the hill to Sapushan.

And so they settled back into their regular station program in Sapushan. Both taught in the Miao Girls' Bible School, Theo also having Bible Classes in the High School, besides the regular nightly meetings in the chapel.

Every Thursday evening Theo and Olive took it in turns to go to one of the Miao homes for a family worship service, and every night except Sunday and Thursday, Olive held classes for the village children.

Most of these were little goatherds—out on the mountains with the animals every day. She taught them the Chinese characters for the numbers, as well as teaching them their Miao script so they would be able to read their own New Testament and Hymnbook. One night was set aside for memorising Scripture. The boys learnt in Chinese, being more likely to already know some Chinese, and the girls in Miao. There were incentives for memorising and the children eagerly enrolled. Forty came along regularly for the chance of winning a pencil with an eraser on the end when they had memorised seventeen verses.

All memorising was done aloud, so with forty strong young children repeating the words out loud, the hubbub was deafening. For those who continued past the seventeen verses, there was a little notebook when they had learnt thirty verses.

The ultimate goal for those who persevered was a book bag, for their Bibles and hymnbooks. For this they had to be able to recite 62 verses,

Some of the Miao girls who memorised Scripture passages[11]
(Photo: WT Simpkin collection)

---

11 A friend has recently met a lady in Yunnan who knew the girls in this photo. Although several have left the faith, there are some who remain believing.

including whole chapters from the Gospel of John. Some had memorised John chapters 1, 3, 4, 10 and 14.

Olive loved hearing them recite Jesus' words: 'Do not let your hearts be troubled. You believe in God; believe also in me' (John 14:1 NIV). Each week they would review the verses they had learnt previously as well as learning new verses. Olive had no idea what the coming days and years would hold for these children, but hoped and believed that God's Word, hidden in their hearts, would guard and bless them, come what may.[12]

Theo's weekly Bible Class was exploring the letters to the seven churches in Revelation chapters 2 and 3.[13] As they read of the various churches of Asia Minor in the first century, and of the persecution they suffered, and the temptations to compromise, it was Theo's heartfelt desire that the Miao believers likewise would be given courage and faith to endure.

Their love for the Lord and for the Scriptures was apparent. Theo thought of a young Miao widow in a distant village who desperately wanted a copy of the Old Testament Stories and a Hymnbook. She had no money to pay for them, but obtained them on credit and then went gleaning in the wheat fields, eventually gathering enough leftover grain to pay for her books. How would her commitment be tested in the coming days?

In Yunnan, life continued to appear peaceful outwardly. Missionary work went on, still largely without outside interference. About thirty tribes-people—Miao, Lisu, Laka and Nosu—asked to do the Scofield Correspondence Bible Study Course, and Theo agreed to facilitate and supervise this. It was heartening to see this desire for Scripture teaching in the local leaders and young people.

At the same time, trouble continued in the church. Some months earlier, the Principal of the Schools had collected money from the students for the purchase of books. Now he was unable to account for half of it. Had he misappropriated it? Although he was not a graduate of any of the Tribes Bible Schools, he had been thought to be a devout Christian.

This incident[14] contributed to the general uneasiness that was threatening the harmony of the church. The political change and uncertainty seemed to be mirrored by stresses and tensions within the church. What would the future hold?

---

12 For this whole section see Olive's letter dated 3 June, 1950.

13 Mentioned in a prayer letter dated 8 June, 1950.

14 See Theo's letter to Mrs Kettle, dated 23 August, 1950.

Chapter 26

NUMBERED DAYS

One beautiful autumn day in September, Theo and a young Miao teacher, made their way down the mountain from Sapushan, along a narrow river valley, across three streams without bridges and through some rice fields to Keti, a village at the foot of a huge precipice[1].

There was no church building in this village, and the believers, mostly women, gathered for the service under the shade of a group of walnut trees. As the service proceeded, it was punctuated by walnuts dropping into the midst of the group. Children scrambled to retrieve them.

Theo's companion shared his own story with the group. He had joined the Bible Club to memorise Scripture. While out hoeing his corn on the mountain side he had his New Testament with him and memorised as he worked.

Unless a man is born again, he cannot see the Kingdom of God.

John 3:3 KJV

He beat the words out as he hoed the corn, and the Lord began to drive the words deep into his mind. They began to worry him. The more he tried

---

1   The details from this story are recounted in an article Theo wrote, dated 25 September, 1950. It may have been intended for *China's Millions*.

to expel them, the stronger the challenge came to him. 'You must be born again...'

Day after day, the words echoed in his mind. At night, he could not sleep. He became miserable. When a message in the church spoke of confessing sin and getting right with the Lord, he would rise and leave the building. But the Shepherd was seeking the lost sheep.

Some time later, while Theo was preaching on the Good Samaritan, the Lord found this lost sheep. That night, the young man called on Theo, trembling, eager to get right with the Lord. Briefly Theo reminded him of the Lord's promise of mercy and forgiveness. 'If we confess our sins, he is faithful and just to forgive us our sins, and to cleanse us from all unrighteousness.' (1 John 1:9 KJV)

Together they knelt in prayer. With tears he prayed confessing sins of which he was ashamed and claiming the promised cleansing. As they rose from their knees, he said, 'My heavy burden has gone', and the look of joy on his face showed it was so.

When Theo asked if he would like to accompany him to Keti he jumped at the idea, and said he could not keep quiet. He felt he *must* tell others what the Lord had done for him.

There were others too, that day at Keti, who needed not only to hear the message of free forgiveness promised by the Lord, but to learn to trust in God's faithfulness.

Some were suffering persecution from unbelieving relatives, such as a husband who smoked opium. Another elderly widow was badly ill-treated by her son because she was a Christian. She was tempted to end her own life. Theo reminded her of the passage he had just read to the group, 'God has called you to his kingdom and glory' (from 1 Thess. 2:12).

'Why, old Granny', said Theo, 'I'm sure your time has almost come, and Jesus may be even preparing to send His angels for you. You are almost at the door of Heaven already, so don't draw back now!'

'Oh, I wish He would send for me quickly, then I would not have to suffer all the pain and hunger and persecution! Oh, my sins must be so great that I suffer like this!'

Theo gave yet another the word of comfort, that her sufferings were not because her sins were so great. Jesus had forgiven her and cleansed her when she believed. She only had to trust him.

As they left that day, Theo's heart ached for this little group of believers.

How could they live through what was ahead? Would they endure to the end? Would he ever have the chance to visit them again?

Yet there was a serenity in their letters home at this time that must have been comforting to their Australian relatives. In a letter to her mother in October 1950, Olive wrote:

> *I do trust you are all well, and are not worrying about us out here. In this last letter of yours you seem to be a bit worried, so what your next letter will have to say, when you know I'd been in bed for a few weeks—I just don't know!! But, just cease from worrying—these are orders! When the Lord opens the way, then it will be time to go, but until then, even if I have got buzzy ears², etc., we must stay on. Our work here is not yet finished, and until it is, we could not be happy to leave.*

News of the children

Letters from the children in the province of Jiangxi hardly ever arrived. When they did, their parents read them and re-read them. They heard of their academic successes, but also of their spiritual development. All three, at one time or another, declared their own decision to follow the Good Shepherd.

They also heard the sad news of the sudden death of the beloved principal of the school, Mr Stanley Houghton, in Guling on 17 July, 1950.

It had been a typical busy day for Mr Houghton in the life of the school. It started with breakfast, School Prayers, administrative duties, lunch and a walk to the Gap to farewell students who were leaving. (As it became possible for some missionaries to leave China, their children would join them in this exodus.) He returned to the school for singing classes, and marking examination papers, after which he went out for a quick game of tennis before the evening meal. He revelled in a hard game of tennis. This is how Marjory Broomhall, one of the teachers, described his passing:

> *He played his long, strong strokes with skill and abandon and infectious enjoyment, eager for more when the first set was over. While playing the second, the Call suddenly came, and with swift, glad step he went in to see the King.*

---

2 Olive was beginning to suffer from tinnitus.

For him there was no sadness of farewell; only deepest grief for us,
bereft of father, counsellor and friend.
'Know ye not that there is a prince and a great man fallen this
day?'[3]

Down on their knees, Olive and Theo prayed persistently that the children might be able to come to Sapushan for the next Christmas, or alternatively that Olive and Theo might be able to visit them in Guling. It would be two years since they had last seen the children.

David was due to return to Australia the following year to continue his education there[4]. He believed God wanted him to train to become a doctor, and would need to be living in Australia for a number of years to be eligible for a Commonwealth scholarship to pay his university fees.

As the situation in China became more unsettled, Olive and Theo contacted the CIM Directors, authorising them to send the three children home to Australia together if the situation worsened. But how could they bear the separation? They took their longings to the Lord in prayer.

As David's fifteenth birthday came in November 1950, Olive and Theo were told the children would definitely be coming to Sapushan for Christmas before David proceeded to Australia. The travel permits had been granted, and now it was just a matter of finding transport. The school was due to 'break up' on 5 December, so they expected the children to arrive about 11 December. There was a new spring in their steps as Olive and Theo went about the business of getting rooms and beds ready, and planning picnics and trips out to nearby villages as a family.

The future of CIM in China[5]

At this time, the government was applying pressure to Chinese church leaders to end their association with missionaries from the West. The Premier, Zhou En Lai, called four Chinese Church leaders to Beijing, warning them to make sure the missionaries left China. At the same period, the government produced a Christian Manifesto, calling on all church members to make the People's Government their first loyalty. It was only later that it became apparent that this loyalty to the government meant

---

3   Martin, G, op. cit., p. 152.

4   See Theo and Olive's prayer letter dated 8 June, 1950.

5   Thompson, P, op. cit., for details in this section.

attending indoctrination classes which were often scheduled on a Sunday at worship time.

Meanwhile the threat of outright war with America, over its support of South Korea could result in another internment of the children at the CIM school in Guling. Should the Mission consider closing the school while it still could? But if that were done, where would the children go? If they were sent back to their home countries for safety, how could they be cared for there? Would the parents have to leave China?

In some places, missionaries were being asked not to attend church meetings. How could they engage in any useful service to the church in this atmosphere?

As these questions were aired within the CIM leadership in Shanghai, and throughout the CIM family, one person wrote the following:

> ...if the Mission has fulfilled the purpose for which God has brought it into being, then let it be dissolved. If it has not, if God's purposes for it have not yet been completely fulfilled, then no one can liquidate it, I believe, either from without or from within.[6]

The end has come

The CIM Directors were realising that in many places, the continued presence of the missionaries was making things too difficult for the local believers.

After many hours of prayer and much soul-searching, the directive went out from the General Director to all CIM members—after 85 years of the Mission in China, they were to withdraw. The CIM was no longer a help, but a hindrance to the local church.

What would become of the Mission? The General Director called an urgent conference for all the Directors to meet in Kalorama (in the Dandenong Ranges, Victoria), Australia. There they would hear the latest news, and pray and seek God's guidance for the future.

Not least would be the question of finance for immediate needs. For this reason as well as other practical considerations, the withdrawal needed to be done in an orderly way. Local CIM Field Superintendents would give approval to each missionary to embark on the process of leaving. First, each missionary must—as far as possible—finalise all ongoing work projects for

---

6   Quoted in Thompson, P, op. cit., p. 52.

which they were responsible. Then there were legal and property matters to be dealt with in such a way that they did not cause further headaches for the local church after the missionaries had gone. It would be a lengthy process.

It would cost a huge amount to withdraw all of the nearly 700 CIM missionaries currently in China and send them back to their home countries. The most straightforward exit route for the majority would be via Hong Kong (at that stage, a British colony) where transport to the four corners of the globe could be sought. But Hong Kong was already filled to capacity with the millions of Chinese refugees who had fled there as the Communists gained control in China. How could these hundreds of missionaries and their children be accommodated and catered for while they sought transport home?

Just as this directive went out, a man came running in to Sapushan with a telegram for Olive and Theo, that left their heads spinning. The telegram said something like this:

'No transport to Yunnan.
All children returning to homelands.
Simpkin trio on way to Hong Kong and Australia.'

While Theo and Olive had been finalising plans for the children's Christmas with them in Sapushan, they had already left Guling and were on their way to Australia.[7]

What a difference a telegram could make.

True, they had authorised the Mission to send the girls home with David if the situation worsened, but they had not expected it to happen so soon.

Would Olive's mother be able to care for them until Theo and Olive could join them? Olive's mother was seventy-two years old. How would she cope with the sudden demands of feeding, clothing and generally caring for her three grandchildren, now fifteen, eleven and nine years old? If the children had to go home, Olive felt strongly that her place was with them. Until she could return, she urged her mother to get help.

In a letter to the children, written the very day the telegram arrived on 13 December 1950, Olive wrote the following (after having received the telegram):

---

7   See Olive's letter to her mother, dated 12 December, 1950.

My Dear David, Dorothy and Helen,

I wonder where you all are tonight? Just after I had gone to lie down after lunch today, a telegram from Mr Martin came. It was dated yesterday, the 12th, and said that you all had just left Kuling for Hong Kong. So, today, the 13th, you will be somewhere between Kuling and Hong Kong, but wherever you are, you are right in your Heavenly Father's care aren't you? You will always remember that, won't you? HE CARETH FOR YOU.

With conditions as they are in China, we felt it would be better for you all to go to Australia. I'm sure you are all glad that you will still be able to be together. David, you will look after your young sisters, won't you? And Dorothy and Helen will be as helpful and wise as you know how to be, won't you? We have written to Grandma, and hope she will be able to care for you.

And I know you will pray for Daddy and Mummy that we may know what the will of the Lord is for us at this time, and that we will be ready to do it. Does He want us to stay on a bit longer in China? You know He sent us out here to preach the gospel and to do His will, didn't He? Does God want us to still stay on out here while you go home? I feel I want to come to you right away now this very minute, and be with you in all your new experiences in Australia, and to look after you because you are my very own children, but, it is quite impossible to come now this very minute, and we must wait until the Lord opens the way, mustn't we? Can we be patient?

We will be praying for you all, and I know you will be praying for us, and I am sure the Lord will bring us all together again in his own good time and way. In the meantime, you will all be good and try wherever you are, to be kind and helpful to one another and those who are caring for you. Let your light shine wherever you are, won't you?

Grandma, I am sure will want to look after you, but remember, she is not as young as she used to be, and, so, if you stay with her, you will have to help her all you can and be obedient. Remember all that you have learned in Scouts, Guides, and Brownies. It will all be helpful to you now. Aunty Mary in Maryborough would love to look after you too, I'm sure, but if Dorothy and Helen went up there, I think David would still have to stay in Melbourne and as we feel sure you will all want to be together, we will first of all think of you all as being with Grandma.

Mrs Metcalf wrote from Kunming today to say that there were no aeroplanes between Kunming and Chungking for a whole month, so that was why no Kuling children could come to Yunnan for the holidays even though your passes had been granted.

Now, you will write regularly to us just as you did in school, won't you, and tell us all about your trip home. Keep regular habits, just as you did in Kuling, and don't forget your quiet times and look to the Lord to guide and help you even in the smallest details.

Now I must not take up too much of the space as I know Daddy will want to have a wee chat to his own three too. So, goodbye for now, and the Lord will watch between us whilst we are absent the one from the other.

Lots and lots of love from Mummy.

Theo's letter to the three children was in similar vein.

Our dear three,

We are all very well here. There seems to be no trouble in these parts, and we are still able to carry on the Lord's work as before. This morning a Chinese man has come to ask for milk for his baby. The mother hasn't any more milk. I think it is our milk which is keeping the baby alive for them.

Yesterday the Glassers sent us a duck for Christmas. They thought you would be here to help us eat it! I wonder what we will do with all the things we were getting ready for Christmas? Give them away I suppose!

The Miao children are practising every day the other special pieces for the Christmas celebrations. A big crowd is to sing the Hallelujah Chorus, I understand. Mummy and I hope to go.

We will both be praying for you all the time. Don't forget to write to us regularly – ordinary mail every week, but an air letter like this you could take in turns to write once a fortnight. We don't want to hear any of the news from the newspapers or the wireless. Just tell us what you are doing at school, and at home. What lessons you are studying. About your schoolmates and about Church and Sunday school.

Tell Grandma you'd like to have Family Prayers every day. We want you to have that too. And of course, don't forget to have your quiet times. So many people at home in Australia are so worldly, and do not love or trust in the Lord Jesus. But you must each remember you belong to Him. And don't forget to pray for us. God will bring us home safely to you in His time I'm sure.

Now another thing I'm sure you will be very good and kind and obedient to Grandma, won't you? Be just as thoughtful as ever you can, and helpful too....

Lots of the school children here are coming nearly every day for cough medicine. It's a good job for them that we are still here, as they have no one else to go to for medicine when they are sick.

So long then, dear ones three. I don't know how long we will still be here, but in the Lord's good time we will all be together again. Lots and lots of love from Daddy.

Theo and Olive had been happy to trust the children to the care of the school staff in Guling. From her months at the school in early 1948, Olive had seen enough to know that they would be well cared for, safe in an environment where their creativity and curiosity would be stimulated and their faith in God encouraged.

But Australia... Olive and Theo had seen enough while home on furlough to tell them that for the majority of Australians, their religion was only skin-deep. The local Methodist church which Olive's mother attended was a fairly staid community. It would do little to stimulate and nurture the children's faith. Few of their schoolmates were likely to be regular church-goers, so how would they influence the children's spiritual growth?

Olive and Theo had to relinquish the children into the hands of the Good Shepherd. They could do no more. What a daily lesson in faith this was!

Unexpected permits

About a week earlier, Theo and Olive had had an unexpected visit from the local police. They said that Theo's application for two exit permits had been approved. Theo was nonplussed. He had made no such application. He could not do so anyway, without the approval of his CIM Field Superintendent.

Because of his long years of service in China, and his good language skills, it fell to Theo to help deal with officials for other missionaries in the Wuding area. There would be property matters to be finalised with the owners from whom they had rented property, and termination of employment to be finalised for locals who had worked for the missionaries in one capacity or another. The current government was encouraging such employees to ask for severance pay, sometimes making exorbitant claims. It required someone with a fine understanding of local culture and good language skills to negotiate all these arrangements peaceably.

This was happening throughout China. In Guling, for instance, the school administration had considerable difficulties with the local Foreign Affairs Bureau over the school property. The officials asserted that the school property still belonged to the Americans. They claimed that the transfer of the property to the CIM had not been registered with the land registration department, and that the US$1 price paid showed that the transaction was spurious.

It was useless for the school principal to explain how often they had tried to register the transfer, but had been repeatedly told that the organisation for registration had not yet been set up. The principal was told he must apologize before the school students and staff could leave. This is how he described it:

So I made my next statement under the heading daoqian ('an apology') and signed it not as 'Headmaster Martin', but as 'the apologizing man Martin'. Soon this document was flung back at me. 'You cannot apologize. Apology is between man and man; you have offended against the State.' So I renewed my statement under the heading huiguo— ('repenting of transgression') and repeated our side of the case...

Little by little they forced me back until they had a blank statement from me which they could use as a confession that I had offended.

This confession was printed in the Central China newspapers, and after that they were prepared to let us depart.[8]

God holds the key

Furthermore, in Sapushan there were some local work programs needing to be finished. Theo had ordered a thousand copies of the Miao New Testament for distribution among the Miao churches. The church's stock had run out some time ago, and Theo did not want to leave until the books had arrived from the printer and he had been able to pass them on to the right people. [9]

Theo told the police he did not want the permits at this time. It was clear however, that their days in China were numbered. When would they be able to make the next move?

They began selling off items they no longer needed, so that when the word came to leave, it would be a simple matter. They realised that they were unlikely to be returning to China for some time; it was no use leaving furniture, clothes or household items in storage. Because of the expense, they did not expect to be able to take many of their possessions with them when they left. So they started disposing of things wherever they could be of some use.

In a letter dated 26 December, 1950, Olive wrote this to her mother:

> *I wish you could see Theo's office, and the tiny room just off his office. This is filled with people for quite a good part of the day, as they are there looking for bargains. Old clothes sell well, and all our old Indian sheets went off like 'hot cakes', but good things that we feel we just cannot sell 'for a song' are still hanging around, and of course things that are essentially foreign, such as cutlery, glass tumblers, etc., and other things that could not be altered to suit the Chinese taste will not sell at all I suppose.*

The process of disposing of their possessions continued for weeks. On the 25 January, Olive wrote the following in a letter to Helen:

> *We sold our two organs – one to the Miao Church here, and the other one to the Da Ch'ing Miao Church. Of course, we did not get very much for them, but, anyway, they will be used in Miao Churches, so*

---

8   Martin, G, op. cit., p. 159.
9   See Olive's letter to David dated 8 January, 1951.

that will be nice to remember, won't it?

Maybe the Girls Bible School will buy my sewing machine. That will have to be sold for less than half of what we need to buy another one at home, I suppose, but it cannot be helped. The Lord has promised to supply all our needs, hasn't He, so we do not need to worry.

Maybe, Wen Hsin Yong will take the gramophone to the Laoba church. The spring is broken and we have not been able to use it for some time, but Wen Hsin Yong thinks he can get it mended, so this morning I divided the gramophone records – half to be left for the church here in case they can buy another gramophone some time, and half for Wen Hsin Yong to take to Laoba.

Later, in a letter to David dated 19 January, 1951, Olive wrote this:

Well, I'm afraid we will just have to forget about lots of things that we once prized, won't we? These days, we are very busy sorting out and deciding what precious little things we would like to take with us – and can't! We will just have to 'take cheerfully the spoiling of our goods', won't we? It does not give one a very nice feeling to see some things go into other hands, but it will be impossible for us to take much with us, so we must just grin and bear it. As I write, two Miao Church leaders are sitting at our dining room table writing out instructions as to how to use the medicines Daddy is handing over to them. All that we have, in the Dispensary, we are giving to the Miao Church, with full instructions as to how to use them. We are very glad that we have this stuff to hand over to them, and only trust that they will use them faithfully. We will need to pray for them, won't we?

Meanwhile, one by one, their fellow missionaries travelled down to Kunming to start the exit process. Already, the Metcalfs in Kunming had received their exit permits.

It was not until the last day of 1950 that a telegram came to the Simpkins from the CIM headquarters in Shanghai, telling them to apply for their exit permits and to leave together as soon as possible. The application could not be done in either Sapushan or Wuding, however. They had to travel to the capital of the province, Kunming, to do that, but—they could not leave Sapushan just yet. There were too many property matters for Theo to finalise. Olive remarked to her mother in a letter dated 31 December, 1950:

It seems one of our missions in life is to clear up after others! We had to do it for the Binks and Dan Smiths and now Theo has gone up to Taku to do it for the Metcalfs and Miss Kemp. When the Grays leave Wuting in a few weeks time, there will be that property to fix up, too, and maybe hand back to the owner. So I can see that that job will fall to Theo too. Well, he said once, he would sooner be the last to leave, than the first, so it looks as though it will be just that. We will be the last in this district to leave anyway, though, doubtless there will be others out West and in Kunming who'll be staying on after we go.

At about the same time, the order of Miao New Testaments arrived in Wuding. When Olive informed the church people, many of the Miao men and boys walked down to Wuding to carry the books up the hill to Sapushan. The excitement of the community was palpable as their hands carried up the hill the precious Word of God in their own language.

What would the future hold? As Theo sat at the little pedal organ, playing it one last time before handing it over to one of the Miao churches, his fingers would have picked out the tunes of songs he had often sung, and he would have been heartened. This may well have been one such song:

God holds the key of all unknown, and I am glad;
If other hands should hold the key, or if He trusted it to me,
I might be sad. I might be sad.

What if tomorrow's cares were here, without its rest?
I'd rather He unlocked the day, and, as the hours swing open, say,
My will is best. My will is best.

The very dimness of my sight makes me secure;
For, groping in my misty way, I feel His hand; I hear Him say,
My help is sure. My help is sure.

I cannot read His future plans; but this I know:
I have the smiling of His face, and all the refuge of His grace
While here below. While here below.

Enough; this covers all my wants; and so I rest;
For what I cannot, He can see, and in His care I saved shall be,
Forever blest. Forever blest.[10]

---

10 Joseph Parker (1830-1902) Public domain.

Chapter 27

LAID ASIDE

What would become of the dear friends they had made from the tribes of Yunnan? To many missionaries it felt like betrayal to be leaving now. How could they think of starting afresh in another country?[1] Yet the order to leave had been given, and they were bound to move. They believed that the Good Shepherd was able to keep his sheep.

Goodbye Sapushan, Goodbye and Goodbye[2]

Olive and Theo set about putting their Sapushan affairs in order, prior to leaving for Kunming. Besides the Miao Bibles there were Hymn books and other books to be handed over to the Miao church. Clothes, furniture and household goods all had to be disposed of. Old Mission documents had to be destroyed. There were last trips to places such as Aguomi and Taogu, where Theo preached farewell sermons.

They made plans to leave in a fortnight, and announced this at the Sapushan church service. The thought that the packing and moving would take them to their children buoyed their spirits. Although they had not yet heard that the children had arrived in Australia, they were picturing them

---

1   Thompson, P, op. cit., pp. 85 ff.
2   See Theo and Olive's letters dated 8, 14, 19, 25, 28 and 31 January, and 4, 7 and 11 February.

there with Olive's mother, making arrangements about schools, uniforms and travel. Letters at last seemed to be getting out from China, though mail in from Australia was sparse and often held up for months.

Theo had long ago learnt how to develop and print his own photographs (probably as a teacher, before he ever went to China) and, besides printing passport photos, and pictures of people and places, was busy teaching the Bible School principal[3] how to do this. Olive and Theo had bought a camera as a Christmas present for David. When the children had not been able to come home for Christmas, the presents lovingly bought and wrapped had to be sold or given away. The Bible School principal bought the camera. Now he was embarking on the next step, learning the developing and printing process from Theo.

As the two weeks passed, many friends called with farewell gifts. One brought a fowl and $10,000[4], while many others brought eggs. Still others came inviting Theo and Olive for a farewell meal in their homes. They could have been eating out twice a day for weeks on all these invitations. No-one wanted them to leave, but they all realised there was no alternative.

Their applications for passes to travel to Kunming were lodged. 'It will take five days to process them', they were told. The five days passed and still there were no travel passes. More days went by, and the delay continued. Another Sunday came and went, and they were farewelled a second time. The waiting went on for still another week.

While at the third Sunday's church service two policemen came into the chapel and gave a message to someone sitting at the back. They had brought the long-awaited travel passes. Theo had to leave the service and locate two passport photos to go on the travel passes. He showed these to the police, who then left.

Theo returned to the service to be asked to give a final word of encouragement to the believers. This time, he directed their attention to Hebrews 13:8 (KJV) 'Jesus Christ—the same yesterday, and today and forever'. Things change; missionaries come and go; nothing in life is certain, just this—Jesus never fails. He never changes. He abides faithful.

---

3 Long Fu Hua is the one Theo was teaching the printing and developing process according to a letter from Olive dated 25 January, 1951. A previous letter from her, dated 3 June, 1950, identifies him as the 'B. S. Principal', however local sources today believe the Principal was Long Fu Hua's brother, Long Fu Yi.

4 At this stage, after massive inflation of the Chinese 'dollar', this was a very tiny sum of money.

Eventually, the day came, 13 February, 1951, when they mounted their horses and rode out of Sapushan. Almost the whole Miao village were out in force to see them off, as well as many from the Chinese village of Sapushan[5]. Numerous women and girls walked along with and behind them, weeping inconsolably. Fifteen of these insisted they would walk all the way to Wuding with them, about five or six miles. Once Theo and Olive were below the precipice, they felt they should not prolong the farewell, and so cantered off ahead of the women. They were never to see them again.

Another night under the stars

It would take them several days to reach Kunming. Towards the evening on the first day, the folk of a Miao village they were passing, begged them to spend the night with them. At first Theo and Olive did not know who they were, and did not feel they should impose on them with so many porters.

The invitation was pressed more urgently as Theo and Olive tried to ride past. Suddenly the penny dropped. They had been in this village before, though travelling from a different direction. The village had been burnt out a few weeks previously, but still the people of the village wanted the Simpkins and their party to stay one night with them.

While the village folk prepared a meal for their visitors, Olive and Theo put up their stretchers in a room with no roof and only mud walls standing. It was a bright moonlit night, and they shared a meal of steamed maize and leafy greens before Theo concluded the evening by leading in family worship.

Two days later in the CIM mission home in Kunming, Theo set about the next step—the business of applying for permits to exit China. He had to call on the police, who required both Theo and Olive to write out detailed family histories in both English and Chinese. All their luggage had to be listed in detail, itemising everything in each piece of luggage, in both Chinese and English.

Theo also helped other missionaries with their applications. His facility with the Chinese language—and his patience—were tested to the limit, as he was repeatedly sent back to clarify something, or answer a question.

---

5   Sapushan consists of two parts: 'large Sapushan' which was a largely Miao village, higher up the hill, and 'small Sapushan'—a mainly Han Chinese village a little lower down the hill.

Often, the officials simply left him standing waiting for hours on end, before closing the office and telling him to come back another day.[6]

Olive and Theo's daily expectation was that, once they had humbly and honestly fulfilled all the official requirements, their exit passes would be supplied, and they could be on their way back to the children in Australia.

At least, they hoped and believed that their children were in Australia. They had still heard nothing, after almost three months, to confirm that they had reached Australia safely.

Letters home from China

In March, Olive and Theo heaved a sigh of relief as they received letters indicating that the children had indeed reached Australia and were now settled with Mrs. Kettle, Olive's mother. David, Dorothy and Helen had all started in school, after a hiccup or two. They were living together with Grandma about as smoothly as one could expect for a group that did not know each other very well and were most unfamiliar with each other's ways.

Letters from Olive and Theo were full of admonition to the children to be good, obedient and helpful to their Grandma, and encouragement to Grandma Kettle to obtain help in the house. Theo's sisters occasionally came to give Mrs Kettle a hand. Many of Theo's letters to David, now a teenager attending a staid Methodist church, and at school in a secular public high school in Melbourne, were laced with instructions to beware of liberal interpretations of Scripture, and to be diligent in his school work.

This was particularly so once they were receiving letters from the children, written from Australia. For example, on 3 May, 1951, Theo wrote this to David:

> Now your 13/3/51 letter! The important thing was about your Bible Class Leaders attitude to the Bible especially some things in the O.T., Job for one.
> (1) The whole story of Job is told as though it is a true story. Job is referred to as an actual man and those were his actual experiences. Anyone who reads the book of Job cannot deny that.
> (2). Ezekiel 14:14-20. These are God's own words, and He refers to

---

6   This was the story we heard our parents tell many times when we were all back in Australia again.

Job as a real person noted for his righteous life.
(3). James 5:11. James refers to Job as a real person and holds them
up as an example. Thus if men say Job is a myth or a folk-yarn we
are setting ourselves up as being wiser than James, or Ezekiel – or
God himself. To me it is a terribly dangerous thing to begin to doubt
God's word in that way. For every such idle word spoken we must
give an account in the day of Judgement.

As they became more aware of the departure process, letters became more and more guarded. Few details were given about what was happening. On 22 March, 1951, Olive told her mother in a letter:

Theo has offered to stay on, if necessary, to finalise up the mission's
affairs, as, for certain reasons which I cannot go into in detail, it
seems wise for someone other than the ones in charge now to be here
at the end.

Before leaving China, each missionary had to have a local person who was willing to stand as guarantor[7]. This person promised to be liable for any unpaid debts and any undisclosed crimes, which included anything the missionary might say or do when back in their homeland that could be detrimental to the government. It amounted to leaving a hostage behind, and ensured the missionaries' silence when they left.

Daily the numbers of the household fluctuated as some missionaries received their passes and left, while others arrived in from outlying stations to commence the exit process. Theo was kept busy helping with the Mission accounts as well as seeing various officials in relation to their exit passes.

He did what he could around the house, mending furniture and fixtures, and cleaning out the yard and box room. On most mornings, there was a Bible Study for those free to attend. Theo took his turn in leading these. Since there were school-aged children of missionaries in the house, Theo started arithmetic classes for them, and their mothers took spelling and writing sessions. (These children were probably those from the Yunnan field who would have been planning to go to the school in Guling, but their plans had been disrupted by the current political situation.)

By the end of March, there was still no sign of their passes. There were

---

7   Thompson, P, op. cit., pp. 66 f.

now thirty-one people in the mission home to be fed and cared for, besides thirty in another house and six in the dental clinic. When the military requisitioned one house occupied by CIM missionaries awaiting exit permits, they had to move out. Somehow, they were squeezed into the already over-crowded mission home. No sooner did one family move out than two or three more arrived.

The missionaries took turns to be housekeeper, to shop, cook, clean, wash up, and provide for the group. Olive's time was filled with baking scones, cakes and biscuits for the large family. She found it hard to accept her enforced delay in Kunming while her elderly mother, thousands of miles away, was becoming exhausted looking after her grandchildren.

Tantalising hints were given by the officials that Theo and Olive, or others, would be given their passes 'soon'. Often, these hints came to nothing.[8]

They all came to experience profoundly[9] the proverb, 'Hope deferred makes the heart sick, but a longing fulfilled is a tree of life' (Proverbs 13:12 NIV). They made the best of the difficult situation, often joking about the non-appearing passes.

When there was a birthday, they celebrated it in as much style as possible. Those among them who could cook would serve up their particular speciality (such as bread rolls while another made muffins or cookies, cakes or scones) when they were rostered to help in the kitchen.

Daily they met for fellowship, Bible study and prayer, often enjoying singing some of their favourite songs of faith. Theo was one of only a few able to accompany the singing on the little pedal organ. Whenever they could, they met with other foreign believers in the city who were also waiting on exit passes. Occasionally there was a sing-song at the German sisters' place (German missionary sisters with whom the CIM missionaries often shared fellowship when in Kunming), where Theo enjoyed singing tenor in a quartet.

In the evenings, the group shared stories of how God had supplied their needs in the past. Those newly arrived in the city would have stories to tell from their particular area—stories of suffering and stories of deliverance.

On other occasions, people gave lectures on topics of interest.

---

8   See, for example, Theo and Olive's letters to family members dated 15 and 25 April, 8, 23 and 29 May and 6 June.

9   See Olive's letter to her mother dated 6 June, 1951.

A Mr. Shipton, who had several times been one of a party climbing Mount Everest, gave a lecture on mountain climbing. Dr Max Gray gave a talk on leprosy. John Kuhn led a study on Daniel, and Dr John Toop also spoke. Those who could play chess developed their skills through many challenging games. Arthur Glasser gave a talk on bridge-building, which was illustrated by Mr Cecil Gracey, an artist in the household. Through it all, each was seeking to learn whatever lessons of patience and trust God was teaching them through this enforced inaction.

In time, the missionaries had to pick up the laundry work as well. Without any washing machine, copper, or ringer, it was very heavy work rubbing, rinsing, squeezing, and hanging out the dozens of sheets, pillowslips and towels needing to be changed weekly, or whenever a family moved out and another moved in.

Days when it was Olive and Theo's turn on kitchen duties were exhausting, and Olive found herself going to bed on those days straight after the evening meal. After one such very heavy turn on duty, Olive developed a bad giddy head, something that was to plague her for the rest of her life. She could not move without everything seeming to go around and around, inducing vomiting. There was nothing for it but to go to bed, which she did for about five or six days. When the giddiness began to subside, she slowly picked up small duties until she was strong enough and back to her usual energetic self.

April came and went, and May, and still there was no news of the travel passes for Theo and Olive.

An urgent petition

People who had come in from other areas seemed to be processed more quickly than those from the Wuding area and were already on their way home. Why was that? What kinds of false accusations were being made against them, that they had no opportunity to counter?

In a letter to her mother, dated 6 June, 1951, Olive wrote in very guarded language:

> Theo has written to Mr Sanders [who became the CIM General Director a few years later], and in terms of Scripture, has given some indication of what has happened here recently, and for the time being, you must be content with that.

> We feel it best not to say more, but the more we think about it all,

and the more time goes by, we realise that there is nothing at all to be worried about. It is probably one of those cases where the devil oversteps himself, and he will gain nothing, but rather lose by it.

We feel it is this because of the way the Lord's work has prospered in the tribal areas from which we have come; and it may perhaps account, in some measure, for the long delay in getting our passes, though even this may not be it at all , and anyway, for ourselves right from the beginning, we have felt it was nothing to worry about, and even now, for the Grays, is nothing either.

It is just an S.O.S. for more prevailing and believing prayer and waiting for the Lord to work for us. In the meantime, we are quite alright here, with all our needs supplied, though of course, we do long to be with you all, and trust it will not be long before we do join you.

They knew others were in a far worse situation. Some had been imprisoned, with few external supports. A letter had just come to hand from Arthur and Wilda Matthews, CIMers who were in Qinghai, a northwest province of China. In a letter dated 25 May, 1951, Olive and Theo quoted from the Matthews' letter:

We cannot write, so please explain to all our friends—the urgent need for sustained prayer. Speaking for the whole Tsinghai group— what happened to the apostle Peter [i.e. he was imprisoned] is before many up here unless the Lord intervene. Peter was kept—but prayer was made unceasing. Pray for endurance, contentment, wisdom. Pray against Satan's power to hinder.

How proud Paul must have felt every time he said 'a prisoner of the Lord Jesus Christ' and we feel the same. We are in His hands, He goes on before and also our rearward.

Before departing, each missionary was required to advertise their wish to leave in the Chinese daily newspapers. This had to be done for seven days. A copy of the seven newspapers must be kept to show the officials as proof that they had, indeed, advertised. This was so any Chinese citizen claiming to have been wronged, or to be owed money by the missionary could institute proceedings against them. Meantime, it was essential to scour the daily papers in case any charge against them requiring an answer was being heard in the local courts. It was a trying and difficult interlude. For people who had always been very busy in the Lord's work, and who knew how much still needed to be done, the inactivity was challenging.

The words of John Wesley's Covenant Prayer, which formed part of the Methodist Church's annual Covenant service, were so relevant:

I am no longer my own, but thine.
Put me to what thou wilt, rank me with whom thou wilt.
Put me to doing, put me to suffering.
Let me be employed for thee or laid aside for thee,
exalted for thee or brought low for thee.
Let me be full, let me be empty.
Let me have all things, let me have nothing.
I freely and heartily yield all things to thy pleasure and disposal.
And now, O glorious and blessed God, Father, Son and Holy Spirit,
thou art mine, and I am thine.
So be it.
And the covenant which I have made on earth,
let it be ratified in heaven.
Amen.[10]

There it was. 'Let me be employed for thee or laid aside for thee'. If it was the Lord's will for them to wait and be still, even for months on end, let it be so. And they found peace in accepting their situation.

May passed and the hot June days came, occasionally cooled down by summer rains. All the Kunming Mission property affairs had been finalised, so there was nothing to keep Theo and Olive in Kunming except their missing exit passes.

Early in June they received an invitation from the British Consulate to join them in drinking the King's health, on the King's birthday weekend. The consulate, like the CIM community, was having to leave China and was disposing of all its possessions, so the invitation came with a request that guests bring their own goblet!

News from CIM headquarters, now in Hong Kong, told them that, of the nearly 700 missionaries in China when the order to evacuate had been given seven months earlier, less than a hundred remained. By ones and

---

10 As used in the Book of Offices of the British Methodist Church, 1936.
    See Huffman, K 2012, The Duke Clergy Health Initiative, *The Connection*,
    'Wesley Covenant Prayer', viewed 2 November, 2018,
    sites.duke.edu/theconnection/2012/08/01/wesley-covenant-prayer/.

twos, the exit passes had been supplied. The iron doors had swung open, releasing the prisoners. Olive and Theo knew that in God's good time, the doors would swing open for them also, 'of their own accord' as happened for the Apostle Peter (Acts 12:10).

Stories were filtering through of the kinds of things the missionaries were being accused of by church members. Some of the believers refused to lay any such charges, but they paid a price for it, sometimes their very lives were forfeit. Some complied with the requirement to accuse by levelling bizarre allegations about missionaries who had already left China, but the officials soon saw through this ploy, and were not satisfied. Others had the idea of making wild and fanciful accusations which no-one who knew the missionary would believe.

Some of these made for sensational headlines in the papers. Yet the fine print might reveal that the date when the so-called crimes had been committed was years before the missionary had arrived in China. Missionaries who had provided medical help were accused of atrocities such as using babies to make their medicines[11]. Reading these charges in the paper without the right to rebut them was deeply hurtful.

Theo wrote to David on 6 June 1951:

> The 9th beatitude[12]—'blessed are ye'—applies to us just now, so pray that the Lord will undertake for us and the Grays, and protect us. Psalm 37 is a very great comfort. Mark the four words commit—trust—rest—wait (in verses 5, 7); that is just what we have to do very really. Commit all to him; Trust in Him and not be afraid; Rest in Him; Wait for Him. And the Lord is faithful. He is able to keep—able to do—able to save to the uttermost!

At last, towards the end of June, they were given permission to start advertising their departure.

---

11 We were told that in 2012, a TV program broadcast in Kunming was still repeating this accusation.

12 Matthew 5:11–12 'Blessed are you when people insult you, persecute you and falsely say all kinds of evil against you because of me. Rejoice and be glad, because great is your reward in heaven, for in the same way they persecuted the prophets who were before you.' (NIV)

Chapter 28

DEPARTURES

I t was on a hot humid July morning, that Theo and Olive were called to go down to the Air Office to buy their plane tickets to Chongqing[1]. Theo rushed out on his bicycle in the rain, to collect their temporary travel passes first and have them approved by the police.

After a frantic morning's packing, they were back at the Air Office that afternoon, with all their baggage, to have it checked—item by item, sealed, weighed up and eventually booked in. They would be joined on the same plane by eight German missionaries and their two children. The plane was flying out the next day, 13 July 1951.

And so, five months after leaving Sapushan, the day came for them to say goodbye to Yunnan.

Too many words!

The flight from Kunming to Chongqing was fairly smooth, and Dr Gray had given Olive some travel pills to take to ease the journey. The plane was above the clouds for most of the way, and Olive was pleased to arrive with

---

1   For this section see Theo and Olive's letters dated 27 June, 3, 12 and 17 July and 5, 6, 14 and 20 August, 1951.

her breakfast still intact. The ride from the Chongqing airport to the air office was nearly her undoing, though, with its bumps and hairpin bends.

At Chongqing airport, all the luggage was laid out in the steamy heat. In spite of having clearly unbroken seals, the officials commenced to open and examine each piece.

This was more than Olive could endure on this long hot day. She remonstrated with the official. 'You can see they are all sealed. They have been passed in Kunming. We have not touched them since they were passed there. Why do you need to open them again?'

After this, the officials were even more meticulous, going through every item in each piece of luggage, including items of intimate apparel, with smiling and studied carefulness and feigned politeness.

Never again did Olive make the mistake of arguing with an official. His retort to Olive went down in family folklore, to be brought out, used and re-used whenever anyone was thought to be talking too much.

'女人.你的话太多了。'

'Nüren. Ni de hua tai duo liao.'

'Woman. Your words are too many!'

Once their luggage had been finally passed they proceeded to the inn in Chongqing where they were to stay while awaiting transport for the next lap of the journey out.

If they thought Kunming was hot, Chongqing was considerably hotter. Local residents thought the weather that day was pleasantly cool. To Olive and Theo and the other score of Yunnan missionaries waiting in Chongqing for transport, it seemed unbearably oppressive. Their accommodation was in a bug-infested Chinese inn. Officials would not permit them to walk around the city. While they waited, they sweltered.

Chongqing was built on the banks of the Yangtze River, and the plan was that they would all go down to Hankou by boat—when one became available. After about ten days in Chongqing, a boat was found, and they set off for Hankou. From Hankou they boarded a train to take them across the border into Hong Kong.

At each junction point, their travel passes, passports, and health and immunisation certificates were checked along with their luggage. Fortunately, they were never questioned.

They learnt later that the three children's experience had been different. Before leaving Guling enroute to Hong Kong, the children had been given smallpox vaccinations at the school. When they reached Guangdong, the officials would not accept the school doctor's certificate, and insisted on re-vaccinating the children. When their train took them over the border, the Hong Kong British authorities would not recognise either of the two previous vaccinations, so the children each had their third smallpox vaccination in just a few days[2]. Fortunately they had no adverse reactions.

Huts in Hong Kong

It was on 30 July that the train carrying Theo and Olive finally pulled into Hong Kong. They were met by CIM folk who took them to the 'camp' on the Kowloon Peninsula, where the missionaries were being housed while transport to their home countries was found[3]. The children had spent some time there as well, seven or eight months earlier, on their way back to Australia.

The camp consisted of a group of old Quonset (Nissen-style) huts that had been renovated and fitted out with plumbing and electricity. Beds and bedding had been obtained, and arrangements put in place for the provision of meals. It was in a very secluded spot, tucked away on the waterfront with the railway at the back, a prison on one side and a cemetery on the other.

Olive and Theo joined nearly a hundred other missionaries, all waiting for transport home. Theo was placed in 'B' Hut with other men, and Olive in 'K' Hut with many younger missionary women and a few older women. Another hut had been set up as the dining room.

There was little insulation in these huts, but Olive and Theo were very grateful for the intermittent sea breezes. Soon after they arrived, there was a typhoon. The winds were tempestuous. They blew and blew. It was hard to keep their feet as they walked between the huts. The rain bucketed down, pouring right into the huts. As the waves crashed onto the ocean wall, the spray flew high over the wall and onto the huts. Everyone got drenched, but no-one minded in the July heat. It was a change from being soaked with perspiration. [4]

---

2   Simpkin, DM, op. cit..

3   See Thompson, P, op. cit., pp. 75–79 for the amazing story of the provision of these huts to house the missionaries being evacuated and their families.

4   See Olive's letter to David from Hong Kong, dated 6 August, 1951.

Olive hoped there would be no further typhoons once they boarded the ship for Australia.

During their three weeks wait in Hong Kong, Theo had several opportunities to speak and preach. He shared with the other missionaries in the camp a carefully edited version of the story of their experiences, as well as giving a Gospel address at the Emmanuel Church. They visited some Chinese refugees from the mainland. One big camp housed 20,000. Many asked about what was going on in China. They had their own appalling stories of thousands being shot for not supporting 'the party', not 'changing their thoughts', or simply for 'being enemies of the people'. Many more were incarcerated. It was a sobering reminder of the need for prayer for believers left behind.[5]

It was late in August that berths were secured on a small liner, the MS *Taiyuan*. As they boarded the ship, they knew a big chapter of their lives was closing. What would the next hold? They were confident that the same Lord who had walked with them over the past few decades was going before them. He would open the way for them.

---

5   See Theo's letter to the family in Australia, dated 20 August, 1951.

Chapter 29

WHAT NEXT?

The family is reunited

It was October 1951 in Carnegie, a south-eastern suburb of Melbourne, where Mrs Kettle lived. Olive and Theo had arrived in Sydney on board the MS *Taiyuan*, just a month earlier, on Monday 3 September.

The ship was not due to sail on to Melbourne for three or four days, and Olive and Theo had been told they would not be able to continue round to Melbourne even if they wanted to. Besides, they could not wait to be reunited with their three children. It was nearly three years since they had last seen them. So they took the train to Melbourne, leaving the bulk of their luggage to continue by boat to Melbourne. They left Sydney on an unusually warm spring day, and arrived in Melbourne on a typically cool, misty, showery afternoon. The contrast for Theo and Olive with what they had left behind in China was dramatic.

The children together with their grandmother, Mrs Kettle, were at the railway station to meet their parents. It was a grand reunion!

And now they were all living together in Mrs Kettle's small weatherboard bungalow, with lead-light windows in the main rooms. There were only two bedrooms, and a closed-in veranda or 'sleep-out' that had been added to the house and was divided into two rooms, making four rooms that could be used as bedrooms. Mrs Kettle's bedroom was the main bedroom, and Dorothy and Helen shared the second bedroom. Theo and Olive slept in the main sleep-out room while David had the tiny one off his parents' room. The kitchen, laundry and bathroom were all quite compact. There was a lounge room, and double doors led through to a small dining-room.

It was a perfectly adequate home for a single elderly lady, and the couple of boarders she had had for some years. The boarders had gone when the children arrived in January 1951. But now, for three adults and three growing children, there were times when the house felt decidedly crowded.

Scenes something like this were both inevitable and frequent.

'Helen! It's time for you to do your piano practice. Dorothy will be home soon, and she'll need to do hers so David can have his turn before supper tonight.'

'You mean 'tea', Mummy. We're in Australia now!'

'I keep forgetting. Just as well I have you to remind me. Now onto the piano quickly. Hop to it!'

'I'm nearly at the end of a chapter, Mummy. I'll go when I finish the chapter.'

Helen was lying on her bed reading the latest 'Anne' book that she had been given for her birthday. While in Guling, she and Dorothy had each been given one of the 'Anne' books; Helen's was *Anne of Green Gables* and Dorothy's was *Anne of Avonlea*. Both had devoured the two books in record time and couldn't wait until the next birthday for another in the series by LM Montgomery. Now Helen had been given *Anne of Windy Willows*, and she was engrossed.

Five minutes later, Olive's mother's voice could be heard.

'Helen, your mother told you to go and do your practice. I can't hear the piano yet.'

Helen shut her book with a snap and stomped into the lounge room where the piano stood. She had thought, when her parents were home, they would be the ones to tell her what to do. Now it seemed there were three resident police.

It took some time for everyone to adjust to the new living situation.

Australia in 1951[1]

In the four years since Theo and Olive had last departed from Australia, there had been changes. Wartime rationing of food, clothing and petrol had all been abolished. Employment was high, and the economy was growing. In striking contrast to China, there was a general air of optimism, and people were encouraged to spend freely. This was the era of the birth of the 'suburban dream', of everyone owning their own detached house and garden. Labour-saving devices were being purchased by many, freeing up more leisure time. A new immigration policy had been put in place with incentives for non-British, but still white, settlers from Europe to emigrate, thus enriching Australian life.

Together with this growing prosperity, there was an increase in secularity in society. Although Christianity was still the stated religion of most Australian citizens, attendance at worship was declining. It was still felt that children should be baptised, and needed religious education, to help them form values and morals for life. Children were encouraged to attend Sunday School, and Christian Religious Instruction was given in the State Primary and some Secondary Schools.

Yet there was anxiety and unease because of the Korean war. Australian forces formed part of the United Nations multinational force defending South Korea from the Communist forces of North Korea, and in some circles, there was fear of World War 3 because of the Korean conflict. During 1950 the Liberal government of Robert Menzies had introduced a bill for the dissolution of the Communist Party in Australia. Parliament passed the bill, but when it was appealed in the High Court, the High Court declared it to be unconstitutional.

Later in 1951, Menzies attempted to outlaw Communism through a referendum to change the Constitution, to allow the banning of the Communist Party. This referendum was held only weeks after Theo and

---

1   See for example van Teeseling, I n.d., *Australia explained: A site for newcomers and old hands*, 'History: Menzies and the 1950s – Part 1', viewed 2 November, 2018, www.australia-explained.com.au/history/menzies-and-the-1950s-part-1, Australian Children's Television Foundation, My Place for Teachers, *Australia in the 1950s*, viewed 2 November, 2018, myplace.edu.au/decades_timeline/1950/decade_landing_5.html, Australian Broadcasting Corporation (ABC): ABC Archives & library services, *1950s*, viewed 2 November, 2018, www.abc.net.au/archives/timeline/1950s.htm and WebsterWorld, Journey into knowledge... Encyclopedia of Australia, *1951*, viewed 2 November, 2018, www.websterworld.com/websterworld/aust/1/1951208.html.

Olive arrived in Australia, fresh from their harrowing experiences under Communist China. The referendum failed, being opposed largely on the grounds of freedom of speech. To Theo and Olive, it seemed that Australia had blinkers on in relation to Communism. Yet they were unable to speak out, hampered by the fact that they had left behind in China believers who would be held responsible for anything Theo and Olive did or said that could discredit the People's Republic of China.

Next steps

The big question Olive and Theo could not put off any longer was 'What now?'. They had felt called to go to China to share the Good News about Jesus with the people of Yunnan, but God had pulled them out of China. What should they do next? Where did God want them to be?

During their long months in China, waiting for exit permits, this question had been at the back of their minds all the time. The CIM believed God was calling the Mission, now that the door into China was decisively shut, to work with Chinese people in other Asian countries.[2] Could this be God's call to Theo and Olive as well? If so, where?

Perhaps they discussed the question along these lines.

'We have been separated from the children for three years. Surely now it's time we accepted our responsibility as parents to guide and care for them personally?'

'It was different in China, where there was such a good school in the same country we were in. We could be confident the children were receiving a good education, and that their spiritual development was being nurtured. But if we go to one of the new fields, we would have to leave them in Australia. They could live in the CIM Hostel for missionaries' children, but they would still have to be educated in the secular State schools. And local churches don't seem very lively. Don't we have a duty to teach our own children first?'

'But how will we support ourselves if we leave the Mission?'

'I could go back to teaching, I suppose', said Theo.

'And I might be able to get a part-time job in an office', suggested Olive.

---

2 Thompson, P, op. cit., pp. 82–87.

Leaving the CIM

The discussions went back and forth, day after day—begun, continued and concluded in prayer. Gradually the conviction grew that God was calling them out of the Mission and to trust him to provide support and opportunities of service within Australia.

Characteristically, they did not wait until the new year to try to find work. Olive made enquiries at the CIM office in Elizabeth Street, Melbourne, to see if there was anything she could do to help. She could take some of the load of typing and book-keeping where needed. For the next twelve months or so, she returned to office work in a greatly changed Melbourne Central Business District. She had last made that regular daily commute into the City back in 1932, about eighteen years ago.

Theo discovered that the Australian Defence Department office in Melbourne was looking for people capable of translating Chinese documents. He applied and was accepted, taking up a brief part-time role there. As the days went by, and Theo pored over military documents with a Chinese dictionary at his elbow, his dissatisfaction grew.

He longed to be teaching people truths from Scripture, not learning new military terms in Chinese. Was this really the place God wanted him to be?

Meanwhile, to help stretch their meagre resources, Theo began planting vegetables and fruit trees in Mrs Kettle's large backyard. She already had a lemon tree, a couple of flowering plums and a lovely old Cootamundra wattle tree. It had almost finished flowering when Theo and Olive arrived in Australia that year, but they looked forward each winter to the sudden bursting of the fluffy golden blossom on the branches of feathery blue-green leaves, heralding the end of winter.

As well as the garden, Theo built a hen-house with roosts and laying boxes, and fenced in a yard for the hens so that soon, they could contribute eggs and vegetables (and very occasionally a 'complete personal commitment' by a hen or rooster!) for their meals. The children were each given their responsibilities of digging, weeding and watering the garden, feeding the chooks and collecting the eggs.

Helen remembers being given the grand sum of one penny per hundred snails she could pick out of the garden for her father to dispatch.

Theo returns to the classroom

In discussions with members of the CIM Home Council, Theo heard that Caulfield Grammar School, a Church of England Boys' Grammar School, had a close connection with China, especially with missionaries to China. From the time of the first headmaster, the school had a close link with the Church Missionary Society. When the second headmaster left the school, he himself went to China as a missionary.[3]

As Theo and Olive prayed about their needs, Theo believed it was right for him to contact the CGS headmaster, and enquire about the possibility of teaching at the school. After a telephone conversation, Theo wrote a formal letter of application for a teaching position. A prompt reply came back offering him a full-time position commencing in 1952. He would be teaching Maths and Science in the middle school, and would also take Scripture classes.

This would provide for all their material needs, as well as give him opportunities to teach from the Scriptures.

In the interim

Over Christmas 1951, the family attended the Belgrave Heights Convention, living on site in tents. The Belgrave Heights Convention is an annual convention run in the style of the English Keswick Convention with its emphasis on Bible teaching and the Deeper Christian Life. It was established first at Upwey, and when the site was required for a local school, a 22 acre property at Belgrave Heights was purchased in 1950. Belgrave Heights is a small township in the Dandenong Ranges, only 40km east of Melbourne. The Convention grounds have a beautiful setting of gum trees, bush and ornamental trees.

The family celebrated with the joyous sound of the kookaburras soaring over the treetops, and the ringing notes of the bell-birds as background, amid the pervasive eucalyptus aroma, while keeping a sharp lookout for snakes in the long grass. What a delight to meet again with large crowds of enthusiastic believers, and to listen to biblical exegesis by eminent Christian teachers from around the globe!

---

3   Welch, I 2003, *Alien Son, The Life and Times of Cheok Hong CHEONG, (Zhang Zhuoxiong) 1851-1928*, Chapter 5 'The Anglican Years: 1885-1928', OpenResearch Repository, Australian National University, viewed 2 November 2018, openresearch-repository.anu.edu.au/bitstream/1885/49261/37/07chapter5.pdf.

Theo and Olive found ways they could help at the convention. Theo and David took turns as ushers in the meetings, and Olive helped at the crèche. In subsequent years, Theo and Olive took responsibility for the tea service, pouring countless cups of tea and coffee for visitors to the convention, often with the help of Dorothy and Helen.

Through one of their prayer partners, Theo heard about orchards in Victoria's north, near Echuca on the Murray, where casual paid work could be found for fruit-pickers. The whole family went up and stayed for some weeks on a friend's farm, so that Theo and David could earn some money by fruit-picking. It was hard, back-breaking work in the hot Australian summer.

On days when they were not working, Theo accepted any invitation he was given to share what he could of the story of the Church in Yunnan with those who would pray. It was a great opportunity to catch up with people who had interceded and had given to support them over their years in China.

While Theo was working in the orchards, he purchased cases of fruit at a discounted rate, and he sent them down to reach Melbourne when the family returned. Olive and Theo co-opted the children to help peel and cut up the fruit, packing it carefully in preserving jars which were then filled with water or syrup. Rubber rings, lids and clips were used to cover the jars before they were placed in the preserving vat of nearly-boiling water to be sealed. This would provide the family with fruit for dessert for most of the year, at a much cheaper cost than if they bought tins of fruit. Preserving became a regular feature for the family, of the late summer and early autumn months for many years.

'Please sir, tell us a China story.'

But soon, the school holidays were at an end, and Theo found himself back in an Australian schoolroom again. Perhaps this is what happened one day in the classroom.

The sun beat down on the school, and the heat in the classroom became oppressive, as it often did in the Australian summer. A fly buzzed incessantly as it tried unsuccessfully to find a way out of the window.

Theo had now been on the Caulfield Grammar School staff for some months, and had settled in to his role there. This was a Maths lesson with twelve and thirteen-year-old boys. The atmosphere was heavy with the repressed energies and characteristic aroma of hot teenage boys. Some were making heavy weather of the linear and quadratic equations.

After a bit of subdued whispering in one corner, a hand shot up.

'Yes Jones? What's the problem?'

'Please sir, will you tell us a China story?'

There was a murmur of approval around the class. Anything was better than Maths on a hot afternoon like this.

For Theo, nothing could replace the people of the Yunnan mountains in his affections. They were daily in his thoughts and prayers. He often took the opportunity to share some of his experiences in China, with the boys in his classes.

Theo looked at the clock. There was only ten minutes until the end of school for the day. He could pick up the lesson next time, and why not strike while the iron was hot?

'Well, your homework for tonight will be to finish the exercises on page 47', he replied, and he made a note on the blackboard.

The boys relaxed and leant back in their desks, ready to enjoy the story, as Theo launched into the account of another of his China experiences.

This is how, many decades later, a past student recalled it:

Nobody who attended CGS at the time could ever forget the intense W.T. Simpkin (who taught 1952-1960) with his constant 'When I was in China' and all of his anecdotes about Chinese life, Chinese culture, and his stories about the kind and gentle nature of the majority of Chinese people.[4]

---

4   Unsigned comment added by 203.206.162.148 (talk), September 2009, under the heading 'Why Nanjing?', Caulfield Grammar School, Wikipedia, viewed 2 November, 2018, en.wikipedia.org/wiki/Talk%3ACaulfield_Grammar_School. by 203.206.162.148 () 03:07, 15 September 2009 (UTC) under the heading 'Why Nanjing?'.

The privileged boys of Caulfield Grammar School were by no means typical of Australia generally. Although it was a Christian school, many of the boys' families had chosen the school for their sons because of its academic reputation rather than its Christian character.

Theo in the classroom at Caulfield Grammar School
(Photo: WT Simpkin collection)

Yet for Theo, being among the boys day after day gave him some insight into Australian values and beliefs. This was the environment in which his children were growing up. Indeed, their school culture was likely to be far more secular.

Besides his regular timetable of Maths and Science classes, Theo was expected to take part in other ways in school life. The school also owned a rural property 65 kilometres east of Melbourne, in the Upper Yarra Valley at Yarra Junction. All middle school boys were expected to spend a week there each year accompanied by teachers.

When it was Theo's class's turn at Yarra Junction, he and Olive went with them. Olive was most impressed with the boys' excellent table manners. She thought her own ex-Guling trio could learn a thing or two from the Caulfield Grammar School boys.

The outdoor education campus at Yarra Junction was opened in 1947, as Cuming House, and was the first of its kind in any school in Australia. So in 1952, when Theo and Olive joined a class of teenage boys there, it was still quite new. It was an opportunity for the boys' education to take place in a new way in a different environment. The boys were encouraged to explore both the environment and their effect on it, as well as to consider their own values and place in the world. There were trips out, to local beauty spots and to the Yarra Dam, and long hikes.

Many of their experiences at Yarra Junction were 'firsts': their first time away from home, first all-day hike, and for some more pampered boys, it was the first time they had been expected to do household chores such as preparing vegetables, setting the tables or sweeping the floor. Even Maths classes were almost enjoyable when held under a gumtree, with the sun shining down.

Crusaders

Another contribution Theo enjoyed making to the life of the school was in helping to plan and run the Crusaders groups. These were voluntary student clubs which met weekly or twice-weekly to consider the challenge to follow Jesus as Lord, to learn more about the work of Christ in the world, and to engage in Bible study and prayer. They were led by the boys, but a staff member was present as adviser. Often there were visiting speakers, and Theo occasionally shared stories about the church among the tribes-people of Yunnan.

His heart was still in China, however. Early in 1962, Theo read in the CIM Home Director's circular about proposed new literature plans. Theo's heart beat quickly. Was there a way here in which he might still be able to serve the people of China through the CIM? Could he do some translating of articles, tracts, leaflets or books that might be able to go where human beings could not? He had behind him the experience of his months of translating for the Defence Department. He had evidently acquitted himself satisfactorily there since they had told him they would have him back at any time. He had been praying earnestly for a way to continue serving the Chinese people.

In no time, Theo had written to JO Sanders, the Australian and New Zealand Home Director, making his offer. Eventually, after correspondence[5] back and forth between Theo, the Home Director and the various Field Directors, Theo was invited to translate some English language material that might be of use to the Chinese church. He found it immensely satisfying to be still part of the work of CIM in this small way. One of the books whose translation he was able to oversee was *The King of Love* by John Deane[6].

However, as the months went by, this translation program was laid aside. Perhaps it became evident that the Church in China needed its own literature, written from within the culture, and by people whose use of language

---

5   Copies of some of these letters are currently held in the Library at Melbourne School of Theology (MST), Victoria, Australia. One of these letters is dated 13 May, 1952.

6   See letter, some years later dated 27 September, 1961, from Cyril Edwards (in the Christian Witness Press, Hong Kong) to Theo, referring to this book.

and idiom—whose expression as a whole—was indigenous to China. Or perhaps they needed literature written by people who were also sharing their current experience. Whatever the reason, Theo had to become reconciled to his new role of school teacher to the relatively wealthy.

Theo believed passionately that the three children were God's gracious gift to him and Olive. It was now their role as parents and teachers of the three children that was most important. How could they nurture the children's Christian faith and commitment in the increasingly secular Australian society?

Home

Initially, the family attended worship with Olive's mother at her church, Glen Huntly Methodist Church, and found a vibrant youth group at another church for David to attend. Every day after the evening meal, the family would read the Scriptures together, sing some hymns (accompanied on the piano, as they were able, by Theo or the children), and pray about matters of concern. Each family member was encouraged to take part in reading the Bible, choosing a hymn, singing or playing, and praying. It became as natural as talking about daily life.

Now that Theo was earning a regular salary, he and Olive began making enquiries about purchasing their own home.

As Melbourne's population grew, more land for residential development was released. Market gardeners growing vegetables on Melbourne's south-eastern edges were pushed out even further as their land was acquired for homes. Housing co-operatives were set up by builders to help first home buyers purchase their own homes.

Theo and Olive heard about one such co-operative and eventually signed up for a simple one-storey new house to be built for them on what had been market gardens in East Bentleigh—at that stage, an outer eastern suburb of Melbourne. How exciting it was for the family to be preparing for their new house. This would be Theo and Olive's first and only home of their own.

As they stood on the abandoned market garden, trying to form a picture of their future home, it was hard to imagine just from the plans what it would look like. Theo had no difficulty visualizing the vegetable garden and orchard he would plant there. The soil must be fertile or it would not have sustained commercial scale agriculture.

The children found it easier to picture the house once the building commenced, and they could walk around the framework on the floor joists.

'This will be our room', said Dorothy to her little sister, imagining glass in the window frame, and a door in the doorway.

At last, David would have a whole room to himself, where he could study without disturbance.

By the time the East Bentleigh house was complete in 1954 and they were ready to move in, about two and a half years had passed since Theo and Olive had left China. They heard very little news from China, and what little they heard was grim. It drove them to pray even more earnestly for the small groups of believers they had left behind in Yunnan, but now they were called to contribute to the life of the church in Australia.

Chapter 30

KANGAROOS OR PANDAS?

Putting down roots[1]

Which church should they attend? They had worked in an interdenomina-
tional organisation for so long that denominational affiliations had paled
into insignificance. The important thing was to find a group of believers
with whom they could worship and have fellowship.

In the end, they threw in their lot with the South Oakleigh Methodist
church which was within walking distance. The June 1954 Leaders' Meeting Minutes of the church note the addition of Theo and Olive Simpkin
as new members, and the three children—David, Dorothy and Helen—as
junior members. Very soon, Theo was asked to join the Leaders' Meeting,
and to take services in the circuit, as a local preacher.

It was a fast-growing area, brimming over with young families. The
church commenced a day kindergarten with encouragement and support from Theo and Olive, and hundreds of local children were enrolled.
Although the families were not all committed to the church, the Sunday
School had more than 500 children on the roll with a weekly attendance

---

1   Details regarding the Simpkin family's involvement at South Oakleigh Methodist Church were
derived from the Archives of the Uniting Church, Synod of Victoria and Tasmania, and from
family memories.

of the order of 200–300. There simply were not enough chairs for all the children. In fact, many teachers taught their classes in their cars. At this stage, it was widely accepted that children would go to Sunday School to be taught about right and wrong, and gain some moral teaching.

Theo and Olive very quickly became Sunday School teachers, and David followed soon after. Even so, class sizes were quite unmanageable, and eventually Theo suggested the church approach the Melbourne Bible Institute, to ask if they could supply some Sunday School Teachers which alleviated the problem a little. By 1956, Theo had accepted the role of Sunday School Superintendent and had also become one of the Trustees of the church.

This was the era of the big Sunday School Anniversaries (perhaps so-called because they marked the anniversary of the start of the Sunday School in the church). In three services, morning, afternoon and evening, on each of two successive Sundays every year, the massed Sunday School performed rousing Gospel songs they had been rehearsing for months.

A huge tiered platform was erected at one end of the Sunday School Hall, large enough to hold hundreds of children and their teachers. The hordes of excited children gathered and were marshalled to their seats on the platform, while their families gathered in the body of the hall. Many of the girls were wearing new dresses, specially made for the occasion, and the older girls were wearing brand-new Sunday hats. Special speakers were invited for these occasions, especially any who were known to have innovative ways of presenting the story of Jesus to children and their families.

At this period, for most families, there was nothing outside the church like these performances. Apart from big private colleges, schools had few if any concerts at which their students performed publicly, so these anniversary services were bright spots on the calendar for the children as well as for their parents.

Bible study group

Theo very quickly became the leader of the small group which met weekly in a member's home for study of the Bible and prayer. The teaching, spiritual reflection and prayer in this group grounded their faith for daily living, and provided them with energising fellowship and community. The members of this group became and remained very close friends and supporters of the Simpkins.

Both Theo and Olive were invited to share about their experiences in China with the Women's Auxiliary of Overseas Missions (WAOM) and the Young Women's Missionary Movement (YWMM), and in turn, they learnt about the Methodist Overseas Missions' work in the Pacific Islands. Olive was a staunch member of these groups all the time they lived in East Bentleigh, taking her turn at leading devotions and speaking about their experiences in China. Dorothy and Helen soon joined the YWMM as well.

Good news for the local community

Quite early in their time at South Oakleigh Methodist church, Theo banded together with other like-minded members to suggest that a group such as Campaigners for Christ be invited to run an evangelistic mission in the area. Ministers of other local churches were approached for their support, and in February 1956 the local Ministers' Fraternal agreed to ask John Robinson (from Campaigners for Christ) to hold a mission. A marquee was erected on a prominent corner, and meetings were held there over the course of a week, and 'the Lord added to their number daily those who were being saved' (as in Acts 2:47 NIV).

Theo also arranged for several missions directed towards children in the area. Pastor Laurie Dyer, a well-known children's missioner led one, and David U'Ren of the Children's Special Service Mission led another.

In 1958, Australian churches began to discuss inviting Billy Graham to come to hold evangelistic missions throughout the country. Theo moved a motion at the Leaders' Meeting, that South Oakleigh Methodist Church would cooperate with other churches in this plan. The whole Methodist church in Australia threw its weight behind the proposal.

Once the decision had been taken to invite Billy Graham, and he had accepted the invitation to come in 1959, a huge program of preparation for the crusade commenced.

Church members were enlisted as choir members, counsellors and advisors. Churches were encouraged to book coaches to transport people from their area to the campaign meetings, and to offer babysitting so parents could attend the meetings together. There were regular prayer meetings arranged, including 24-hour prayer meetings as the starting date approached. Theo and Olive were heavily involved in this, helping to select and train local counsellors, advisors and people to work in the Follow-Up department besides running prayer meetings.

The three children were involved, too, as they were able. David was nearing the end of his medical course at Melbourne University. Dorothy was well into nursing training, and Helen had just started a science degree course at Melbourne University. Both Dorothy and Helen volunteered to join the choir as well as being trained as counsellors and helping in the Follow-Up department after the crusade. It was a heady time for Australian churches when conversations about following Jesus made headlines in the media.

Undimmed passion

Theo's passion for Chinese people never dimmed, and in Melbourne, to which large numbers of Asian students flocked for an education, there were many opportunities to meet them. The Overseas Christian Fellowship—a group geared towards friendship for and Christian witness to Asian students—was soon to be formed. Theo jumped at the chance to meet and converse in Chinese with these students, sharing in leading Bible studies with them, and occasionally giving them hospitality in the family home.

He and Olive faithfully attended CIMOMF[2] prayer and fellowship meetings. Now their prayer focus widened beyond the Chinese to those being contacted in the 'new fields'—Malaya, Thailand, Indonesia, the Philippines, Singapore, Taiwan and Japan. As new workers applied to join the Mission, Theo and Olive would often invite them into their home for a meal and fellowship with the family. The three children grew up seeing missionary work as a natural part of the church's life and witness, engaging bright young people as well as those of their parents' age. It was not surprising that all three were thinking about the possibility of missionary service themselves, if that was how God's calling came to them.

Theo's eyes still looked longingly towards China. He made overtures again to the CIMOMF. Wasn't there some way in which he and Olive could still serve the Lord among the Chinese, say in Hong Kong?

But the door to overseas service closed. Olive's health had become patchy. Much of the time she was quite well, but the tinnitus (head noises) she had begun to experience in Yunnan was increasing with the accompanying loss

---

2   After withdrawing from China in 1951, the China Inland Mission became known as the China Inland Mission Overseas Missionary Fellowship (CIMOMF) until 1964, when the 'CIM' was dropped and the Mission became known simply as the Overseas Missionary Fellowship (OMF). It is now known as OMF International.

of hearing and incapacitating bouts of giddiness. An operation designed to improve her hearing had minimal effects. She was diagnosed with diabetes. Various other health problems arose as the years passed, which meant her time and energy could stretch only to home, family and church responsibilities.

Olive did not get a good health report in the required medical[3], and instead, the Mission leaders asked Olive and Theo if they would be willing to take into their home for up to a year, three children whose parents were still on the Mission field. The hostel for missionaries' children in Melbourne would probably close since it would not be economical to run the hostel just for these three for the coming year. If Olive and Theo could take them and care for them like their own children, it would be a real contribution to the Lord's work, and would give the parents confidence that their three were being loved and nurtured in the faith, until they were due to take furlough, later in the year.

Consequently, for about a year, Theo and Olive became Aunty and Uncle to the three Tarrant schoolchildren (twin teenage girls and a younger boy), as well as Mum and Dad to their own three. A 'sleep-out' (a small old single-roomed relocatable bungalow) was purchased and set up in the back yard in East Bentleigh to accommodate the larger family. The twin girls took Dorothy and Helen's room in the house while Dorothy and Helen moved into the sleep-out, and David shared his room with the younger boy. At this stage David was in his mid-twenties and studying medicine at Melbourne University, Dorothy was about twenty and Helen about eighteen.

Back to China again?

However, Theo's conviction strengthened that their service within CIMOMF was not over. He believed that Olive's health issues were totally manageable, as witness her ability to handle the extra work entailed during that year when they temporarily 'adopted' the three Tarrant children. Together they prayed and discussed what the future might hold for them, now that the Tarrant children' parents had returned from the mission field and the children had gone back to stay with their parents. They often heard about how busy the folk running the Christian Witness Press office in Hong Kong were, and how they were receiving requests for significant Christian works

---

3   A copy of this medical report is in the MST Library.

to be translated into Chinese. Olive could help in the office, and Theo could help check some of the translations.

Theo wrote to Cyril Edwards and Ron Roberts, both responsible for the Christian Witness Press (CWP) work in Hong Kong. Could he help check translations of works they were planning to publish? He was also in contact with Alfred Chow of the Hong Kong Bible Institute to sound out the possibility of taking on some teaching responsibilities there. Cyril had told Theo of some other CIMOMF members who had helped the Bible Institute in this way.

They wrote again to the OMF directors, offering to go to Hong Kong to help wherever they could be used. Again they were required to take a medical, and although Theo passed, Olive did not. The letter[4] from the Home Director was clear.

> Dear Theo and Olive,
> The doctor's report is now to hand and I regret to inform you that he is unable to recommend Olive for overseas service on account of evidence of diabetes. This will come as a disappointment to you I know but I think you must accept it that the Lord's sphere of service for you now is in the home land. I know He is using you and will continue to do so, all the more because of your willingness to go overseas again.

Accepting this reply as God's will for them was something Theo could not do. They both spent much time praying, thinking and talking about it. Perhaps it was the possibility that Olive might need to be flown home for medical treatment because of the diabetes, that tipped the scales against her. Could they tip the scales back by offering to bear all the travel costs themselves for the journey out to Hong Kong, and back again if Olive needed to come home early? Could they afford to do this? The house was not yet paid off, though Theo's salary at Caulfield Grammar School meant they had no trouble with the monthly payments. Without that salary, how could the payments be made?

Theo and Olive called the family together and explained the situation. They had sufficient savings to make the offer of travelling to Hong Kong at their own expense, but did the children (each of whom was now earning) have any suggestion about the house payments?

By this time, the children were all young adults. David had now graduated

---

4   A copy of this letter, dated 5 October, 1961, is in the Library of MST.

as a doctor and was working as a surgical registrar at Prince Henry's Hospital. Dorothy was continuing her nursing training, adding additional certificates that might be useful if she were to become a missionary. Helen also had finished school and was studying science at Melbourne University in preparation for teaching.

They quickly responded. 'If we were not living here, we would have considerable rent to pay. We can keep up the payments for you, so you can return to Hong Kong, if the OMF will have you and this is what God is calling you to.'

Theo and Olive wrote an answer to the Home Director's letter, making their new offer. Within a week they had a reply[5] that gladdened their hearts.

> Dear Theo and Olive,
> As you know there has been further reference to the field of matters concerning your medical clearance and I have now heard from the General Director that in view of the fact that you are prepared to travel out without cost to the Mission for passages and to pay the return fare if such a need should arise, he has agreed to your going to HongKong as soon as you can be free from present commitments.
> I rejoice with you in this re-opening of an apparently closed door. Perhaps you had better come and see me as soon as possible to confer about arrangements for travel to HongKong. I enclose two copies of the revised P&P[6] for your signatures.

Their hearts sang as they read.

They began to make preparations without delay. Theo wrote to the Caulfield Grammar School principal, asking for leave of absence for an undefined period (in case it became necessary for Theo and Olive to return to Melbourne). The reply contained warm-hearted appreciation of Theo's service in the school community, and the school's very best wishes for this new assignment. Resignations from the positions in the local church also elicited deep regret that the church community would be losing their fellowship and participation, but trust that God would continue to use and bless them as they returned to China.

Now Theo and Olive could look towards a new future, in the land of

---

5   Letter dated 23 October, 1961. A copy of this letter is held in the MST Library.

6   The *Principles and Practices* of CIMOMF.

the panda instead of the land of the kangaroo. What they might lack in physical energy—both being now fifty-eight years of age—they more than made up in maturity. With so much experience behind them, both in China and Australia, a greater confidence replaced any diffidence or uncertainty they may have felt as junior missionaries—yet their trust was not in any abilities of their own, but in their Master who was sending them out, and would equip them as he had before.

Chapter 31

RETURNING TO CHINA

Olive stood in the doorway, looking back into the East Bentleigh house. For a fleeting moment she saw the children as they had been about nine years ago when they first moved in—Helen still a child, Dorothy just entering her teens and David embarking on adult life and responsibilities. Then they were replaced in her mind's eye by images of the three Tarrant children—a typical little boy, and the teenage twins, who had come in to their lives for a year. And now, she was leaving the house.

She shook her head, and came back to the present. Yes, they had done the dishes and swept the floor. The biscuit barrel was full of the family's favourite 'overnight' biscuits which she had made. There was a casserole in the refrigerator, as well as milk, bread, fruit and vegetables that would feed David, Dorothy and Helen for a couple of days. That would give them some breathing space before having to take over all their own shopping, cooking and cleaning. How would they get on, she wondered.

David was now a medical intern at Melbourne's Prince Henry's Hospital and was often at the hospital for meals as well as overnight. Dorothy was in the middle of her nursing training and would also often be at work in the Alfred Hospital where she was training, or in the Nurses'

Home overnight. Helen would be the only one regularly living and sleeping in the East Bentleigh home.

Olive was not a sentimental person. She thought of herself as the practical one in the partnership, the one with her feet firmly on the ground. As she pulled the door closed behind her however, she acknowledged that it had been, for the family, a good decade since they returned from China.

There had been big changes as Theo returned to school teaching, and they moved into their own home. The three children had grown up and all had now left school. They had taken active roles in the life of their local Methodist church. The three children had joined Christian groups in their current areas of training—David joining the Christian Medical and Dental Fellowship, Dorothy the Australian Nurses Christian Movement, and Helen the Evangelical Union at Melbourne University. Their faith was maturing as they grew older. How grateful Olive and Theo were for God's goodness to them as a family!

> Olive's eyes darted quickly around the front garden. That had been her area, while Theo's domain had been the backyard vegetable garden and orchard. Bright smiling pansy faces nodded at her; gaudy hibiscus blooms showed off in the sunshine. The glossy toothed leaves of the liquidambar tree in the corner of the garden danced in the warm breeze. Already, the prickly fruits were forming, promising a lawn full of the spiky woody seedpods in autumn. 'It will be up to the children to deal with those this year', she thought. But Theo and the children were waiting for her in the car in the driveway, as was Theo's nephew and wife with the two aunties in a second car. She turned away towards another year of unknown experiences.

Instead of flying directly to Hong Kong, Theo and Olive dropped in briefly enroute to some of CIMOMF's new fields. Their first stop was to the new Headquarters of CIMOMF in Singapore, where they met the staff and some of the directors, and began to get a feel for the even more international flavour of the fellowship. Then they flew on to Kuala Lumpur in Malaya, and Bangkok, Thailand, for several days. Finally they were on the last leg of the trip to Hong Kong. At each place Theo took photos and made notes to send home to friends and family who were praying. God's work depended as

Olive and Theo with family, some of Theo's sisters and nephew as they prepared to leave for the airport, 1962. Theo's sisters Mary (next to Theo) and Mabel are the two ladies on the extreme right of the picture.
(Photo: WT Simpkin collection)

much on the faithful prayers and support of these allies as on the workers in the field.

Back in Hong Kong[1]

How Hong Kong had changed since they had last been there over ten years ago! At that time, Olive and Theo knew there were thousands of refugees from mainland China escaping to Hong Kong. Their brief stay in Hong Kong in 1951 had been too short for them to discover the extent of the problem. As many as 100,000 reached Hong Kong monthly at the peak of the flight from China, so that Hong Kong's population increased dramatically to over two million by the mid-1950s, many being accommodated in improvised huts on the outskirts of the city. A disastrous fire in the Shek Kip Mei shantytown on Christmas Day 1953 left over 50,000 people homeless[2]. Something had to be done quickly. The Governor of Hong Kong developed a huge building program featuring multi-storey buildings, each

---

1   Information relating to this section was derived from Theo and Olive's scores of letters from Hong Kong, dated from January 1962 to August 1963.

2   Hong Kong Housing Authority, History of Estates, *Historical Background of Shek Kip Mei Estate,* n.d., viewed 2 November, 2018, www.housingauthority.gov.hk/hdw/en/aboutus/events/community/heritage/about.html.

capable of housing two-and-a-half thousand people. Hong Kong's population density rivalled the highest in the world.

As Theo and Olive's plane dropped down to the runway in January 1962, the city below was bristling with these high-rise developments.

Working for the Press

Theo understood that he would join the Christian Witness Press (CWP) editorial department, under the leadership of Ron Roberts. The Christian Witness Press had been set up by the CIM when it was expelled from China. Literature was seen as the best means of sharing the story of Jesus with people in mainland China. Gospels and tracts were being published by the CWP for dissemination in China.

This soon ceased to be possible, and the CWP refocused on producing literature for Chinese prisoners of war in Hong Kong and other countries, and then for Mandarin-speaking populations in other Asian countries. By the time Theo joined the Hong Kong team, the CWP had distributed scores of millions of Gospels and tracts throughout East Asia[3]. Theo believed it to be a strategic program and he and Olive were keen to be part of it.

They rented a small, two-bedroom flat on the sixth floor of a 13-storey block in a good part of Kowloon. The layout of their flat was such that they had at least one window facing each of the four points of the compass. This had the great advantage—at least in Olive's eyes—of meaning whatever breeze there was, they would be able to catch some of it. Their apartment block was surrounded by many more multi-storeyed buildings.

Theo would work mostly in the Christian Witness Press office, but there wasn't room for Olive to work there, so they brought a big office desk up to the Simpkins' flat so Olive could work from there.

Theo's role

One definite task for Theo would be for him to check the Chinese translations of significant English books the CWP had decided to publish in Chinese. The translations had been done by Chinese translators, and Theo's role would be to check that the Chinese faithfully represented the meaning of

---

3   Miller, AJ 2015, *Pioneers in Exile: The China Inland Mission and Missionary Mobility in China and Southeast Asia, 1943-1989,* University of Kentucky, UKnowledge, viewed 2 November, 2018, uknowledge.uky.edu/cgi/viewcontent.cgi?article=1027&context=history_etds.

the English text. (Chinese translators may be able to produce fluent translations and yet misinterpret unfamiliar idioms in the English.) Other roles might include pre-editing English books before sending them to translators, corresponding with foreign publishers regarding publication rights etc., and assessing the value of various books proposed for translating[4].

Theo threw himself into his translation-checking with enthusiasm. He started with John Thompson's *Archaeology and the Old Testament.* This was followed by *Mary Slessor—White Queen of the Cannibals, William Booth, The Life of Henry Martin, Heresies & Cults* by J O Sanders, *Upon this Rock,* Hugh Redwood's book, *Practical Prayer,* and others.

The translations were in hand-written Chinese, and he soon began to have great sympathy for those who complained that a doctor's handwriting was illegible. He found it a bit slow at first. There were times when even the English original was not totally clear. It was a strain to keep at the right pitch of concentration to do a good job. Because of this, Theo needed a change occasionally. He was asked to write the CWP Christmas Tract, his first foray into being a published writer.

Initially he thought to focus the tract on 'Christmas Gifts' since he had seen the immense needs of the Chinese refugees in Hong Kong. This showed how his thinking had unconsciously shifted during his decade in Australia. He had forgotten that the giving and receiving of gifts at Christmas was a very Western custom, not practised by many rural Chinese at all. He had to find another theme for the tract.

He was also asked to prepare a series of messages to be radio-broadcast into China. As he wrote them, he pictured the believers he had left behind in the various villages and towns of Yunnan, and he wrote from his heart to them.

When Ken Budge, the Local CIMOMF Secretary in Hong Kong, was away or otherwise engaged, he asked Theo to deputise for him. In this role, Theo had to keep track of the local accounts. Sometimes he was required to collect visitors from the airport or the wharf. If the Mission Home was full, he would arrange for one of the other missionaries to be host/hostess to the visitors in their own unit.

The Simpkins also found their second bedroom being occasionally occupied in this way. It was a great opportunity to hear about what was happening in some of the mission's new fields. Every time they had such

---

4   Letter from Ron Roberts to Theo dated 4 October, 1961.

CWP Staff Conference, May 1963, Mr Williamson gives annual report
Theo and Olive have backs to the camera and are immediately to the left
of the gap in the circle. (Photo: WT Simpkin collection)

CWP Staff Conference 1963. Olive is second from the left in the front row,
and Theo is at the extreme right of the back row.
(Photo: WT Simpkin collection)

visitors, Theo would invite them to record a brief message for him on a tape recorder. These he would send home to Australia, to be played at prayer meetings, where the messages gave fuel for the prayers.

There were CIMOMF Staff conferences for the Hong Kong CIMOMFers, and Theo might be asked to lead a session, or lead the Staff Prayer Meeting. He was so happy to be part of the CIMOMF family again, and gladly offered to do any job that needed doing, including mending furniture, putting up a shelf, fixing leaky taps and so on.

Another task that came their way after they had been in Hong Kong for some months was to prepare a window display for CWP at the Emmanuel Book Store. This space was regularly made available for a presentation of books and leaflets available from the CWP. Such window dressing was a first for both Olive and Theo.

Still, all of this did not fill his days, so Theo began to look around and pray about other opportunities to serve in Hong Kong. He received many invitations to preach or teach, such as at a local tuberculosis hospital, in the New Territories (one of the three main regions of Hong Kong) where there were Mandarin-speaking groups, or in groups connected with their church. They had discovered that many of their fellow workers attended the English-speaking services at the Emmanuel Church in Nathan Road, and Theo and Olive joined them.

It was not long before both were teaching in the Sunday School, and Theo soon became Superintendent. He spoke frequently at the Emmanuel Young People's group the 'Bible Explorers', and he and Olive were asked to attend the Bible Explorers' conference as counsellors, with Theo giving the opening and closing addresses. They led the daily Bible studies for the young people too. Olive did not feel that preparing such studies was her forte, especially since she had been out of the routine of running such sessions for the past decade, but gladly typed up Theo's notes for them both to use.

Although Emmanuel was an English-speaking church, much of

Theo serving as guest speaker at Elim Church Bible Club for children
(Photo: WT Simpkin collection)

the Bible Explorers' conference was conducted in Cantonese which was almost incomprehensible to Theo and Olive who spoke Mandarin. Several of the more capable young people had planned a children's program each afternoon of the conference, for local children. About a hundred streamed in, hot, sweaty and dirty, but full of enthusiasm for the activities being run. They quickly learnt the choruses, and sang (or was it 'yelled'?) them at the top of their voices.

By September 1962 Theo had also been invited to teach classes of up to thirty or forty second- and third-year students at the Hong Kong Bible Institute. This was a Bible College, similar in style to the Melbourne Bible Institute, catering for local young people who wanted to study the Bible in depth.

It had been nearly twelve years since Theo had had to teach or preach in Chinese. He was rusty! To begin with, his preparation time took many hours longer than otherwise would have been the case, but his fluency gradually returned. There was another additional complication. Theo and Olive's version of Mandarin was that commonly used in Yunnan, but it had a very provincial sound to the Hong Kong students. Theo had to try to modify his spoken language for these classes.

In his first term at the college, Theo had classes on 1 and 2 Timothy and Titus, three mornings a week, and the following term, Ephesians was his subject. It was good to be again teaching the Bible to enthusiastic young Chinese people, but this was all work outside the CIMOMF. Should Theo be thinking about moving more fully into teaching in the Bible college?

Following the publicity surrounding Billy Graham's ministry through-out the world, the Hong Kong churches also banded together to invite Dr Graham to conduct a crusade in their area. Having lived through the experience of Dr Graham's 1959 Australian crusade, Theo and Olive were familiar with much of the process and quickly became involved in preparations.

Olive's role

In contrast to Theo who was always looking for another avenue of service, Olive never had the luxury of wondering what she should do next. Once they were settled into their flat, various office jobs began to come her way. There wasn't enough room in the CWP office for Olive to work there, so she set her typewriter up in the living room of their small flat. The first job was to write daily the thank you letters to people who sent donations for the

Olive with some CWP ladies: Mrs Wong, Jocelyn Budge (daughter of the Hong Kong Local Secretary for the CIMOMF), Olive, Mrs Mak
(Photo: WT Simpkin collection)

work of the Christian Witness Press. Some months after commencing this, Olive became dissatisfied with the way these donors' letters were filed, and contrived her own more efficient system.

There were regular Field Bulletins, giving news from each CIMOMF field, to be prepared for posting. She had to maintain their own personal accounts for the mission, and was soon asked by Ken Budge, the CIMOMF Local Secretary for Hong Kong, to check and then type up the Local Secretary's accounts. She was always relieved and pleased when the trial balance came out right at her first attempt.

Her secretarial skills were so good she found herself in heavy demand to type up letters, notes and reports for various members of the CIMOMF team in Hong Kong. Whenever the CIMOMF Directory was updated, Olive was given the job of checking that mistakes in the old directory had been corrected, and that all details were up-to-date. On another occasion she was asked to do a stock-take, first gathering information from every CWP Book Store around East Asia. Then she had to list all the items in CWP stocks on hand in each place, noting the number and cost of each item, and adding up the totals.

Several times, she was asked to help prepare a book to be sent to the translator. One book, JO Sanders' *Problems of Christian Discipleship*, needed Biblical references added for any Scripture verses quoted, as well as references for hymns mentioned—quite a difficult task in the days before internet search engines!

A big job was to go through the new Bible Handbook that they had just printed, indexing all the proper names of people and places, to get some uniformity in the transliteration of proper names mentioned in English. Then another book also needed to have proper names indexed, and so the list went on.

Health issues

Despite the pre-Hong Kong medical reports Olive and Theo had to submit before being provisionally accepted for service in Hong Kong, it's interesting that Theo was the first of the two to encounter a health-related problem. When they had been in Hong Kong for a couple of months, he began to suffer from severe sinusitis. The doctor sent him to a Chinese Ear Nose and Throat specialist who dealt with some nasal polyps that Theo had. Some days later he had a nasty chest pain. ECGs and X-rays were completely normal, and after a few days the pain subsided.

Another day, Olive stepped off the kerb—not noticing there was a manhole in the gutter just there and its cover was cracked. She managed to fall through the filthy rusty manhole cover. As a result, her leg swelled up and came out in all the colours of the rainbow.

Some time later she developed a march (stress) fracture of a small bone in the foot which, once again, confined Olive to bed. She continued working with the typewriter on a board balanced on two drawers, rigged up across her legs. She was very glad when, after a couple of weeks, she was able to put some weight on her foot, and get back to normal life.

A couple of times in the hotter months especially, Olive was laid low with a giddy head. She learnt that the only solution was to go to bed and lie still for a few days until the world stopped rotating around her.

Just after Olive had started on a new task, she had a painful attack of shingles that laid her low, and took her out of the office for six weeks. All these problems underlined for them the importance of praying for the health of their fellow workers as well as for themselves.

Refugees in Hong Kong

Whenever Theo and Olive drove out of the city towards the resettlement areas, they were horrified at the extent of the refugee problem in Hong Kong. The numbers of refugees who had escaped from Communist China was huge, and their living conditions were appalling. Theo believed that Christians should be doing far more practically to show the love of Christ to such needy people, and since he had the time available, he should do something.

He wrote home to the South Oakleigh Methodist Sunday School as well as other groups of the church, inviting them to gather donations of clothing, blankets and gifts to be shipped to Hong Kong for distribution to these people. There was a very prompt response from friends in the South Oakleigh church. One lady—Marge Growcott—took a lead in the project, setting up a bank account in which to deposit donations to be transferred to an account Olive set up in Hong Kong. At the same time, Marge started collecting clothes and gifts, and making enquiries about the cheapest way to freight them to Hong Kong. Some of the church members knitted woollen jumpers and caps for the refugee children.

This seems to have begun a family life-long care for refugees that was evident at the funeral service for Marge's husband, Jack Growcott, over fifty years later. Helen attended this service and was pleasantly surprised to see a large number of Vietnamese, Cambodian and Lao people in the congregation at Coatesville Uniting Church (formerly South Oakleigh Methodist Church). Helen was told this was because of Jack's strong involvement in the local Moorabbin Refugee Resettlement program over the previous few decades. Theo and Olive would have been delighted to see his continuing interest in caring for refugees who were accepted for resettlement in Melbourne.

Theo and Olive also wrote to relatives in Maryborough and Thornbury, inviting their contributions as well. The result was described by Olive as a 'ship-full of clothes' for them to pass on to the grateful recipients. Olive, who in so many respects, was a person of conservative opinions, spoke forcefully of her belief that the Australian Government should dispense with its 'White Australia Policy' for immigration.

When she heard that the Hong Kong government was beginning to send back some of these 'illegal immigrants' into China because it was unable to provide even enough water for so many, she wrote in a letter to the family dated 25 May, 1962:

> But when you see the crowded state of the resettlement areas NOW, you cannot wonder that the government is loath to take more people in. It is quite time Australia scrapped their White Australia Policy, and took in a million or two from Communist Governed Countries, such as these Chinese.

However, the problem continued, and was exacerbated when a typhoon struck in September 1962. There had been numerous warnings over the previous few months of possible typhoons heading towards Hong Kong, but none had actually struck the colony. This was the first typhoon that Olive and Theo had experienced since returning to Hong Kong, and was something they never hoped to have to live through again.

In a desperate hour

Typhoon Wanda[5] formed late in August 1962 as a tropical depression, over 2,000 km east-southeast of Hong Kong, over the Pacific Ocean. It gradually strengthened as it moved west-northwest towards the colony of Hong Kong. It was the most intense tropical cyclone ever recorded in the colony and made landfall on 1 September 1962. What a day! The winds of the previous night strengthened to gales, lashing everything in their path.

Just after Olive and Theo had finished breakfast the typhoon struck. Rain came down in torrents and the strong winds forced it under every tightly-closed window. Soon their living room was flooded. All they could do was use towels to mop it up and squeeze them out into buckets, emptying the water down the sink. As fast as they could mop it up, more rain pushed through. Altogether over 300 mm (over 11 inches) of rain fell. And the noise was terrific as the wind screamed for hours. The buildings felt as though they were swaying under the force of wind and rain. A maximum gust of 140 knots was registered at the Royal Observatory. Experiencing it, even in the relative safety of their flat, was both frightening and exhausting.

At the same time, huge surges in tides occurred. In Tolo Harbour, the tide rose more than five metres above what had been forecast. Predictably

---

5 Hong Kong Observatory, (extracted from the Observatory's publication *Supplement to Meteorological Results 1962*), 'Typhoon Wanda August 27 to September 2, 1962', viewed 2 November, 2018, www.hko.gov.hk/informtc/no10/wanda/wanda.htm.

there was immense damage and loss of life in the colony, with 434 people killed and 72,000 left homeless as shanties and houses were swept away. Nobody went to work that day. No shops opened, no buses or ferries ran.

The one blessing was that the typhoon added much-needed water to the colony's water storages. Previously, water had only been available in their taps for a few hours each day. (In fact, when Theo and Olive had had a week's holiday on Cheung Chau Island, water was rationed to only run in the taps for half an hour each day.)

Olive and Theo were so grateful when the many boxes of clothing arrived from their friends and relatives in Australia. They prayed that the recipients of these items might also experience something of the love of God as they were warmed and clothed. It was a pleasure to pass the gifts on. Even so, there were many needy people for whom they had nothing.

Most of what Olive and Theo collected was distributed by Mrs Gladys Donnithorne[6], the wife of an Archdeacon, who ministered, by whatever means available, to those existing in the most squalid conditions in alleyways and rooftops. 'She was prepared to go anywhere, however distressing...'[7] It had not taken Theo and Olive long to hear about Mrs Donnithorne and what she was doing, and to make contact with her. 'I can take all the donations you have been given, and pass them on to those in desperate need', she told Olive.

Theo and Olive reported back with gratitude to their friends and prayer partners in Australia who had sent over the supplies:[8]

> Since then [i.e. Typhoon Wanda], we have received six boxes of clothes sent from South Oakleigh, and two more parcels from Thornbury. These will be of great help, but don't forget to back them up with prayer, that through these gifts the recipients may come to know something of the Love of God and His Gift to them. Miss Groce and Mrs Donnithorne—working in 2 different areas—will distribute the articles where they are most needed, and where none will be wasted.

---

6   Madokor, L 2012, Vancouver, *Unwanted Refugees: Chinese Migration and the Making of a Global Humanitarian Agenda, 1949-1989,* viewed 2 November 2018, www.collectionscanada.gc.ca/obj/thesescanada/vol2/BVAU/TC-BVAU-43061.pdf, referring to Black, M. 1992, Oxford, *A Cause for our Times: Oxfam—the first 50 years*, pub. Oxfam and Oxford University Press.

7   Black, M, op. cit., p. 49.

8   See Theo and Olive's prayer letter dated 25 October 1962.

Chapter 32

ACROSS A CONTINENT

From East to West[1]

As their second year in Hong Kong drew on, Theo's CWP work was drying up, although Olive continued to be fully occupied with accounts and office work. Months went by when there was no translation checking for him. He was deeply concerned about this. It was not a good use of the CIMOMF resources for him to be having to seek opportunities outside the CWP, but was that the direction in which God was leading him? Should he again be looking beyond working with the CIMOMF?

As the CIM had been affectionately described as *Constantly In Motion*, the renewed OMF was further portrayed as *Only More Frequently!* And so it was for Theo and Olive.

A challenge came to them to consider leaving Hong Kong and taking over the role of Local Secretary for CIMOMF in Western Australia. Once they got over their surprise (neither had ever been to Western Australia), they began to see how God had been preparing them for precisely this role over the past two years.

From the time they left Melbourne in January 1961, Theo had been

---

1   Information for this chapter comes largely from Theo and Olive's many letters dated November 1963 to November 1968.

taking every opportunity to gather first-hand information and news from the various new CIMOMF fields (such as Thailand, Indonesia, Malaysia, the Philippines, Laos, Japan and Taiwan), often tape-recording interviews with missionaries passing through Hong Kong so he could send the tapes back as fuel for prayer meetings he knew about in Melbourne. In Hong Kong, the constant stream of new and returning missionaries passing through was a rich source of news and reports

They had given hospitality to so many in Hong Kong, and now, having met these workers from the new fields, they would be well placed to share their concerns with interested supporters in Western Australia.

Olive had already learnt in Hong Kong about the record-keeping required of the Local Secretary. Besides providing for guests passing through Perth on their way to or from the South East Asian fields, she would be able to keep the accounts, while Theo travelled around the state, helping with meetings and encouraging more support for the missionaries. And although Perth could have high temperatures, it did not have Hong Kong's humidity. There was the added bonus that it was in the same country as their three children. The possibility of visits between them would be greater despite Melbourne being about 3500 km from Perth.

Olive and Theo both recognised this was God's perfect appointment for them. It had always been thus. When they were shut up in what seemed a dead-end road, if they took the situation to God in patient prayer, God invariably opened a new pathway for them.

Over the plains

Their last months in Hong Kong were very busy. In preparation for the new role, Theo made a whistle-stop tour of the CIMOMF Japan and Taiwan fields. Over three weeks he visited sixteen mission stations, met sixty missionaries, and took scores of photos to be made into slides with a commentary, to use at prayer and missionary meetings in and around Perth. Hearing about it was enough to make Olive's head spin. She was happy to be quietly getting on with the packing in Hong Kong.

Then they boarded the SS *Oronsay* in Hong Kong on 10 October, 1963. They were reunited with their family in Melbourne eleven days later. They had about six weeks to catch up with relatives and friends. It was good to see how the 'children' had matured and grown in independence since their parents' move to Hong Kong eighteen months earlier. Although there had been many letters to and from Theo and Olive over that time, it was good for them to hear in person about Helen's twenty-first birthday and birthday party the previous year.

They also spoke at 34 meetings at various places in Melbourne and northern Victoria, about the CIMOMF work. Then they boarded a train for their new assignment, stopping off in Adelaide for six days and staying with Mrs Nicholls, whom they had known in Yunnan. While there, Theo spoke at seven more meetings, and this proved to be a foretaste of things to come in the west.

The miles of desert plain, stretching out to the far horizon in all directions, flew past the window for hour upon hour. Cradled in the cocoon of their railway carriage, Olive and Theo relaxed back into their seats with a sigh of gratitude. Nothing was required of them for the next few days— just to sit back and be transported from one side of the Australian continent to the other.

The Trans-Australia Train, bound for Western Australia, crosses the Nullarbor Plain[2], a vast semi-arid desert with scarcely a tree, as the name suggests. The vegetation is sparse, consisting largely of saltbush and bluebush scrub. The Nullarbor, thought to have been originally a shallow seabed, comprises the world's largest exposure of limestone bedrock, and stretches nearly 700 miles from east to west across the border between South Australia and Western Australia. The railway track across the Nullarbor includes a dead-straight span of just over 300 mile—again, the longest anywhere in the world.

It's not surprising that Theo and Olive found themselves nodding off now and then to the clickety-clack of the diesel train on the rails.

Two days later they pulled into Kalgoorlie, a goldfields town about 370 miles east-northeast of Perth. They were glad to meet up with Don and Valda Byrne, CIMOMF workers on furlough from the Philippines, who took them to a meeting at which Theo was invited to give a brief message. From Kalgoorlie they changed to the bone-shaking 'Kalgoorlie Rattler' for the last night of the journey to Perth. There they settled into the CIMOMF Mission Home at 33 Brewer Street East Perth.

They were very quickly in the thick of things. A 'Welcome Dinner' was

---

2 Penberthy, Natsumi 2016, *Hidden Nullarbor,* viewed 4 November 2018, www.australiangeographic.com.au/travel/destinations/2016/04/hidden-nullarbor/, originally published in the Jan-Feb 2016 edition of *Australian Geographic.*

arranged for CIMOMF friends and family to meet Theo and Olive. They were taking over the role from Mrs Eveline Binks who, with her husband Tom (who had since died), had been stationed in Aguomi, Yunnan, when Theo first was designated to that province, and then at the Taogu Bible School, so it was good to renew their friendship with Mrs Binks. Mrs Binks was now retiring from this post in Perth into a home of her own.

The Kalamunda Keswick-style Convention followed over the Christmas and New Year period, and Theo was asked to lead the daily 7 am Prayer Meetings at the convention. He spoke at the Missionary Day as well as at a Children's Meeting, and looked after the Mission's bookstall in one of the marquees at the convention.

All of this gave them a good way of meeting and becoming known by the Perth Christian community. Invitations followed to preach in various churches, and Theo and Olive began to see more of this vast Australian state. Theo was invited to join the Christian Business Men's Crusade Team and to share in the crusade to Geraldton, a town 300 miles north of Perth. He was also invited to give weekly lectures on the Gospel of Mark at the Perth Bible Institute. Theo was delighted to be able to renew his connection with the Overseas Christian Fellowship which had just commenced in Melbourne before Theo and Olive moved to Hong Kong. He was invited to speak at some of the OCF meetings in Perth, too.

And there were the usual Mission groups in homes and churches to keep fuelled with information and missionary speakers, where possible. The Youth for Asia group met monthly in the Mission Home where Olive provided a light meal, and a meeting followed. Other prayer groups needed to be given up-to-date information about the Western Australian CIMOMF missionaries.

Whenever any of these missionaries were home on furlough, meetings were organised at which they could share their own personal story of what God was doing in the country where they served. Very often, these missionaries would be met at airport, wharf or railway station, and transported to the meeting. Sometimes Olive prepared the spare room for such passing guests.

Every year there was a Prayer Conference, a live-in weekend program of meetings to hear from and about missionaries, and to pray for them. This they believed was the vital core of CIMOMF work—prayer and a trusting dependence on God. Publicity had to be produced and disseminated so interested people would register for the event and be galvanised to pray. Being a live-in conference, food had to be provided, so Olive worked together with the cook to devise a menu and to make purchases for the conference.

When young people began to consider whether God was calling them to missionary service in one of the CIMOMF new fields, Theo and Olive became their mentors and advisors. Their decades of experience in missionary work in China meant they had a lot to share. And it was always a joy when one or other of these young people applied to the Mission and was accepted.

While Theo was often involved in travelling and speaking at meetings, Olive dealt with the routine office work, as she had done in Hong Kong. There were donors' thank-you letters to write, accounts and other records to keep, and Theo's notes for addresses to be typed up. They worked well together as a team.

Paths to mission

Meanwhile, all three Simpkin children seemed on the path to mission. While Theo and Olive were in Hong Kong, David had completed his medical course, and spent three years as a surgical intern in the Prince Henry's Hospital in Melbourne, before going on to Sydney University to take the Graduate Diploma in Tropical Medicine and Hygiene. He was planning to go to the Melbourne Bible Institute in 1964 in preparation for medical missionary service in Asia. Dorothy was nursing at the Alfred Hospital in Melbourne and added a Theatre Nursing qualification to her resume. Helen was teaching senior Physics and Maths at MacRobertson Girls' High School.

By the time Theo and Olive had reached Perth, David had spent a year studying the Scriptures at the Melbourne Bible Institute. He then applied to do medical missionary work with the CIMOMF somewhere in South East Asia. Dorothy was continuing to gain more nursing experience, doing a midwifery course at the Queen Victoria Hospital, a Melbourne hospital for women and operated by women. Helen continued her teaching while completing a Bachelor of Education degree at Melbourne University.

At the end of 1964, Dorothy and Helen travelled by train to Perth for a holiday with their parents, after which Dorothy commenced a two-year course at the Melbourne Bible Institute. Helen joined her at MBI in 1966, commencing a three-year course leading to a Bachelor of Divinity (with Honours in Old Testament) degree. Her interests were leaning towards doing some kind of Christian work among Asian students.

CIMOMF Centennial year

The year 1965 was a memorable year for the CIMOMF—their Centennial year. It was an occasion for numerous special meetings, including some in Perth at which the General Director, J Oswald Sanders, was the speaker. David Bentley-Taylor also shared about his student work in Indonesia, and Mr & Mrs Paul Contento brought news from South Vietnam. At the Centennial Prayer Conference Mr Rowland Butler, the CIMOMF Overseas Director and Acting Home Director for Australia, spoke.

There were also testimonies from out-going Western Australian missionary, Miss Evelyn Bayly, and from David Simpkin—for in this Centennial year, David had applied to the CIMOMF and had been accepted for service in the CIMOMF hospital at Saiburi, South Thailand. After completing the Candidates' Course in Melbourne, he was on his way to Singapore to join the next group in the Orientation and Language Centre. He had been accompanied to Perth by a very close nurse friend, Miss Marjorie Jenkins, who hoped also to be serving God as a medical missionary somewhere in South East Asia, and was currently studying at the Melbourne Bible Institute.

It had always been Mission policy that each person must separately believe God had called them to missionary service, and be able to convince the Council of this, before being accepted. It was not satisfactory for one of the couple to be called, and the other accepted simply as their spouse. As with Theo and Olive, David had already travelled to the field and commenced language training, knowing that if Marjorie were not to apply to the Mission, or were turned down, they would not be able to be together. God must come first in their lives.

When Marjorie Jenkins applied and was accepted by CIMOMF to attend the Melbourne Candidates Course, and then proceed to Singapore, she and David became engaged.

Now that David was in Asia, he followed Theo's example in taking photos and adding a commentary to post home to Australia to be used in missionary and prayer meetings there. Theo's letters to David at this time were full of encouragement to David to continue this practice, as well as a lot of advice regarding how to make the slide and commentary sets more effective. Since Theo was often the one to use these sets in meetings, he knew where the hearers misunderstood, or missed the point, and where their hearts were touched.

This is how he put his advice to David in a letter to him dated 5 December, 1966:

> It was very interesting to read about your visit to the Floating Market, Temple of the Dawn & other places—and we'll be looking forward to seeing pictures of them in due time. A well-thought-out and much-prayed-for Commentary amply justifies the use of time, & thought, & energy. And of course an occasional one of yourself either studying, or doing a medical job, or giving out tracts, or preaching etc., etc., would give a sharper edge to requests for prayer for such tasks.
>
> We were very much amused to find three of you serenading Derek & his fiancée. I'm sure it is good for all who took part—(good—medically speaking)—as it would help to release tensions building up with the long hours of concentrated language study etc. Release—relax—rest—renew—are important words all along the line of Christian workers. When do you go to Manorom? I trust you have a very blessed & profitable time up there. Make sure you get some good photos of the preaching, & teaching of the Word, of personal work—as well as of 'ops' [i.e. surgical operations] and the result of 'ops' etc.

And, on another occasion, Theo suggested to David in a letter dated 7 November, 1967, 'The *personal* or *human-interest* in the story about a slide or the subject of the slide is what grips people'.

Another move

The year 1967 marked another bend in the road for CIMOMF in Perth. It had become increasingly clear over the past couple of years that the Mission Home being rented in East Perth was not suitable. Its rooms were too small to be able to cater for the groups meeting there. In a letter on 11 August, 1967, Theo wrote to his Western Australia supporters:

> What were we to do? Where could we go? Where could you rent a suitable place at a modest rental in these days when houses are snapped up at any price immediately they are vacant? Our only

resource, as all ways was GOD HIMSELF. As we brought the need to Him in prayer, His message was Mat. 6:23—'Seek ye first the Kingdom of God...and all these things shall be added unto you'. So we continued with the ministry of His Word and left it to Him to provide. We had looked at a few places which we thought would not place too big a burden on Mission finance, but the Lord confronted me with Ephesians 3:20—He seemed to say, 'Cannot you trust ME to do exceeding abundantly above all that you ask or think?' 'Yes, Lord' was the answer, and this was followed by complete freedom from all anxiety.

Many of you had joined us in prayer for this much-needed provision. The first telephone call on our return to Perth informed us that one of the Lord's stewards, who wishes to remain anonymous, had offered to buy a suitable house and let it to the mission at a nominal rental... Join us in thankful praise to the Lord Who once again has shown that 'HE is faithful that promised.' Our sincere thanks and gratitude are due, too, to this generous donor.

The move from East Perth to Mount Lawley entailed a lot of work. Although the two properties were only a few kilometres apart, all the household equipment and furniture, as well as mission supplies and personal possessions had to be packed up and transported. Then the house had to be thoroughly cleaned.

It was, perhaps, not surprising that the chest pain Theo had suffered on one occasion in Hong Kong returned. After a couple of days of rest, it subsided, and he gave no more thought to it. By the end of 1967 Theo had totalled up a thousand messages he had preached since moving to Western Australia.

Chapter 33

SERVICE TO THE END

Theo and Olive continued with their work in Western Australia throughout 1968 until they both reached retiring age—sixty-five years. George and Dorothy Tarrant, whose three children had been part of the Simpkins' family for a year before they went to Hong Kong, were then asked to take over the Western Australian office temporarily, until Percy and Amy Moore had had their furlough and could take on the WA Office permanently.

By this time, David and Marjorie had married in Saiburi, South Thailand, following a civil ceremony in Bangkok. Dorothy had also sensed God's call to her to serve in medical missionary work in South East Asia. She applied to the CIMOMF on completion of her MBI course and was accepted into the Melbourne Candidates' Course for 1969. It was probable that she would proceed to Singapore in the middle of 1969. Meanwhile, Helen had completed her Bachelor of Divinity with Honours in Old Testament.

Theo and Olive returned to their East Bentleigh home. Theo continued to serve as a Local Preacher, regularly taking services in the various churches in the Methodist Circuit. Helen was now an accredited Local Preacher as well and had commenced work on a Master of Arts degree in Biblical Studies at Melbourne University. She had enjoyed her introduction to Biblical Hebrew in her BD studies and looked forward to taking it further. Her thesis, 'The Character of Yahweh in the First Book of Psalms', was based on a study of the Hebrew verbs used of the Lord (Yahweh) in those psalms.

Tying up loose ends

Over the next decade, Olive and Theo quietly served the Lord wherever opportunity presented itself. Olive helped Dorothy prepare all she would need to take to Singapore. Theo accepted requests to preach in the Chinese Church of Christ, Queensberry Street Carlton. Whenever they heard significant information from David and Marjorie, or from Dorothy, they shared it with local prayer groups.

They renewed relationships, as they were able, with their relatives. Sadly, they had little time left with Olive's mother, who had a stroke soon after they returned home. Mrs Kettle died in June 1970, aged 92. Theo's sister, Mary, was still living in Maryborough, and Theo and Olive visited her and other relatives periodically, as they were able.

To the second and third generation

David and Marjorie had two children, Joy and Timothy, both born at the Saiburi Christian Hospital in Thailand. Dorothy surprised the family, and herself, by becoming engaged and then married to a fellow missionary, David Strachan, from Belfast in Northern Ireland. Although she had quite a wicked sense of humour, Dorothy was never self-assertive, nor did she court the attentions of the opposite sex (as some single missionaries were tempted to do).

Helen was happy to travel to Thailand via Indonesia, Singapore, and Malaysia, for Dorothy's wedding, and to be one of Dorothy's bridesmaids. Dorothy and David had previously travelled to Bangkok for the civil ceremony, but the church wedding—the real wedding, in their minds—was to take place at the Saiburi Christian church.

Although neither Theo nor Olive felt able to make the journey, it came at a time when Helen was able to afford both the time and the expense. (At that time, international air travel was neither as common nor as economical as it is now.) David and Marjorie would also be present, since they were stationed at the Saiburi Christian Hospital in South Thailand.

Helen had expected that this visit to South East Asia would underline a call from God to engage in Christian service somewhere in Asia, but it was not so. She returned home uncertain about the direction her life should take. She continued studying, going on to do a PhD based on a twelfth century Syriac commentary on the Psalms. Perhaps this could lead to theological ministry within Australia if not in Asia.

Dorothy and David Strachan moved into village work in Yala, South Thailand, after their marriage on 25 September, 1972. Like David and Marjorie, they also had two children, Alistair and Adele, both born in Saiburi. All four of these children, like David (Simpkin) and Dorothy, had to leave their parents to start their schooling—at the Chefoo-style boarding school which the CIMOMF set up in the Cameron Highlands, in Malaysia. They were all learning, this time from a different perspective, what Theo and Olive must have experienced when they sent their young children away to boarding school.

The Mission later asked Dorothy and David (Strachan) to relocate to Manila, the Philippines, to run the Mission Home there, which they did. Their children were now old enough to go to Faith Academy in Manila, the school which the CIMOMF children in the Philippines attended. This had the benefit of being in the same city as the Mission Home, so the children did not have to board at the school.

Helen became involved in the Melbourne Youth for Asia group, taking a turn cooking at their Easter camp at Belgrave Heights. The group was run by Val and Keith Butler (Keith's father was Rowland Butler who had served with CIM in China and then as one of the Mission's Directors). Val's brother, Robert Joynt, started attending the YFA group and ultimately, he and Helen became engaged in 1974.

Theo proudly walked Helen down the aisle at South Oakleigh Methodist Church on 8 February, 1975. This was the only wedding of their three children which Olive and Theo were able to attend. David and Marjorie with little Joy and Timothy were also able to be present since they were home on furlough. (Dorothy and David Strachan were not due for furlough, so were unable to be present.) Theo was proud to nurse his youngest granddaughter when Helen gave birth to Sandra in 1976, just the day before Olive's birthday.

Last days

During the late 1960s Olive and Theo both faced health problems requiring surgery. Olive's was simply gynaecological 'repair' work, but Theo's uncovered a bowel cancer in the very early stages. This was long before the era of common chemotherapy and radio-therapy. Still, both made complete recoveries after their operations, grateful for God's goodness to them.

Just three and a half years after their daughter Helen's wedding, Theo began to experience quite severe giddiness. Many visits to the doctor and various tests provided no diagnosis. Apparently he had also suffered from shortness of breath, being unable to walk far without having to stop. Cardiology was still at an early stage in the 1970s. In retrospect, it seems clear that he was suffering from blocked arteries, which had caused his chest pain both in Hong Kong, and in Perth. The ability to detect such blockages was still some time off in 1978. ECGs only showed that there was no heart attack occurring at that precise moment.

At this time, Dorothy and David Strachan with their two children were on furlough, sharing the East Bentleigh home with Olive and Theo. When Olive's brother in Mount Waverley mentioned that he was going away for a few weeks, he suggested Olive and Theo might like to go and stay in their house in his absence.

It was a quiet respite for the Simpkins, but Theo's symptoms showed no improvement. Olive was very concerned about his worsening condition and rang Dorothy, her nurse daughter, who dropped everything to go quickly to be with her mother and father. She put her mother to bed in another room and herself stayed in Theo's room for the night.

Very early on the morning of 23 July, 1978, as a result of a massive heart attack, Theo 'went in to see the King'. He had passed into the immediate Presence of the Lord he had served so faithfully for most of his nearly seventy-five years.

That same day, Olive went to stay a few nights with Helen and Robert and their wee daughter Sandra. 'I didn't expect it would be so soon', faltered Olive through her tears to Helen that night. She later confided the following to one of Helen's friends, 'I am so glad God left me one child to stay at home with me'—for to her own surprise, Helen had not sensed any call of God to go overseas to serve Him. She was glad to be at home to support her mother when Dorothy and her husband David returned to the mission field.

Olive continued to live in the East Bentleigh home, but soon began to realise that it was more than she wanted to care for—or could care for on her own. The OMF had by this stage built a small retirement hostel, 'Cherith'[1], in Kew, Victoria, for its retired missionaries.

Olive sold the Barrington Street house and moved into a single room in 'Cherith'. Here again she was in a small CIMOMF community, where she felt at home. Helen and Robert were often able to visit her there with their children, as could David and Dorothy when they were in Melbourne. The boundaries of Olive's life had contracted sharply, but she did not complain. God was caring for her and would continue to provide for all her needs.

After some years, Olive's physical needs were greater than could be adequately managed by the few staff OMF could employ at 'Cherith'. Reluctantly she had to be moved to a nursing home, becoming a resident at the Uniting Church Aged Care facility, Carnsworth Garoopna, also in Kew.

The move triggered a quick decline into dementia for Olive, and in two more years (1988), she also passed on to receive her Lord's undoubted greeting: 'Well done, good and faithful servant! ... Come and share your master's happiness!' (Matthew 25:21–23 NIV).

Little did we know then how many people still remembered Olive and Theo and thanked God for their selfless and Christ-focused service both in Australia and in China.

---

1   'Cherith' was named after the brook beside which Elijah was fed by the ravens (see 1 Kings 17:2-6.).

Epilogue

ENDURING HARVEST

'Robert! Look at this!'

I passed him my copy of *The Chefoo Magazine¹*, 2011. It was open at a page reporting on the inaugural Lushan Institute for Language and Culture's summer program and was advertising the 2012 program. Lushan is the name by which the Lu mountain range is known now, and it includes the town that was known to our family (and many other missionary families) as Guling, the home for the CIM boarding school for missionaries' children in the late 1940s.

The article described the Institute's program, designed to give students from all nations:

> *...the opportunity to learn the Chinese language and study China's rich history and culture, to build lasting friendships, and to experience the mystique and majesty of Lushan.*

The four-week course included accommodation in Lushan, and tuition by teachers from Nanjing University at a very reasonable rate. A cultural program incorporating Chinese Art and Calligraphy, Paper-cutting, Tai Chi, as well as various local tourist excursions to places whose names were so familiar to me, all served to increase the attractiveness of the program.

---

1   *The Chefoo Magazine,* 2011, publ. by the Chefoo Schools Association, 2011, Canada, p. 28.

I had not been back into China since the family's enforced evacuation in 1951. How I would love to go back! At first it had been out of the question since China, or at least the parts of China I wanted to see, were not open to Western travellers. Later, as China began to open up, my home and family responsibilities precluded such travel.

But now—our children had all grown up and left home; China was open—could we go back? And if we were to go, could we include trips to some of the places in Yunnan where Theo and Olive had lived and worked?

Could I persuade my sister, Dorothy, to accompany us to China also? I knew I had little hope of enticing my brother, David (who enjoyed travel even less than our mother had), to come with us.

Over recent years, as I had re-read the hundreds of letters Theo and Olive had written, I had become convinced theirs was a story worth telling. Now, if I were to travel to Yunnan, perhaps I would have a means of gathering more information for such a story.

Ultimately, Dorothy did agree to meet us in China and shared our pilgrimage to both Lushan and Yunnan.

Land of millions

Had we thought Melbourne a large city, with its population of nearly four million souls? As our aeroplane landed in Shanghai, and then as we were driven to our hotel, we saw hundreds if not thousands of clusters of skyscrapers, together providing accommodation to millions of people. In fact, the population of Shanghai[2] exceeded the whole Australian population[3].

It was a dramatic first introduction to China for my husband Robert, and a sober reminder to me of the different human scale in this populous country.

Our parents' legacy

We spent a few days in Shanghai first, walking along the famous waterside Bund, ascending the iconic Oriental Pearl Tower and wandering through the beautiful Yu Garden.

---

2   Shanghai Municipal People's Government, *Shanghai*, 'City News', 2012, viewed 2 November 2018, www.shanghai.gov.cn/shanghai/node27118/node27818/u22ai68540.html.

3   Australia's population at December 2012 was 22.9 million. Australian Bureau of Statistics, *3101.0 - Australian Demographic Statistics, Dec 2012*, 2013, viewed 4 November 2018, www.abs.gov.au/AUSSTATS/abs@.nsf/Lookup/3101.0Main+Features1Dec%202012.

From Shanghai, we flew on to Nanchang in Jiangxi province. From the airport we were driven up to Lushan where Dorothy joined us.

The car wended its way up and up the windy mountain road with sublime disregard for drivers possibly coming the other way. I was on the edge of my seat, apprehension contending with eagerness as I gazed out the window at the mountain and its trees and bushes which I had last seen over six decades earlier.

Would we arrive intact at our destination that day, and if so, would I recognize anything after such a long absence, especially since I had been so young when I left?

During the following four-week summer school, memories buried by the dust of the decades stirred and began to awaken. Phrases in Mandarin long forgotten through lack of use began to re-surface. The sound of rain pouring down on the roof, and the ever-present music of running water in the gutters and streams tugged at recollections too indistinct to define.

The summer school in Lushan was followed by the heart of our China visit—to Yunnan where my parents spent so many years. After a few days in the Yunnan capital, Kunming, we went by bus to Dali, seeing the very church Theo would have preached in, and meeting some long-term church members. This church is now one of the government-registered churches.

On our way back to the province capital, Kunming, we sought a driver who might help us find the town of my birth, Guanglu Zhen. At the last moment, someone agreed to drive us.

The town was right off the main road, and not another foreigner was there that day, but we found friendly residents who were intrigued to meet these elderly foreigners, one of whom claimed to have been born in their town.

Dali Christian Church in 2012 (Photo: H Joynt) and 2014 (Photo: S Joynt)

The road sign directing us to
Guanglu Ancient (Gu) Village
(i.e. Guanglu Zhen) in 2012
(Photo: H Joynt)

The main road in Guanglu Zhen
in 2012
(Photo: H Joynt)

Wuding County

After a few days back in Kunming, we set off for Wuding and Sapushan.

In Wuding we learnt that the unsurfaced roads to Taogu and Aguomi would be impassable because of all the rain, but we might be able to get through to Sapushan.

Robert outside the Wuding
state-registered Church
(Photo: H Joynt)

Lisa was a resident of Yunnan with a lifelong interest in the history of missionary work. She had offered to take us to some of the towns and villages where Theo and Olive had lived and worked, so she went out into the marketplace to find a driver willing to guarantee to get us all the way up the mountain.

It was the middle of the rainy season and in places this road too was a quagmire. Only a week or two earlier, Lisa had hired a driver to take her up the mountain, but he had been defeated by the mud in which he was continually bogged and had to turn back.

A FOOT WIDE ON THE EDGE OF NOWHERE

'Have you found a driver?' I asked anxiously when Lisa returned from the bus station. How disappointing it would be to have come all this way to be defeated by a muddy road.

'Yes', replied Lisa. 'He has agreed (reluctantly) that he will be paid only if he can get us right up to Sapushan. He will have to stop on the way to collect a hoe though, in case he needs to dig us out of the mud.'

Very soon we were on the way. The road crossed the valley at the foot of the mountain before commencing the climb up. The air was heavy with moisture from the recent downpours, and the leaves and flowers by the roadside and on the steep cliffs, were glistening in the sun. Occasionally the familiar scent of eucalypts filled the air, as we bumped past rice fields, and crops of maize and tobacco.

What would we find when we arrived? Would there be any church members around? Lisa had warned us that the church in Sapushan had suffered greatly over the decades, and was struggling to survive. We should not expect to find a thriving fellowship there.

Would Dorothy and I recognise anything? We had only stayed in Sapushan a few short weeks during the 1948 Christmas school holidays. Would there be any sign of the vibrant Miao church that had been there so long ago? I remembered the church packed with many hundreds of Miao

The Wuding valley seen from the road to Sapushan (Photo: H Joynt)

believers, joyfully singing praises to God in the Christmas services. But numerous years of persecution had intervened, and there had been conflict between those believers who joined the government-registered TSPM church (Three Selfs Patriotic Movement) and those who remained in the underground church. I had been told not to expect many people at all near the church.

These thoughts were in my mind as the vehicle lurched and slid and bumped along the steep, winding road up the mountain from Wuding. Periodically when it got bogged, the driver got out and used his hoe to try to free the car's wheels from the mud while we took the opportunity to walk on.

Finally, the car rounded the last corner and came to a halt next to a high mudbrick wall surrounding the church.

We opened the gate on an unforgettable sight. Scores of Miao young people, many in their colourful Miao traditional skirts and tops, were milling around huge pots of rice, vegetables and meat.

A summer school for Miao young people was being conducted in the local church with the assistance of a visiting teacher. A group from a Chinese church in another province were also sitting in on the summer school that day.

L to R: Helen, Dorothy and Robert proceed on foot as the driver digs the van free

(Photo: Joynt collection)

All of us visitors had arrived at lunch time, and we were quickly invited to share the meal. After lunch, we sat inside with the students for a short time. Although we could not understand the words, there was no mistaking the enthusiasm of the young people as they eagerly searched their Bibles for answers to questions, or as they prayed and sang hymns of praise.

The young people and the summer school leaders were intrigued by the foreign visitors, and moved almost to tears to hear of my

Inside the walls around the Sapushan church (Photo: H Joynt)

Some young ladies sang and danced for us (Photo: H Joynt)

The young people at the summer school (Photo: H Joynt)

parents' connection with the local church. They crowded round, poring over copies of old photos I had brought with me.

While the summer school continued, several of the Miao took Robert and me for a walk through the village. They showed us the house where our parents had lived for three years. Not far from the house (now unoccupied and falling into disrepair) was a monument to Wang Zhiming.

Pastor Wang had been the Miao Church leader in Sapushan when our parents were there. He was ordained soon after they left Sapushan, while they were still waiting for exit permits in Kunming. Like so many of the church leaders, he tried to accommodate the government's demands, signing the Christian Manifesto that had been drawn up under the fledgling Three Selfs Patriotic Movement.

He was unwilling, however, to attend and participate in the accusation meetings. The Cultural Revolution of 1969–1976 aimed to purge Chinese society of any remaining capitalist or traditional elements. Following accusations levelled against him by some locals trying to gain favour with the government, Pastor Wang was declared a counter-revolutionary and imprisoned. In 1973, he was executed in a stadium in front of more than 10,000 people.

The Miao community was incensed. Seeking to placate them, the government eventually paid a small compensation to Wang's family, and, in 1981, erected a monument to Wang in Sapushan. It is the only monument known to commemorate a Christian killed in the Cultural Revolution. At its foot may be found the words, 'As the Scripture says of the Saints, "They will rest from their labours for their deeds follow them."(Revelation 14:13)'[4]

Pastor Wang's suffering, seen as representative of so many who suffered in China during the Cultural Revolution, became the inspiration for his inclusion in a group of ten modern martyrs whose statues were unveiled in 1989, over the western entrance to Westminster Abbey.

The monument to Wang Zhiming in Sapushan (Photo: H Joynt)

The statue of Wang Zhiming at Westminster Abbey
(Photo: Dean & Chapter of Westminster Used with permission)

---

4   As quoted in Westminster Abbey, *Wang Zhiming, Priest,* n.d., viewed 2 November, 2018, www.westminster-abbey.org/our-history/people/wang-zhiming.

A Miao language hymn book
(Photo: S Joynt)

As we turned to go home from Sapushan, one Miao lady, through her tears, whispered a message to me, which Lisa translated: 'Thank you for bringing the Gospel to us'.

She was not the only one in tears that day.

Triumph of the Cross

The reality of the challenges being experienced by the Church in China were brought home to me not long after Robert and I returned home to Australia, when we received an email from a friend in Yunnan, telling us the following story.

The very day after our visit to Sapushan, a carload of police and government officials drove up to Sapushan. An elderly Miao man living in the village, Long Fu Hua[5], had informed the police of the unusual goings on at the church. He told them that a foreigner was leading a summer school there.

The local government sent about a dozen inspectors from the Public Security Bureau, People's Bureau, Safety Bureau and Bureau of Religious Affairs up to Sapushan. They parked their van outside the village with the intention of surprising the teachers at the summer school.

For some reason they commenced searching in the dormitory block next door to the church property. They were seen by some local believers who alerted the summer school leaders. The visiting teacher quickly hid, and the local leaders took up the teaching.

When the officials burst into the church, they found a large group of enthusiastic young people being taught by a young Miao man. They interrogated the leaders, searching fruitlessly for a foreign teacher. It seemed to all that God had smitten them with blindness that day. After being invited to share lunch with the young people, the officials departed empty-handed.

Some weeks after hearing of this, Robert and I received the following

---

5   This is the same man (now deceased), who is reputed to have been the one to denounce Pastor Wang Zhiming to the Communist officials, leading to Wang's martyrdom in 1973. Long Fu Hua, who had been a leader in the Sapushan church in Theo and Olive's time, had thrown his lot in with the Communists after the missionaries were evicted, thus gaining for himself a position of some power in this small community.

email from one of the believers who had been present on the day of our visit. Translated, it said:

> *Dear Esteemed Helen and Robert,*
>
> *I am Brother Long from Sapushan. Thank you for sending us the photos. I have looked at all of them, and was very moved. For many decades, the church brothers and sisters have wished to see photos of Rev. and Mrs Simpkin. Now our wishes have finally been fulfilled. We know that they sowed the seeds of the Gospel in Sapushan, and the Yunnan Miao churches of today are their Gospel fruit. Therefore, not only were they your parents, but also our spiritual parents here at Sapushan Church.*
>
> *We are very thankful to you for providing the photos, and for travelling so far to come and visit us. We will pray for each other. May the Lord bless you.[6]*

How thankful Theo and Olive would have been to know that there were still living churches in the areas where they had worked. My parents died without knowing anything about the fate of the believers they had left behind when they had to leave in 1951. Many did give way under the persecution directed at believers and renounced their faith. It has always been so. There is a faithful remnant. Others suffered long years of imprisonment and hard labour rather than deny their Lord. Some paid the ultimate price.

Nevertheless, the church survives today. The fruit that is born out of the selfless sacrifices of those who give up a comfortable life in order to follow where they believe their Master is leading them may not be seen at once. It may not be seen for decades or more. But God's Word is powerful.

There are indeed difficulties facing the church in China, but God is not defeated by human power and philosophy. The forces antagonistic to the Gospel do not have the last word. In spite of persecution and hardship, God's Word continues to bear fruit.

---

6   Email dated 15 September, 2012 forwarded to Helen and translated by the foreign friend.

APPENDIX
The SSOOS Spotlight[1]

---

1   These scans of the SSOOS *Spotlight* are included to give an insight into the character of the new workers and the relationships within the CIM group in Dali 1939-40.

                                  A FOOT WIDE ON THE EDGE OF NOWHERE

THE CHARTER OF THE SSOOS

1. For all time and by all people the Language School for Men in west China shall be known as the SSOOS which letters signify, the Simpkin School of Oriental Studies.

2. The Principal shall always be a Simpkin or, alternatively, another Simpkin.

3. The wife of the Principal shall always be known, unless she hits you for it, as the Mother Superior.

4. There shall be no rules except good rules. All rules shall be made by the students.

5. The SSOOS uniform shall be a black leather jacket and trousers (pants) of a gray material. Shorts may be worn provided that students do not have knobbly knees.

6. Charades shall be held at least once every two months or, alternatively, when the full moon and a birthday coincide.

7. Frames and string will be provided from which students will construct their own beds.

8. All doors shall be wire doors.

9. Vegetables shall be made to rotate in a clock-wise direction or even an anti-clock wise direction, at meals, but never in both directions simultaneously.

GLOSSARY OF SSOOS TERMS

Bleacher: A difficulty; an awkward situation; an unfair question in the Primer.

Bertie: A small carnivorous animal fitted with powerful molars and whose night life consists of revelling and feasting. Last seen going rapidly north.

Bloke: A Sax. 'bluke'. A good fellow, a gentleman of the first quality; a friend of Harry's.

Boscar: *OOSuper-splendid : marvellous; the best New Zealand can produce.

Corker: Australian version of 'boscar' which see.

Curley: Read in forth tone, twisted or coiled. Read on third tone, a future event.

Fiddlin': Mucking about, making a row, irritating the other fellow.

Jolly guy: A gentleman whose merry quips and cheerful countenance cause him to be an asset to society in general.

Shucks: What you say when you get your examination paper back.

St. nk. r : Undiscyphered hieroglyphic: thought to have a slightly derogatory meaning.

Tutti-fruity: Luscious fruit, cream, juice, nuts and just a little bit of something else undefinable, all brought into imminent juxtaposition.

Whack-o: Lat. 'Acquio—I give a yell.' Good: bad: small; large; all up; punishment. What you give people in Australia.

Ah!-ah!: What you say when you haven't been listening to the other feller and want a reply that means 'yes' or 'no' to make him buzz off.

WAR NEWS.

For six months there has been serious fighting on three fronts and although the position has not changed we have accounted for many enemy losses with only the loss of a little blood.

The enemy attacked with Mechanised Bertie units and large Louis tanks which succeeded in entering our camp. The Louis tanks were too slow and were easily caught but the Mechanised Berties caused much irritation until the new wet finger was introduced and this rendered them helpless.

The morale of the troops is good but we are sorry to say that two of our most successful Bertie catchers from Canada who have only one name between them lost courage and forsook the men holding the street.

WAR IN THE AIR. We have not yet succeeded in beating off enemy flycraft. After much weighty thought and many a frown Prof. Simpkin evolved the fly-proof door and large consignments have been rushed to the front. The early consignments have not proved very successful and the Prof. is now knitting his brows over one to fit over the entire compound. If the Prof. fails to find workmen sufficiently intelligent to follow his intricate drawings he intends to fit wire mesh over the moon gate just to annoy the enemy by making them fly over the top.

AMERICA. President Wagner is deeply shocked and has already sent four cases of moral support. The Tali Press suggests that four cases of Keating's would have been much more to the point.

TO-DAY'S MARKET

The government to-day announced new designations and frantic activity ensued in the street. Heavy selling in Australian stocks followed the rumour of foodstuffs being transferred to Anhwei. Speculators rushed the market with a view to hoarding but it is expected that the government will take action against this. There is also a danger that the reds may enter the market.

Oil to-day remained steady in spite of an attack by the foreign group which tried to influence prices by spreading rumours of increased transport charges. Heavy stocks are still on hand but there is little demand.

In the fruit and foodstuff market there was a slump following the recent rush on berries and ice-cream. Expert watchers predict that the slump is only temporary. Many prominent buyers were not seen in the fruit exchange to-day.

Money market. Rapid rises in the cost of living and heavy demands of the postal authorities caused unsteadiness in the market and capitalists made a hurried attempt to rally the market. Later in the day the Tight Club entered the field and the day finished at a steady level. The ratio between the silver and the national currency remained the same. The level however is still considerably higher than those which prevailed in the old Wuting market.

FAVOURITE SSOOS RECIPES

Plain overnight cookies (English—biscuits)

4 cups brown sugar
1 cup butter
4 eggs
1 tablespoon soda bicarb.
1 cup hot water

1 tablespoon cream of tartar
1 teaspoon salt
1 teaspoon flavouring essence
7 cups flour
(little more if necessary)

Method. Cream sugar and butter. Beat eggs separately and add. Dissolve soda in cup of water. Sift cream of tartar with flour. Knead well with hands. Form into long narrow loaf shape. Let stand over night.

Next morning. Slice thin and bake in quick oven.

N. B. When slicing, one straight un-interrupted cut with knife will give the crinkled surface for the biscuits. For smaller quantities use half amounts.

Aunty's drop cakes (Quickly made tea-cakes)

4 oz. flour sifted with 1 teaspoon baking powder.
2 oz. butter or lard rubbed into flour until it is like fine bread crumbs.

1 dessert spoon cinnamon.

Pinch of salt. 2 eggs well beaten and enough milk to make a dough that will drop from a spoon. Drop onto buttered baking tin and bake for 15 minutes in fairly hot oven.

Peanuts chopped up, instead of cinnamon, make a nice variation.

Lemon honey or lemon curd.

6 eggs well beaten. Place in double saucepan.
Add :—

½ lb. sugar. 2 oz. butter (or lard) 1 teaspoon of citric acid.

Put on fire to boil and stir until it thickens. Take off fire and add 1 teaspoon of lemon essence.

Caramel fudge

1 tin condensed milk
2 cups sugar
2 tablespoons syrup (or honey)

Butter, the size of a walnut
½ teaspoon of salt
2 teaspoons Vanilla essence

Method : Put all ingredients into a saucepan and bring steadily to the boil stirring *all the time.* Boil steadily for 17 minutes stirring all the time. Turn onto a buttered dish and make into squares before it is cold.

Mincemeat

1 cup of apple (Or pear)
1 cup raisins (Prunes are good cut up if no raisins)
1 cup currants

1 cup brown sugar
1 cup nuts (Walnuts are good)
1 cup syrup (or honey)
2 big teaspoons of cinnamon.

Method: Chop up apple or pear into small pieces. Wash currants in hot water. Chop up raisins and nuts. Mix all ingredients together and boil lightly for 10 minutes. Enough for 4 8" tarts.

Salad dressing

Mix together :—

½ teaspoon mustard
2 heaped teaspoons flour
½ teaspoon salt
1 teaspoon sugar
½ cup milk
1 egg well beaten.

Bring to boil and beat while adding ¼ cup vinegar. Cream added improves dressing greatly.

SSOOS SPECIAL

A liberal supply of floral decorations
2 long tables full of new recruits
As many sparkling "prupearong" cocktails,
Equal amounts of scotch eggs and french fried, in home-
    grown lettuce nests.
Plenty of appreciation sprinkled over,
SSOOS tutti fruties.
Perfect trust and confidence in the housekeeper
1 pinch of unselfishness
Buckets of cheerfulness
Spicy debates
Rather more than a sprinkling of interest in the fellow cut-
    ting the birthday cake and
3 loud cheers when the aforesaid is finally distributed over
    a large area.
Makes a very pleasant evening.
To be repeated as often as a fellow reveals his 生日

Signed:— D. E. Kemp
SSOOS housekeeper.

TO-DAY'S RADIO PROGRAM

3.00 p.m. Gardening Talk by T. Simpkin 'Cabbages and
    their ways.'

3.15 p.m. Music that Makes History.   Selections by the
    Dadufranstev Quartet.

3.30 p.m. Talks to mothers, by Mrs. T. Simpkin.   "The
    care of the child."

3.40 p.m. Running commentary on the Hua Chung v. SSOOS
    Soccer Match by Cheer-leader Gould.

4.30 p.m. "Recollections of old Wuting"
    A short talk by T. Simpkin

4.45 p.m. "My adventures with the Reds."
    A short talk by T. Simpkin

4.55 p.m. "Memories of Tom."
    A short talk by T. Simpkin

5.30 p.m. News, weather and time.

6.00 p.m. Time weather and news.

7.15 p.m. "Old favourites' hour." The cast will include:—
    Mr. Binks, Tom Mulholland, Jack Graham, Albert
    Allen and the tall consul.

8.00 p.m. New Heresies by Canon Gunn.

8.30 p.m. "Quest and Conquest". Reminiscences by that
    great hunter Frank White.

9.00 p.m. Bed-time music on the violin by G. Malins.

The above program is liable to change without previous intimation. If the Savage's have sent the battery to
Hua Chung or the Wiggy-Wags haven't got their new set
in time, there will be no program at all.

PIPPITY IPPITY

Pippity Ippity
Lived in a house
It seemed to be known
For its little brown mouse
    (rat, burty luey or louse)

It had small windows
Of paper so thin
And at every door was
A small openin'.

Pippity Ippity
Painted it red
He wished he had washed it
All over instead.

His tiny doorstep was
Round smooth and low
He scrubbed it so hard
But no one would know.

And his wee garden had
One little tree
From it a clothes line went
Brilliant to see.

Pippity Ippity
Loved his wee house
He ate and he slept in it
So did the l————

    Prankie Dank.

UNCLE DANK'S CORNER OF PRANKS

My Dear Boys and Girls,

How are all my little boys and girls today? My me o' my, my family is so large I don't know whether to laugh or cry. Let me see now, there is Donnie Cunnie white and funny, Artie Gunnie always sunny, Hector Gothard ring the bell hard, and Davie Junny promising tummy. And there is Harold Gould properly schooled, Stevie Knights looking for bites, Geoffie "Bath" Malin who counts every pail in, and Bessie, Burtie's chum who writes to "Dad and Mom". There is Willie Hilly Billie and Wyley Red White and our own nursie Kemp we cannot exempt.

Now Children Dear, come very very near, and each morning clear you will always hear a snoring noise from all the boys. But listen well and you can tell that greater noise comes not from boys. Though "Baby" is small she knows how to bawl. Baby brother is another. But in comes Poppa-Theo-bop-ya, and out comes tears followed by tears. Children Dear take not great fear, from an advanced year, these small appear. Be good and cheerie like Poppa's "Dearie" — never weary, never fearie. Learn from Uncle Dank who never played a prank, but what his poppa on his track, never failed to give a smack.

    Goodbye from Uncle Dank,

    Who does not ask for you to thank.

THE MAGIC MOUNTAIN

Long, long ago, before ever people became so clever that they ceased to believe in fairies, and gnomes and hob-goblins, there was a magic mountain. At least people who ought to have known, said it was a magic one in spite of the fact that it looked just like any other mountain. Well, one day, two bold, dashing travellers came to the city of Ilad which was the city nearest to the magic mountain. They had come from as far away as possible and they told the citizens living in the joint that they were going to have a go at the mountain.

The first thing to do was to sneak some grub and then sneak off before the good fairy whose name was Sadie, could forbid them. And very early, while all the good people were still asleep they sneaked off and the grub. Up they went, and up and up, and I'm not so sure there wasn't another up. The snow grew deeper and the magic bushes plucked at them and tore pieces of their clothes off until it became a question whether they would be wearing any-thing at all when they arrived at the top. However the top did come. And they knew they were there because when they tried to go a bit higher there was nothing to go up.

Now near the top there was a lake, deep mysterious and very magic. "What about it?" they asked each other in their vulgar way. And believe me or believe me not, I don't care, before you could say 'Snakes alive' they found themselves in the lake and their clothes on the bank. The water looked just like the water they had once had in a bath when they were tiny. But it wasn't the same it was solid magic. And they were soon under a spell. They got out and dressed. And then the magic began to work.

In just about as long as it takes the Mother Superior to add 3 and 4 together correctly, they found they were lost. That sounds a bit funny but what is meant is they were in a horrible forest of bamboo that prodded them and mucked about with those who blokes so much they would have cried if they had been alone instead of together. Then

one of them had a brain wave. He remembered a magic word he had once heard when he was eating grubs in the bush. "Tutti-fruity," he said so softly to himself he could hardly hear what he said. And there they were out of the bamboo winding their way down the most beautiful valley you have ever seen, even if you have lived in Australia.

But that wasn't the end. Oh no, there's a bit more if your are not sick of listening. But anyway you needn't listen if you don't want to. I don't care. Well they went down that valley until suddenly the valley did a queer thing. It dropped, it just wasn't there: it was below them, miles below and the only way to go on was to fall over and they weren't sure how you pulled up when you dropped like that. So they thought they would go back to the path that they would have been on all the time if they had not been bewitched. You see the magic was beginning to wear off a little and they were as nearly sensible as they had ever been in their lives. It made them feel quite excited.

But would you credit it, Boys and Girls, no sooner did they try to climb up to the right path than the sky grew black and dark and they couldn't see and they didn't know what to do and they hadn't got the magic light that all the people of Ilad used to have whenever they went for a walk in the dark or anything like that. All the birds and the beasts laughed like mad at them and came along to have a free smell as these two adventurers fell asleep in the bamboo. What you say? Oh, yes, they had got back to the bamboo again.

That night long after Mummy has tucked you up in bed, four good fairies set out with a glow worm to try to find the missing links but the dark magic of the night drove them back. The next morning the citizens of Ilad had a meeting and from their number they chose the four bravest and nicest and most handsome and best liked citizens and sent them off on the search. But that is another story.

P.S. The two travellers got back all right. But during the night they turned into little baa-lambs and that is why their smiles were sheepish.

OUR SPORTS COLUMN

BASKET BALL

"Play the man and not the game", shouts Harry.

"Saay, what do yer think yer doing", sez Doug, "this is the way to shoot goals, to demonstrate (ah! hold your breath boys!) Tung ch'i hsi lo, but in the cabbage patch not in the basket.

"Time", bawls Theo. Time for what? Time for the scrubbing-brush, time for tea, and time for— "You fellows sure put the dirt in", growls Don.

"Nothing of the sort" replies Geoff, "I haven't disabled anybody yet".

"Pretty close though", pipes up Hec, showing a black eye.

"Well the best side won".

"Be ——(censored)——" yell the losers, "wait till we get you next time".

VOLLEY-BALL

"Spike her Frank!" What 'spike'?

Rail-road spike, running-shoe spike, Spike Murphy— no, not these spikes, but the spike, a famous spike, a leap-in-the-air-smash-her-down spike. (May be) And who is 'her'. I hope got a lady. Well perhaps, in which case the real word should be "tap the ball girls". We can all understand that.

OTHER SPORT.

1. Rooting up weeds (?) — Old Geoff (shih-la)
2. Shooting squirrels, imaginative only — Frank W. (This matter has been reported to the Tali S.P.C.A).
3. Trapping flies in student's rooms. The Principal. (also reported).
4. Incessant tramping to a distant Mission Compound (and back) Steve & Dave or Dave & Steve?
5. Miscellaneous, calling for great skill. Bill Pape.

DO YOU KNOW?

Test your intelligence by these questions to which answers will be found in the next issue of this periodical. No prizes are offered for correct replies received so don't waste time sending 'em in.

1. Whose birthday is the same day as the anniversary of the battle of Waterloo?
2. If the average amount of food eaten by one student in 6 months is 2 ton 3 cwt. $9\frac{3}{4}$ lb excluding pepper and salt, how much would a Muir eat in a similar period?
3. Try and name three people who are nearly as nice as you are.
4. How long is a piece of string, and, if so, which?
5. Why have all the tigers and snakes left Kweichow and gone to Anhwei?
6. Taking the Mother Superior as standard, who are the most beautiful women in China?
7. What will you do when you are made General Director?

Candidates must only write on one side of the paper at a time. Any color ink may be used except red which is infuriating. No other student must be in the room at the same time nor must there be any furniture about. All books must be handed in to the warden. The candidate will be sealed up in a box until he has finished. To ensure there is no cheating, candidates will be bathed by an official before commencing the paper and will be expected to wear only a bathing costume while answering the questions.

PERSONALITY PAGE.

Jeff: To be seen every day carrying two buckets of water from south to north or two cans from north to south. Wardrobe: a hat, one sock, pair of pants (trousers) and a jacket. Vocabulary: the single word 'Shla'.

Two-patch: Guardian of all in the east wing. Shows persistance at entering any room at any time. Wears her clothes vice-versa.

Hudson & George.   Erstwhile vivious beasts now tamed by the quiet gentleness of the student members of the SSOOS.

Mi-mi: Dropped from the heavens by an eagle, this feline friend found herself in a veritable Canaan. Now possesses fur, fatness and fun. Owes her life to Harry.

Hopeful Annie: Queen of the beggars. Wears a Paris hat and goes to business each day with a smile and a basket.

Jigger Li: Holds the 'jigger' record with 61 out of a possible 65 in a 25 minutes shoot.

Wiggy-wags: An affectionate name used secretly for some very good friends across the way. Noted for ice-cream, a gramaphone, and laughter.

Big Sister, Yang Ta Ma ('Holey Nose') Yang Wu and Wang Pe Yung never got popular names but they all made themselves notorious by looking after us for 6 months without ever letting us fall by the way through lack of nourishment. Big Sister sometimes rose to great culinary heights.

SNIPPETS

The "Knights-Muir" Barber Shop and Touch-Up Corner offer the following suggestions to graduates and under-graduates of the SSOOS, who might benefit by our good name.

1. Time is saved by placing a pail on the customers' head and making a chalk line to indicate the extreme limits of the proposed operations. Working to a chalk line is also less dangerous.

2. Advise customers to bring clippers, scissors, comb, whisk and sheet, and you must provide the rest yourself.

3. Suggested subjects for conversations:—

    a. If customer appears to be henpecked, speak of Tsingtao.

    b. If he has aboriginal characteristics speak of kangaroos, gum trees, cactus and other luxurious growth.

    c. If his "chief" theme is hard times, console him by speaking of the institutes satisfactory "turn-out."

4. Make sure of the denominational persuasion of the customer. It makes it embarrassing for both parties if you only dampen his hair with a bottle when he prefers submersion.

LOOK YOUR BEST!

Knights & Muir. Beauty fixer-upers.
Prices depend on the nature of the hair.

    Our motto
Come early, come late
Bring snippers, bring clippers.
From grown-ups to nippers
We're sure to elate.

Address:—Next door to the Humane Society, Tali.

ADVERTISEMENTS

LETTERS TO THE EDITOR.

Dear Sir,

On behalf of the Tali branch of the Red International, of which I am a member I am raising my voice against the wanton aggression, intolerable suppression and infernal oppression of certain of the foreign mu sers and cho sers. We workers must rise and snap our chains.

There is the matter of Nieh Mu Ser. We are treated as dumb animals, but sir, we have our feelings, and it was a deep shock to my sensitive nature to see the aforesaid Mu ser undress in my presence. The matter of the carrot-patch and the dastardly spying of Mao Hsien Seng also deeply grieved me. And may I say sir, that the question of scrubbing-brush versus floor-cloth is entirely a matter for self-opinionated, self-determined independent workers to decide. The aggresive Si mu gets my goat.

In conclusion my message to the departing hsien sengs is to beware of the blood-stained foot-print planted high on the first wall inside the city gate of Tsu Hsung. Or rather don't beware of it. It is your sign of doom.

I remain,

Yours till your tires burst

Tu Patch (X) her mark.

(Translated by Old Geoff)

Dear Mr. Editor,

It is with much regret that I find it necessary to make the following complaint to your honoured paper.

Being part of my duties in the SSOOS to get the weekly bath water I find it necessary to grouse about the amount of water used by each person. It seems absolutely ridiculous that any student shall be so excessive as to take one whole pail of hot water. Surely his lily white anatomy could be washed with, at the most, a small jug of water.

Trusting action will be taken by your paper to 'keep the funds down'.

Yours 'oping you'll 'ave an 'art

Shuo la ma.

(We suggest a joint committee be set up immediately to report on the relative surface areas of representative anatomies. Ed.)

C. I. M.
London

Dear Mr. Editor,

Many thanks for the Proofs which I have read with great interest.

We in England understand that the main purpose of the training home in Tali has been to have meetings in English in the guest-room I cannot therefore understand why these do not feature in your magazine. From your syllabus it would seem that you have had between seventy and eighty meetings and this makes the omission all the more remarkable.

Believe me,

Yours sincerely,

N. W. Bakfun.

KAO HSIEN SENG TI P'ENG YU

One winter's day, in heaven's heights,
The SSOOS beheld an awesome sight
As eagle's wings did bear to them
A little cat all torn and thin.
One gallant student, Kao by name
Kindled his heart into a flame
And pent up love went out anew
So puss became his old peng yu.

Such tender care he showed for her.
He sacrificed beyond compare,
And from the SSOOS's table fare
He took his puss her little share.
With loving eyes he watched her grow
Until Kao's heart began to glow
With love and zeal, till all beside
Has lost its place in Harry's pride.

To-day puss lives to pester us
But 'ssh!', else Kao will make a fuss
Yet still his very life declares
His love for cats is very rare.

A sufferer at Kao's hands.

STOP PRESS NEWS

The SSOOS, a mysterious organisation in West China, was to-day disbanded by the government who declared the society illegal and members outlaws. Harry 'owled.

AMBITION

In many of our schools ambition is upheld as the great incentive to encourage the students to do their best. "Get to the top". "Be the best you can!". "Nothing good enough but the best!" "Hitch your waggon to the stars!" These are some of the slogans we hear. The Chinese counterpart of these is 把你的燈籠掛高些 "Hang your lantern a bit higher!"

Ambition has been one of the curses of the world. It made Napoleon plunge Europe into war; and even now it is bathing Flanders in blood. And yet ambition, rightly directed, is a most important factor in a Christian's life. Paul says, "We are ambitious"—as the A. V. says "We labour"; while the R.V. says "we make it our aim." But the Greek puts it: "We are ambitious" What then is our ambition? To get to the top? No! To be chief among the Lord's servants? No! To take the uppermost seat and on His right hand and on his left! No! No! We are but servants; and having done our best are to consider ourselves unprofitable servants, for we have merely done what was our duty to do.

What then is our ambition? 2 Cor. 5:9 "To be well-pleasing unto Him": This is to be the motivating thought, and the ambition that spurs us on. To be well-pleasing unto Him! To "please Him who hath chosen him (us) to be a soldier".

Alas, of so many it may be said: "For they all seek their own, not the things of Jesus Christ". Their own glory; not His. Their own comfort; not His honour, Their own wealth; not diadems for His brow. But, oh let *us* be ambitious to be well-pleasing unto Him; in study, and prayer, and Bible Study and personal work. That Christ may be magnified in my body whether by life or by death.

T. S.

VALETE

Many times laughter has transformed a moment of time during the hours of the days that have made the last six months: many a time laughter has broken the stillness of the quiet evening hours. Sometimes it was a whimsical thought of short life that caused our merriment: sometimes a family joke that even repetition failed to blunt. And therein lies the truth of the matter for it is always in a family that laughter is most innocent and most simple of cause. And herein lies a reason why we should pause to make witness to the goodness of our God which we have most particularly enjoyed these days at Tali.

If we did but remember each day separately, we should recall the grace given us that day, but as it is we can only review the period as a whole. The result is the same. There has been peace that is rare in this troubled world, there has been the daily bread and the daily strength: often times prayer made on our behalf has been answered, all unknown, perhaps, to the maker of it; and there has been given us the Father's best gift which is love, making us a family indeed.

We came to study Chinese intensively and that task has been accomplished in it's first stage by the grace of God. What we know now, we know because His help was given in a common task. We know that the Lord Himself will reward Mr. & Mrs. Simpkin for every help they gave to us and compared with that our thanks have but little value. But each of us is grateful and although 'thank you' are trite and conventional words they best express what each sincerely wants to express.

We are all glad Miss Kemp came to be a Mary to us and day by day contrive to satisfy the demands of 11 hungry men. If anyone was not satisfied he has never said so nor is he normal. We shall miss 'Dear Sister', too not only because of what she did for us but also because she was one of the fellowship.

THE SSOOS SPOTLIGHT.

TALI 1940.

Our visitors each brought a contribution to the family life. We remember Mr. Kuhn, Orville Carlson, Dan Smith, Miss Chang, Mrs. Christianson, Miss Clarke and our neighbor Miss DeWaard who also fed us well and truly for the first month of our time here. It will seem strange not to have brother Ted about the place, too. But at the Throne over which is written grace our prayers will mingle and if in the 'house of many mansions' tales are told, we will there relate the story of the matchless that was here begun below.

WE SHALL REMEMBER

Mr. & Mrs. Simpkin staying on at Tali for a while.
Miss Kemp who will sooner or later find herself at Wuting.
Harry Gould off to Chengyangkwan which is not far from Shanghai.

Arthur Gunn ⎫
Doug. Muir ⎬ who will all stay at Tali and be thinking
Frank Muir ⎭ of the tribesmen.

David Johnson travelling down to Chengkiang to prepare
to take the Evangel to the Moslems of Yunnan.

Goff Malins ⎫ who will soon be in Kwanhsien and later
Frank White ⎬ on in Shansi.

Stephen Knights ⎫ bound for Luhsin. Bill with his face
Don Cunningham ⎬ towards the Kiarung tribe on the Sze-
Bill Pape ⎭ chwan border.

Ted Holmes working in Tali and the villages of the plain.

SELECTED BIBLIOGRAPHY

Andrews, M 2012, *My China Mystery,* Even Before Publishing, Australia

Dunn, G 1984, 'The Martyrdom of John and Betty Stam', first published in *East Asia's Millions,* November/December 1984, as 'For the Stams No Deliverance', OMF International, viewed 2 November 2018, omf.org/us/the-martyrdom-of-john-and-betty-stam/.

McGilchrist, Stevenson 1968, *William Robertson, Victorian Pioneer, 1837-1890,* Melbourne.

Martin, G 1990, *Chefoo School 1881-1951,* Merlin Books Ltd., Braunton Devon

Miller, AJ 2015, *Pioneers in Exile: The China Inland Mission and Missionary Mobility in China and Southeast Asia, 1943-1989,* University of Kentucky, UKnowledge, viewed 2 November 2018, uknowledge.uky.edu/cgi/viewcontent.cgi?article=1027&context=history_etds.

Moran, MG 2015, *Someone to be with Roxie,* Lulu Publishing Services.

OMF International, *Chefoo Reconsidered—The Story Continues,* October 2016, viewed 2 November 2018, omf.org/blog/2016/10/11/chefoo-reconsidered-story-continues/.

Oulton, M 1995, *A Valley of the Finest Description – A History of the Shire of Lexton,* Australian Print Group, Maryborough

Simpkin, WT 1935, 'Pursued...yet not forsaken' possibly for *China's Millions* August 1935.

Simpkin, WT 1940, 'A prosperous journey', *China's Millions* 1 April 1940, p. 52.

Simpkin, WT 1940, 'Six months with the students', *China's Millions,* 1 September 1940, p. 134.

Simpkin, WT 1941, 'Moving to a new sphere', *China's Millions,* 1 May 1941, p. 72.

Simpkin, WT 1941, 'What God hath wrought among the tribes', *China's Millions,* 1 July 1941, p. 104.

Simpkin, WT 1941, 'An uncomfortable journey', *China's Millions,* 1 September 1941, p. 135.

Simpkin, WT 1943, 'A Tribal Bible Institute', in *According to plan, Part of the story of the China Inland Mission in 1943,* compiled by Bishop Frank Houghton, St John Bacon, Melbourne.

Smith, P, *Dwellers at the holly, The life and times of William Hollis (1841-1921).*

Taylor, Mrs Howard 1935, *The triumph of John and Betty Stam,* CIM.

Thompson, LC 2014, *Missionary Children in China: The Chefoo School and a Japanese Prison,* Academia.edu, viewed 2 November 2018, www.academia.edu/8994079/Missionary_Children_in_China_The_Chefoo_School_and_a_Japanese_Prison.

Thompson, P 2000, *China: The Reluctant Exodus, The story of the China Inland Mission's Withdrawal from Communist China,* ed. Tewksbury, ME, OMF International, Littleton, Colorado, USA

The Chefoo Magazine, 2011, publ. by the Chefoo Schools Association, Canada

Westminster Abbey, *Wang Zhiming, Priest,* n.d., viewed 2 November 2018, www.westminster-abbey.org/abbey-commemorations/commemorations/wang-zhiming/.

CPSIA information can be obtained
at www.ICGtesting.com
Printed in the USA
LVHW071623280520
656402LV00007BA/578

9 780648 384908